FAME

How to Build an Iconic Personal
Brand in Any Industry

Andrew Wood

Copyright © 2019 by Andrew Wood Inc.

All rights reserved. This book or any portion thereof may not be reproduced or used in any manner whatsoever without the express written permission of the publisher except for the use of brief quotations in a book review.

Printed in the United States of America

First Printing, 2019

ISBN 9781795138550

Legendary Publishing Group
3729 S Lecanto Hwy.
Lecanto, FL 34461

www.fameattracts.com

TABLE OF CONTENTS

1. Your Creation Myth
2. Claiming Your Position & Putting "Luck" On Your Side
3. Confidence & Competence - The Bedrock of Fame
4. The Sounds of Fame
5. Creating an Iconic Look - "Your Look!"
6. Is a Picture Worth a Thousand Words?
7. Symbols, Icons, Rituals and Communities that Turbo Charge Your Fame
8. Creating Legendary Charisma
9. The Ying and the Yang - Finding the Perfect Enemy!
10. The Famous Don't Leave Their Publicity or Legacy to Chance
11. Showtime - Delivering a Legendary Performance
12. Persistence, the Turning Point to Fame
13. Final Thoughts

FREE VIDEO

From rock stars to realtors, entrepreneurs to athletes, having a personal style, color, signature, gesture or accessory can help build your personal brand quickly, bringing the additional opportunities and income along with it.

What's your signature look going to be?

Visit www.fameattracts.com/download to receive a free video **"Fame – Creating an Iconic Look for Your Personal Brand"**

This video will show you how to coordinate all the elements of an iconic look to create a look that is uniquely YOU!

IN EVERY CITY THERE'S SOMEONE FAMOUS IN YOUR PROFESSION. MAKE THAT SOMEONE YOU!

Chances are good you have heard of famous martial artists Bruce Lee, Jackie Chan, Jean-Claude Van Damme and Chuck Norris. Chances are equally good you have never heard of me, Andrew Wood. [That's my picture on the cover of Martial Arts Business!] I was never a great black-belt tournament fighter or in any Kung Fu movies, but in the 90s I was famous in the "business of martial arts." That is to say, almost every one of the 15,000 instructors running commercial martial arts schools in the United States and Canada at the time knew my name. At one point Chuck Norris even asked me to help market him!

Fast forward twenty plus years and the same is true of me in the golf industry. The vast majority of the 28,000 golf professionals in the US know my name, along with several thousand golf course owners and club managers at more than 50,000 golf clubs around the world. In the golf business niche, *I am famous*. That niche fame brings business to me, sells my books and gets me speaking invitations all over the world. I make a fine living on my own terms and often get invitations to stay and play for free at the world's best resorts. There are hundreds and perhaps thousands of other people who do golf marketing. None of them are famous!

Becoming famous is no mere ego trip. It is the simplest most effective way to create exponential growth and demand for your professional skills, products or services. In every city in the world, there is already someone who is the most famous lawyer, Realtor, golf instructor, plastic surgeon, jeweler, artist, politician, builder, consultant, CEO, landscaper and so forth. The faster you make that someone you, the more business, money, opportunity, recognition and invitations will come your way. Getting famous and building an iconic personal brand is not frivolous; it's essential for maximizing your personal success.

INTRODUCTION

GRABBING YOUR 15 MINUTES OF FAME AND TURNING IT INTO A **LIFETIME OF PROFESSIONAL SUCCESS**

Famed pop culture artist Andy Warhol coined the phrase "15 minutes of fame" in 1968. What he actually said was, "In the future, everyone will be world-famous for 15 minutes."

There are those who are famous only for their murderous acts: Billy the Kid, John Hinckley, John Wilkes Booth, Peter Sutcliffe, Ted Bundy and many more. Others such as Jesse James, Bonnie and Clyde, or Butch Cassidy and Sundance were famous only for robbing banks.

Others, such as Paris Hilton, the Kardashians and whoever is staring in the latest "reality show," are only famous for being famous.

"Jackie O" was famous for whom she married rather than anything she ever did. So too was Yoko Ono, once the most famous Japanese person anyone could name. Still is...

Then there are those who have become so famous they need only one name.

For example, the likes of Ali, Madonna, Ronaldo, Dali, Pele and Adele, Sting, Cher, Bono, Björk, Coolio, Moby, Morrissey, Fabio, Liberace, Prince, Shakira and so on.

But to get famous this way assumes not only some good fortune but also genuine world-class talent.

Dying, especially before your time, is another great way to create an iconic personal brand

Elvis was worth far more dead than alive. Presley's death in August 1977 meant that business was even better than usual for his manager Colonel Tom Parker. After all, Elvis had been in worsening health for years, and he and the Colonel had grown estranged. In death, Presley could be repackaged and sold as a timeless pop icon, and fans would no longer have to look at the sick and bloated caricature the once gorgeous singer had become. Posthumous sales of Elvis records and tawdry memorabilia boomed. "Elvis didn't die," the Colonel told callers in the days following Presley's death, "the body did. We're keeping Elvis alive." I suspect the same was true of James Dean, Sid Vicious, Buddy Holly, Ayrton Senna and many others.

But dying to get famous has little future. No, we need a simpler, more predictable path to fame than outrageous talent, fortune, crime or death - something that can be replicated predictably in whatever profession, industry, niche and geography applies to you.

1
YOUR CREATION MYTH

Your fame starts with your story that answers the basic questions of why you do what you do and where it all began. You will want to explain how you found your calling and how you developed your talents. Your fans will be interested in your aha moment and what challenges you conquered along the way. Once you are happy with your story, tweak it and enhance it so it resonates with your audience in an emotional and empowering way to grow your fame!

Study the Best

In all walks of life if you want to be great, you study the best. In this book you are going to hang out with the world's most famous people and study their business DNA, their unique code, and the little things they did that others missed. You'll find the things you can copy to rapidly build your personal brand. Together we will make you famous and make your brand iconic in whatever city, niche and profession in which you operate. The opportunities, recognition and money will flow from there!

All great stories of famous people have some common characteristics: a time, a place, a protagonist, some setbacks and an aha moment that was the catalyst to all their successes. Like a great book or movie, your fame will start with a story, your story. Some call it a back story or, in many cases, a creation myth because over time fact is blended with fiction until no one really knows the truth but the story lives on. The more engaging that story, the more successful you will be.

Here are a few more edited stories of a famous persons who were just ordinary folks until that aha moment hit them. Fame comes to a few by chance, but to most by persistence and design.

Unknown Pamela Anderson was at at a BC Lions football game when the Jumbotron caught a glimpse of her wearing a cut-off Labatt Blue T-shirt. The beer company got so many phone calls inquiring about whom she was that they hired her as their spokesmodel! She's best known as a babe on the TV show "Baywatch."

Steve Jobs and Steve Wozniak built computers in Job's parents' Palo Alto, California, garage. In 1976, Wozniak developed the computer that eventually made him famous. He alone designed the hardware, circuit boards, and operating system for the Apple 1. Wozniak originally offered the design to Hewlett Packard while working there, but was turned down by the company on five different occasions. Jobs instead had the idea to sell the Apple 1 with Wozniak as a fully assembled printed circuit board. Wozniak, at first skeptical, was later convinced by Jobs that even if they were not successful they could at least say to their grandkids they had had their own company.

Mother of Canadian Justin Bieber uploaded a video to YouTube of him singing. Bieber's mother Pattie Mallette, who was underage at the time of giving birth, raised her son with the help of her mother and stepfather. Pattie worked a series of low-paying office jobs, raising Bieber as a single mother in low-income housing. In early 2007, aged 12, Bieber sang for a local singing competition in Stratford and was placed second. Mallette posted a video of the performance on YouTube for their family and friends to see. She continued to upload videos of Bieber singing covers of various R&B songs, and Bieber's popularity on the site grew. When searching for videos of a different singer, Scooter Braun, a former marketing executive of So So Def Recordings, clicked on one of Bieber's 2007 videos by accident. Impressed, Braun tracked down Bieber and his mom and eventually signed him to a contract. Bieber released his debut EP, My World, in late 2009. It was certified platinum in the U.S. and he became the first artist to have seven songs from a debut record chart on the Billboard Hot 100.

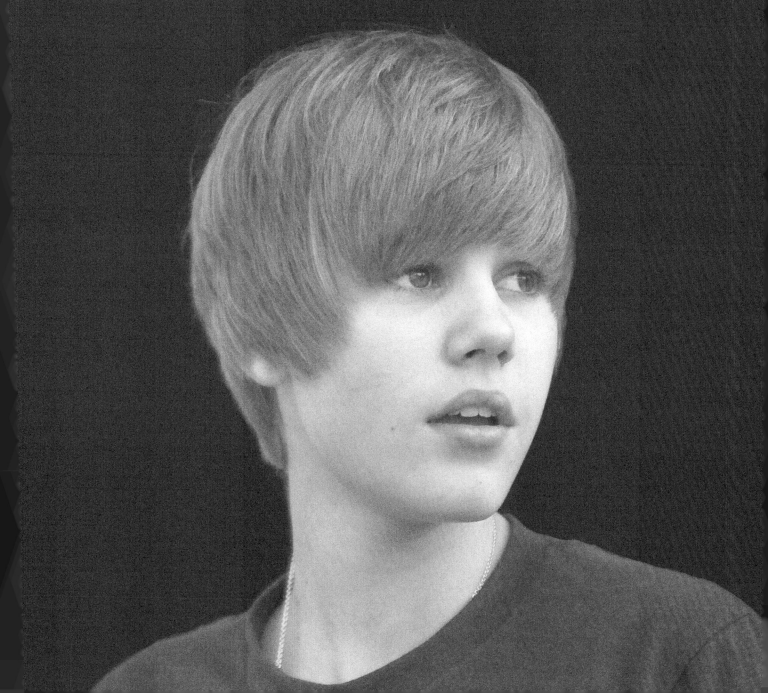

Replica of Ray Kroc's original McDonald's

Ray Kroc

Paper cup salesman Ray Kroc was amazed by the efficiency of the McDonald brothers' hamburger store in San Bernardino, California. Having been in approximately a thousand kitchens, Kroc believed the McDonald brothers had the best-run operation he had ever seen. It had a very simple menu, cheap prices, and tons of business. Procedures were set up with simple systems that got good results every time. The restaurant was clean, modern, mechanized, and the staff professional and well-groomed.

Roadside hamburger restaurants were more often than not hangouts for motorcycle gangs and rebellious teenagers, and Kroc saw in McDonald's a better vision for a restaurant. Kroc opened the first McDonald's franchised under his partnership with the McDonald brothers in Des Plaines, Illinois.

A little-known part of the McDonald's story is that the brothers had already sold franchises to other people! But those people didn't carry through all the difficult steps that Ray Kroc had to go through to really get multiple franchises running successfully.

Richard Branson started a magazine, in London and sold T-shirts and records by mail. He made a fortune and sold his record company for a billion dollars to start an airline - and then just about every other business known to man including health clubs, cell phone service, cola sodas, railways and more under the Virgin brand.

Harrison Ford had just about given up on his acting dream and took part-time work as a stage hand and carpenter so he could support his family. Then he was called out to George Lucas's home to build some cabinets. Lucas not only paid him, but he also offered Ford a role in his next feature film, American Graffiti. The rest is galactic history!

Colonel Sanders believed that his little restaurant would remain successful indefinitely, but at age 65 he had to sell it after the new Interstate 75 reduced customer traffic to a trickle. Left only with his savings and $105 a month from Social Security, Sanders decided to begin to franchise his fried chicken concept in earnest.

He traveled the US looking for restaurants who would use his secret recipe. Often sleeping in the back of his car, Sanders visited thousands of restaurants at which he offered to cook his chicken. If the owners liked it, he negotiated franchise rights of four cents a chicken. It took him offering the deal to hundreds of restaurants before anyone took him up on the offer!

Two students at Harvard University, Mark Zuckerberg and his college roommate Eduardo Saverin started a social media network. Originally set up for people to upload pictures and rate them, Facebook was an overnight success.

Bruce Jenner got a double dose of fame. First he became famous as the world's greatest male athlete when he won the gold medal in the Olympics decathalon event.

Then 40 years later he became famous again, this time for becoming a woman!

THE TEN ELEMENTS OF A GREAT CREATION STORY

There are ten key elements to a great creation story. While some miss a few, you will find these elements in almost all. Think how your story can be enhanced using this formula. Some are simple descriptions, but they help clarify who you are in people's minds. This example of the 10 points is an actual case. See if you can guess who.

1. Location: Where did it all begin, once upon a time... Detroit, Michigan, 8 Mile Street.

2. A problem needs to be solved: Poor kid, no father.

3. Protagonist: Drug dependent mother lives in trailer home, has to get out of poverty, has to be someone!

4. Aha moment: Discover he's good at rhyming words and singing songs.

5. A dream is dreamed: A goal is set, a position taken. There will be a famous white rapper who lasts longer than the one hit wonder Vanilla Ice.

6. Talent development: Practice night and day. Author Malcolm Gladwell found that to become really good at something takes 10,000 hours. This doesn't mean you can't make money along the way. Gladwell pointed out that the Beatles played in dives in Germany for thousands of hours before they got famous back in England.

7. Challenges must be overcome: "White guys can't rap." Drugs, crime, poverty, negative feedback, no support: you're on your own to believe in yourself!

8. Setbacks occur: Finishes second in a major rap battle, disappointment.

9. The regroup, retry and persist: He keeps going, getting better and better at his raps.

10. Success: Others including Dr. Dre, recognize Eminem's talent and sign him to a record deal. The rest as they say is history.

THE FORMULA DOESN'T CHANGE MUCH NO MATTER WHAT PROFESSION YOU HAPPEN TO BE IN, LET'S LOOK AT ANOTHER FAMOUS CREATION STORY.

1. Location: Portland Oregon, University Campus.

2. A problem needs to be solved: Running shoes are poor quality.

3. Protagonist: Initially a lack of funds and a dodgy supplier; later the giant German might of Adidas and Puma.

4. Aha moment: A waffle iron shoe sole produced in Coach Bill Bowerman's garage.

5. A dream is dreamed: Instead of selling Tiger brand shoes we will create our own. Phil Knight sells shoes out of the trunk of his car at track meets.

6. Talent development: In many areas -- design, sales, marketing, negotiation, funding -- all tasks initially fall on Phil Knight.

7. Challenges must be overcome: No money, spotty supply, long lead times.

8. Setbacks occur: Initial supplier cuts them off, bank kills credit line.

9. The regroup, retry and persist: New bank found, company saved from the brink.

10. Success: After securing new funding, Nike takes off and becomes the world's leading seller of athletic shoes.

As you see the formula is pretty consistent. In fact the closer you stay to that formula the easier it will be. All you have to do is add the juicy details of your life and journey. The more vividly you paint them, the better.

Now let's look at some other stories in more detail. See what style and plot elements you can take from them to apply to your story.

NEVER JUDGE THE BOOK BY THE COVER

Sometime in the mid '90s I was sitting in seat 1A on a flight from Dallas to Orange County, California. Next to me, already seated in 1B, was a large, middle-aged woman with a giant handbag. From it, poked out copies of National Inquirer, Star and The Sun -- all sensationalist rags of the first order. I stole a glance at her, another glance at the bag of magazines and quickly buried myself in a book, thinking that I couldn't possibly have anything in common with this person.

About half way through the flight, she asked me if she could get out to use the restroom. I said something polite and got up to let her out. She said something polite in return and we exchanged a few words more. When she came back and sat down she turned directly to me, looked me in the eye and challenged, "You weren't going to talk to me were you?" Without waiting for answer, she went on, "Just because I'm a fat, middle-aged women with copies of the National Inquirer, Star and the The Sun in her bag does not mean I'm not worth talking to."

There was nothing to do but admit she had me nailed! She went on without missing a beat, and thankfully not chastising me any further, and asked what I did? At the time I was running my martial arts empire but I had just written my first book, Making it Big in America, so I wanted to focus on that, so I told her I was an author.

"Oh," she said, "that sounds interesting. How is your book doing?" she asked.
"Quite well," I said proudly "It's sold 5,000 copies in six months."
"What do you do?" I asked.
"I write books too," she said.
"How is your book doing?" I asked politely.
"Quite well," she said modestly. "I have just come from a book signing in Dallas where my agent said we have sold 260,000 copies this year!"

Talked about being smoked!

"What kind of books do you write?" I inquired.
"True crime," she said.
"And how did you get into that?" I asked?

She went on to tell me that she lived in Seattle and that as a middle-aged housewife, her husband left her with kids and no job. She was unsure of her future and felt quite depressed. Someone suggested that a way to help her feel better about herself was to volunteer to help others and so she volunteered for the suicide hotline. Seattle, as you may or may not know, is the suicide capital of America. The work as you may imagine was taxing, so taxing in fact that that during her first few months several of her co-volunteers actually committed suicide themselves. Shocked at this disturbing trend, the organizers of the program decided to pair up their volunteers so they could support and motivate each other. Ann was about to get a shock of her own.

Her partner on the suicide hotline was Theodore Bundy, who later became America's most notorious serial killer, and the topic of her first bestselling book. Can you imagine feeling so depressed that you call the suicide hotline and get Ted Bundy as your counselor?

Needless to say, the rest of the trip went quickly and contained more equally fascinating stories, she was delightful company. When I got home I sent her a copy of my personal growth book for her son, while she sent me a copy of two of her best-selling crime books.

Now that's a back story that launched an amazing career that included 33 best-selling books for Ann Rule.

Former PGA Tour star and CBS Announcer Bobby Clampett Runs One of the World's Best Golf School's With his Own Unique Method of Instruction.

A STORY OF TRUTH: "IMPACT IS THE ONLY THING THAT MATTERS"

In the 1980s my friend Bobby Clampett was the PGA Tour's new golden boy, a whiz kid from California who was the "next Jack Nicklaus," only it never quite worked out that way. While he did have a long and profitable career on both the PGA and Champions Tour, the predicted success never quite materialized and he was left with just one PGA Tour victory to his name. Then came a successful career at CBS commentating on golf while running one of the country's premier golf schools.

Clampett's aha moment came when he was in the middle of his career at CBS where they had developed a new technology known in the business as "swing vision." Super slow-motion cameras provided the ability to look at golf swings under the microscope. As Bobby started to watch a lot of this footage and study the golf club impact of the best players of the game. He suddenly realized their hits were all virtually the same regardless of how they swung the club! He came to the conclusion that "The only things that matters in the golf swing are the two inches before the ball and the four inches afterwards!"

"So why then," he asked "is every golf pro trying to teach you to get in a certain position at the top or adopt a certain swing that may be totally unsuited to your body style?"

Did Jack Nicklaus swing like Arnie? Or Watson swing like Seve? Tiger like Faldo? Rory like DJ? How about Jim Furyk, he's like 3rd or 4th on the all-time money list - come on, who else on tour swings like him? The only one thing that all great players have in common, says Clampett, "is that they all create great impact." Golf is simply a game of impact, It's how this ball meets the clubface, that's the secret. When you discover it, golf gets fun fast!

For years PGA professionals have been trying to teach players a certain style of swing based on the average golfer. The trouble is, this style of swing doesn't fit everybody... and in fact, trying to retrofit YOUR unique swing into someone else's "mold" is the worst mistake you could make.

Jim Furyk won over 100 million dollars with a swing only his mother could love and no one will ever copy!

Players are all different. Height. Weight. Posture. Natural rhythm. Everything about you and the way you handle the club differs in a million ways from the guy you tee it up with every Saturday. And that's the way it's supposed to be, no matter how hard someone tries to fit you into a standardized and approved "golf swing template." Because the golf ball doesn't care what your swing looks like. It doesn't care what your physical abilities are or how athletic you are. If you can learn to make great impact, you can learn to play great golf. The problem is, nobody's been teaching this truth until now!

That fundamental truth is the creation story behind Impact Zone Golf, Clampett's million-dollar golf school headquartered in Naples, Florida. As an avid golfer, Clampett's story is one I connect with immediately!

When I work with instructors of any kind I try to help them find that moment when they knew their calling was to help others. I try to find a success story from one of their students. I magnify the anguish of the decision to give up their own dream of playing golf or riding in the Olympics to help others so the story creates an emotional element that attracts.

THE WORLD'S #1 HORSEMAN WHO INVENTED A NEW WAY OF TEACHING, "NATURAL HORSEMANSHIP"

When I met Pat Parelli in 2009, he had already become the world's most famous horseman. I was fascinated by his story and it follows the classic formula I've outlined for building a famous profile and persona.

Parelli was born in California and spent the summers with old timers who taught him the way of animals. He had no idea how this would guide his career in the future, let alone his rise to fame. He loved horses and, living in the west, it wasn't long before he started riding in rodeos.

Pat enjoyed successful career as a bareback rodeo, earning Rookie of the Year in 1981. But life after rodeo was tough. He thought training horses for a living would be easy, especially given his rodeo skills but nothing could have been further from the truth. He was lucky to meet his mentor and studied and worked with him for five years. After Troy Henry passed away, Pat was left with his legacy of principles in the psychology of horse training and Pat launched his career as a trainer and competitor in the Reined Cow Horse world. But, a few years later, Pat woke up to find that he was broke. Something had to change.

Pat hit the road, driving around California and offering his help to fix horse behavior problems... and his reputation quickly grew. Not only could he impressively fix all kinds of issues with horses, his personality was infectious and he started to attract small audiences as word got around.

A prominent veterinarian friend started sending business his way and telling him how much to charge, and then his blacksmith and good friend encouraged him to give his first seminar and helped him consolidate the Eight Principles of horse training that he still uses to this day. Pat was witty, charismatic and very good at what he did. His engaging rhetoric, mustache, cowboy hat, boots, spurs and chaps were instantly recognizable and he wore that wherever he went - even in Europe.

Pat's ambition was strong. He knew he was going to be somebody but hadn't quite figured who - or how to do that. He got a big leg up when a famous veterinarian, Dr. R.M. Miller, wrote an article about this young, talented horseman and published it in the #1 western magazine at the time: The Western Horseman. "A New Look At Old Methods" put Pat on the map and the phone rang off the hook - still for horse training.

Shortly after that, an ex-rodeo entrepreneur friend of Pat's invited him to do a seminar tour in Australia and this is where his talent for teaching seminars was born.

Pat's ability to transform horses while entertaining a crowd was unique. He was not a trick trainer or show act, he was the consummate horseman who liked people as much as he liked horses. This was not normal in the 1980s and he was heavily criticized by his peers who were not so good with people.

Pat somehow knew that his future success lay with teaching, by sharing what he knew and that served to widen the gap between him and other trainers. They were jealous of his success and intimidated by his willingness to share the 'insider secrets' of horse training.

Furthermore, he shunned the cruel techniques so often used and was not afraid to make a stance about the ethical treatment of horses. He made a lot of enemies with his outspoken condemnation of harsh training techniques and so began his mission to change the world and make it a better place for horses.

In Sydney in 1989, Pat met the woman who would help him to change the world. Linda Paterson brought her challenging horse to a Pat Parelli clinic. Not only did he teach her how to calm her horse and win its trust, his techniques were something Linda wanted to help promote in Australia. She established a business for him in Australia and three years later he asked her to move to the USA and help him to change the world.

Linda arrived in the USA to find Pat deeply in debt after his divorce. They traveled the country in a motorhome with a horse trailer behind it, living at Kinko's to print their flyers and educational materials as they staged small horsemanship clinics and his reputation grew. Audiences grew, word got around, Pat's reputation spread to Europe and continued to grow in Australia, and in the USA - its' always harder in your own back yard!

Business grew, then Parelli's created a Savvy Club which was the first membership concept in the horse industry, developed instructors, produced multiple DVDs, training manuals and Parelli Centers in Colorado and Florida. Pat Parelli started a movement that became known as Natural Horsemanship and is a significant part of the horse industry, influencing trainers and riders in all disciplines, at all levels from recreational to Olympic level who want to use horse psychology and relationship skills as the basis for success.

All I Ever Wanted to be Was a Golf Pro Instead I Ended up with a National Chain of Karate Schools

MY STORY - BIRTH OF A MARKETING LEGEND

This is full version of the creation story I have used in my seminars, online programs and books for almost, 30 years. There are shorter versions for different occasions and uses but in a full day seminar this one always connects!

I told this story hundreds of times in the martial arts world and told the exact same story when I went into the golf business. The fact is, the story works in any business because the basic story of frustration and failure, persistence and redemption is one most of us understand or have lived through. Over time I grew bored with my own story, thinking it too far in the past to be meaningful to my audience. I shorted the story, left out key details and glossed over the jokes and the punch lines. This proved to be a huge mistake. While I had grown tired of the story, my audience had not and leaving out that vital connection at the start meant less of a bond with them.

I worried about telling the same story and jokes to people who came back a second or third time to a seminar. But they were waiting for them like you wait for your favorite rock band to play their big hits in a concert. Rather than moving on from your story, you should do all you can to protect it, nurture it, and add details and emotion to it. This book will show you how to put together your story and convey it to others. Your story is the bedrock of your fame. Get it it right and stick to it! It will attract others and build your success.

All I ever wanted to be was golf pro, but one small detail held me back from a career on the PGA Tour: lack of talent. I quit school at 15, the year my parents moved from England to Scotland. I stayed in a small 15-foot caravan (trailer) in the field next to Lilleshall Hall golf club. There, for the next three years, I played golf from dawn to dusk, hitting 500 balls and playing 63 holes every day it was light enough to do so. I got down to scratch (par golf) but still needed to be much better. When I turned 18 I asked my parents for a ticket to America, and the day before Thanksgiving in 1980, I landed in Washington DC where my dad had a college friend. I was mainly making the move for better weather and playing conditions, but in December Washington, DC, did not fit that bill. So, I hitched a ride to Florida. There I got a walk-on golf scholarship at Palm Beach College and a job at a golf club. After two years I decided I did not have the game to play PGA Tour-caliber golf. As fate would have it, I ended up giving a golf lesson to a karate master and soon after was accidentally thrust into a new career in the martial arts world.

In 1987 I bought a small karate school in Irvine, California, with no money down. The first month, the business lost $1,000; the second month, it lost $1,000.

At that point I was running my school the same way every other karate school operated. I ran ads in the local paper that looked exactly like the ads all my competitors were running. What I didn't know then was that all those ads were terrible to begin with. When I copied them and made alterations, I only made them worse. I never really questioned if there was a better way. I was, as Henry David Thoreau so aptly put it, "Living a life of quiet desperation!" Sure, the phone rang occasionally or someone walked in with a coupon, but the weeks came and went with little real progress and zero profits.

Finally, I sat down with a yellow pad and began some serious soul searching. First, I asked myself what I was doing wrong. Second, and perhaps most important, I wondered what I was going to do about it. The simple act of writing questions down on paper can bring amazing clarity. I quickly realized (surprise, surprise) that the first thing I needed was paying customers. I also realized that since the phone wasn't ringing, my ads were not working.

Please understand what kind of "quantum leap" thinking was going on at this point. Most business owners or managers don't ever consider such simple issues. Instead, they are more likely to subscribe to the Professor Slutsky theory.

The Professor Slutsky Theory

For those of you not familiar with the good Professor Slutsky's work, allow me to digress a moment. The noted professor did pioneer work with frogs. He started his experiments with a perfectly healthy frog. He yelled "jump" until the frog moved. He then measured the leap. Then, under anesthesia (in the most humane way possible), he amputated one of the frog's front legs and repeated the "jump" experiment. After measuring again, he amputated the frog's other front leg, yelled "jump" and measured the leaps, which, as you can guess, were decreasing in length. The frog's back left leg was cut off and again the professor yelled "jump." The frog's wobbly attempt was duly measured, whereupon the final leg was removed. The professor yelled "jump" once more but the frog did not respond. Professor Slutsky concluded that, "After amputation of all four legs...the frog became deaf."

I mention this story because whenever marketing doesn't work, most business owners immediately point to the medium rather than the marketing itself. The newspaper doesn't work, TV doesn't work, radio doesn't work, the website doesn't work, and social media is just worthless hype!

Rarely if ever do they consider the simple fact that their marketing is at fault!

EUREKA!

I came to that exact realization one December morning in late 1987. What followed was a decision that changed my life forever. After acknowledging that I didn't really know the first thing about marketing, I rushed to the local bookstore and bought all eight of their marketing books. The first was David Ogilvy's classic Ogilvy on Advertising. I was amazed to learn how changing a simple headline could produce a 500 percent increase in response...how adding a picture of scissors next to a coupon could increase redemption by up to 35 percent...how reverse type (white letters on black) sharply decreases readership, and so on. Before I finished the second book, I ordered twenty more books! I was like a man possessed...highlighting, underlining, and taking notes for 30 straight days. All through the Christmas holiday I soaked up marketing information like a sponge.

Up until then, all the ads that I had seen for karate schools were pictures of people flying through the air and kicking somebody in the face. What I didn't realize was that 80 percent of the world gravitates towards the negative. So when most people looked at these ads, they saw themselves as the one getting kicked! Instead of running in to sign up for karate, most ran the other way!

After reading the books, I designed some new ads. I began putting pictures of smiling women and children in the ads. I listed the benefits and changed the headlines to Build Your Child's Confidence and Build Your Self-Esteem. I changed the whole focus of my advertising to let people know that the martial arts were fun!

BINGO!

The phone rang off the hook. I signed up 30 new students in a single month as opposed to the five I typically signed up! I was ecstatic but realized there was still work to be done. If I could get such a massive increase in response just by studying the gurus of marketing, perhaps I could capitalize on these leads even more by improving my sales skills. I purchased tapes from the likes of Dale Carnegie, Tom Hopkins, Joe Girard, and Zig Ziglar.

Suddenly, instead of closing two out of ten leads, I was closing eight out of ten and it didn't cost me a dime more to do it!

Next, I turned my attention to customer retention, newsletters, thank-you cards, and follow up. I adopted the tactics I found in books like Carl Sewall's Customers for Life. By the end of the year, customers were staying an average of six months instead of three!

Nationwide franchise from scratch in just six years!

At 28 years of age, in my second year in business, I walked out of a 1,148 square foot karate school in a suburban strip mall with $128,000 in my pocket-a net gain of $121,000 over my previous year's income. And this was in the 1980s.

Six years later, I had 156 franchise schools, plus 275 affiliates nationwide. Later I went on to found a successful ad agency specializing in golf and resort marketing.

Elon Musk's story is that of a visionary business tycoon.

STORY ANGLES

There are lots of angles on your story you could choose to take that might fit with your life experiences.

Whichever angle you choose start with the long version that covers everything like a magazine feature story then, create a one-page versions a half-page version and a paragraph version to use in different circumstances.

Here are a few examples:

1. The Business Tycoon, - Jeff Bezos, Elon Musk
2. The Eccentric Entrepreneur - Richard Branson
3. The Researcher - Malcolm Gladwell
4. The Puppet Master - Henry Kissinger, Malcolm Forbes
5. The Self-Made Man/Woman - Oprah
6. The Evangelist - Pat Parelli, Bobby Clampett, Martin Luther King
7. The Contrarian - Winston Churchill, Boris Johnson
8. The Angry Man - Jim Cramer
9. The Boy Genius - Bill Gates, Mozart, Tiger Woods
10. The Optimist - Ronald Reagan
11. The Creative Genius - Madonna, Bowie, Steve Jobs
12. The Outcast - Eminem
13. The Common Man - Bruce Springsteen
14. The Futurist - Jeremy Gutsche
15. The Intellect - Barack Obama
16. The Advocate - Richard Simmons, Suze Orman
17. The Fixer - Lee Iacocca
18. The Maximizer - Jack Welch
19. The Mad Scientist - Dave Pelz, (world's highest paid golf instructor.)
20. The Adventurer - Buffalo Bill, Evel Knievel

Pick a story angle that suits your profession and tell it using the 10-step formula I shared with you in as much detail as possible first. Then go back and edit so you have versions of different lengths for use in different situations.

SUMMARY

The more famous you are in your profession, niche or geographic location the more opportunities will come your way. The more respect and recognition you will gain from you peers and the more money you will make. Get famous and business comes to you!

Great stories are at the heart of every great brand including yours. They always include key elements like where you are from, the problem that needs solving and the Ah Ha moment when you knew this path was for you. This discovery is followed by the big dream you set out to accomplish. You will detail some of the many challenges you faced along the way before your talent, creativity and persistence win through and finally forge the successful person you are today!

Unable to catch his break, Harrison Ford took up carpentry to pay the bills before ultimately landing the role of beloved smuggler Han Solo in *Star Wars*.

ACTION PLAN

Your back story is a critical part of your fame formula and it's far better that you write it than let some random reporter or blogger do it for you.

- Where are you from?
- What is your social, economic, religious, emotional background?
- How did your early life, military service or corporate position impact your thinking?
- Where does your motivation, your passion, come from?
- What was your big goal or dream?
- How did you get into your current profession?
- Why is it important to you?
- What was your aha moment?
- What obstacles have you had to overcome?
- Who tried to stop you or got in your way?
- Detail some of the challenges and how you conquered them?
- Who helped or mentored you?
- Where do you go from here?
- Write, read, edit, read again, rewrite.

Continue with this process until you get this right. As your fame grows, this story will be retold a thousand times. Make sure it's the story you want told!

"Luck is the residue of design." - **Branch Rickey**

2

CLAIMING YOUR POSITION & PUTTING "LUCK" ON YOUR SIDE!

It would be foolish to pretend that luck does not play a part in the attainment of fame for some people. While the "will of the gods," is fickle you can, through planning and persistence, stack the cards of fate in your favor. You often hear people say:

"The main way to get ahead in life is to meet the right people."

"You have to be in the right place at the right time."

"You have to be very lucky to get promoted, become famous or acquire wealth."

In fact, many people feel they have very little control over the events in their lives. They feel fate has dealt them a losing hand and that, in effect, luck is simply not on their side. Luck to these people is a strange and mystic phenomenon that avoids them like the plague and bestows itself on others. This, of course, is just not true. **There are things beyond your control, but 95% of luck lies directly in your hands.**

WHAT IS LUCK?

The definition of luck as preparation meeting opportunity goes back at least 2000 years to the Roman philosopher Seneca. More modern research has been done by Spanish professors and businessmen Alex Rovira and Fernando Trias de Bes. Their book *Good Luck: Create the Conditions for Success in Life & Business,* outlines **five keys successful people have used to creating business luck:**

Taking responsibility for your own actions. Sure, you can't control everything, but feeling responsible changes your actions and encourages you to analyze and look for new actions.

Learning from mistakes. Forget feelings of failure. Mistakes give you the most opportunity to learn. When things go well you hardly notice the details. Mistakes focus your attention and encourage you to try new things. Edison and his light bulb is the classic example of 1000 "mistakes" plus persistence leading to a breakthrough.

Perseverance and quickness. Notice that Edison also persevered. But don't add each task to your to-do list. Do them immediately whenever possible. The trick is to move fast so you don't lose track of your learning and you keep your momentum.

Two parts of confidence. Self-confidence helps in most things. But confidence or trust in others is often overlooked. This helps build your network and inspires others to do their best. Most of your opportunities will involve others throughout the process.

Cooperation. Trust in others leads to a solid network of work colleagues and friends, which, in turn, provides more resources to carry out projects. Many people have ideas and would like to see them developed, but few people follow through. You can help them be part of your success.

Luck, in short, is the crossroads where planning meets opportunity.

If you miss an important event because your car develops a flat tire en route is it bad luck? Not if you've been driving around on bald tires without a spare for six weeks. Not if you didn't leave early enough to get a taxi or hitch a ride in case of an emergency. Not if you have no money in your pocket to pay a cab. In these cases it is just poor planning and judgment, not bad luck.

If you have developed no plan, have set forth no strategies complete with back-up plans, and have taken no positive action to move toward your goals, it's very unlikely that you will meet opportunity. Inaction and a lack of planning do nothing to improve your chances of being **lucky**. If, on the other hand, you have planned and taken action towards your goals, then your chances of being lucky are greatly enhanced.

SOME THINGS IN LIFE ARE JUST LUCKY

South African-born actress, Charlize Theron won a best actress Academy Award for her portrayal of serial killer Aileen Wuornos in the 2003 film Monster. She's experienced quite a lot of drama in her own life. Her mother shot and killed her abusive, alcoholic father in self-defense. Theron was bullied as a teen and never finished high school. Her study with the Joffrey Ballet ended after a knee injury. At 19 she headed to Hollywood with only a suitcase. She was living in a gross, pay-by-the-hour hotel, trying to survive on the paychecks she had received from modeling in New York. One day, she was trying to cash her very last check, but the bank teller wouldn't accept it because it was from out of state. From there, things got very heated.

In an interview with Oprah, Theron said, "I'm like, 'It's survival, people.' If I didn't cash that check, I wouldn't have had a place to sleep that night. I said to the teller, 'You don't understand-please!' I was begging and pleading, and a gentleman came over and tried to help." It turned out that the helpful man was also a talent agent, and he offered to represent her. John Crosby organized acting classes for Theron. Within months she made her acting debut in Children of the Corn III.

Oprah Winfrey herself didn't get a lucky start in life. She was born into poverty in rural Mississippi to a teenage single mother and later raised in an inner-city Milwaukee neighborhood. She has stated that she was molested during her childhood and early teens and became pregnant at 14; her son died in infancy.

Oprah's lucky break came at 17, when a Nashville, Tennessee, radio station chose her as its entry in a local beauty pageant based on her spunk during a radio interview. "I was the only Negro in a pageant of all red-haired girls, and it's the 'Miss Fire Prevention' contest. So the Lord knows, I'm not going to win. So I was very relaxed about it. I thought, 'Well, I got a new gown, and this is

great," she told the Academy of Achievement. When asked about her career aspirations, Winfrey shocked the crowd again by saying she hoped to become a broadcast journalist. When she returned to the radio station to receive her Longines watch, it was Winfrey's turn to be surprised - they offered her a job. By 19 she began co-anchoring the local evening news. Her emotional, ad-lib delivery eventually got her transferred to the daytime talk show arena. After boosting a third-rated, local Chicago talk show to first place, she launched her own production company and became internationally syndicated.

In his book, *How to Get Rich*, billionaire British entrepreneur Felix Dennis, founder of Maxim magazine and current publisher of MacUser, The Week, and many other publications, tells how luck in timing jump started his career. After seeing some Kung Fu movies, he and a friend, both journalism students in their early twenties, decided to write a biography of Bruce Lee. They talked someone in their local pub into lending them the plane fare and flew from London to Hong Kong. Having no idea where he lived they eventually found his address and showed up at his apartment unannounced! He graciously let them in and talked to them for several hours.

They returned to London and started writing. They tried to sell their manuscript, a 95-page book titled Bruce Lee, King of Kung-Fu.

The two young and unpublished authors had no luck finding a publisher for their yet unfinished work and were turned down by over twenty.

Then came an amazing twist of fortune -- or misfortune --depending on your point of view: Bruce Lee died.

The book from two unknown authors became the number-one best-selling book in the world a few days after its publication. Dennis went on to become a billionaire.

There was an amazing amount of good fortune involved in this event: the timing, someone lending them the money for the tickets, finding Bruce's apartment at all, then being let in and hosted for several hours. Still had Dennis and his friend not come up with the idea and flown

to Hong Kong you can be sure his chances of eventually becoming a billionaire would have dropped significantly!

Had Oprah not entered the beauty contest, or Theron not moved to LA, neither would have had the "lucky" encounter that changed their lives!

They all put themselves in places where opportunity could come along, PLUS they acted on their opportunities.

LUCKY PLAYER?

You are unlikely to get really lucky, so a far better approach is that of golfer Gary Player. When Gary Player arrived in the United States in the late 1950s, he was already becoming known as a "world traveler." His schedule was at first limited; nevertheless, he quickly made an impression on many of the home-grown pros, and developed a reputation among them as a "lucky" golfer. As is common when faced with someone who is more successful, many of the regular Tour players decided Player was winning because he was luckier than they were. (Incidentally, this same excuse would also be hung around the neck of Steve Ballesteros when he burst upon the tournament golf scene.)

Rumors of Player's luck were circulating in the clubhouse after he had won a PGA tournament and a less than tactful reporter asked him to comment on the matter. He summed up his feelings about luck by paraphrasing Thomas Jefferson. **"Sure, I'm lucky," he told the journalist, "and the more I practice, the luckier I get."**

THE KEYS TO IMPROVING YOUR LUCK

Make no mistake about it, the keys to dramatically improving your "luck" are planning, practice, persistence and positive action. Other pro golfers of the day were reluctant to admit, even to themselves, that Gary Player practiced harder than they, hitting thousands more balls as he grooved and fine-tuned his swing. Or that he showed up before dawn and stayed after dusk, then went to bed early, avoiding parties and hangovers. They also ignored the fact that he compensated for his small stature with a rigorous program of exercises and muscle building, long before it became fashionable to do so. Player was almost fanatical about his diet, his body and his physical conditioning, all with the objective of playing better golf. Other pros dismissed his fine performance as "lucky" because it was more comfortable than facing the cold, hard truth. He was better than most of them because he worked harder and tried harder.

HE GOT LUCKY

People are no different today than they were forty years ago. Ask a struggling musician how rock star Bruce Springsteen became so big that, in the music business, he is now simply referred to as **The Boss.** Most will dismiss any further thought on the subject with a quick, "Well, his music is good, but he just got lucky." Ask a writer of novels, trying to make it to the top of his craft, how Stephen King became such a huge success, and the majority will quickly answer with that simple word again -- **luck.**

Ask a corporate vice-president why he or she was passed over for promotion, and they will quickly rationalize that so and so was simply **lucky** because of their connections. Rarely does it occur to ask why the competitor had inside connections and they did not. It is simply easier to put it down to luck, or the lack of it, than to admit failure to develop contacts was the real reason the opportunity was lost. Once you realize and accept the simple fact that you can make your own luck, you can improve your path to fame. In fact, your eyes will suddenly be opened to a host of different ways in which you can accomplish this on an everyday basis.

BE IN THE RIGHT PLACE AT THE RIGHT TIME

In coastal California, every teenager knows if you want to meet girls, you go to the beach. But let's suppose you have a great script for a movie, then where do you go? If you want to meet movie people, you hang out in the Polo Lounge at The Beverly Hills Hotel. That doesn't mean that by hanging out there for a week you are going to meet Stephen Spielberg, but if you eat lunch there once a week, take a drink at the bar, make friends with the bartender and make it one of your regular hangouts, sooner or later you are going to meet someone who will look at your script or at least knows someone else who will. *Hollywood Reporter* lists 25 hot spots to meet agents and producers. *Business Insider* lists hots spots for NYC journalists "*Forbes* employees like to hang out at El Cantinero, a tequila bar on University Place that's really, really cheap. *New York Magazine* staff goes for Toad Hall on Grand St."

Hollywood super-agent and former head of Disney, Michael Ovitz, worked as a tour guide at Universal studios in his teens. He went in early and stayed late every day roaming the 400-acre lot from end to end soaking up everything he could about the movie business.

Stephen Spielberg's first practical exposure to the workings of Hollywood studios came in a similar fashion when the summers just before and after he graduated from high school, he apprenticed at Universal Studios as an unpaid assistant in the studio's television department.

Find out where the movers and shakers in your target field hang out, and then make their place your place. Use Google, LinkedIn and Facebook. Ask friends, coworkers, secretaries, and competitors. Find out something personal about the people you need to meet. Read trade blogs and local news to determine their interests. Play Sherlock Holmes with their hobbies, recreations, and hangouts. Once you have discovered what you need to know, take the direct action that gives you the opportunity to cross their paths in a business or social situation. You'll at least meet someone who knows someone who can move you ahead. Here is a simple and practical example of this type of **luck** in action. Recently while chatting with a neighbor, I discovered that a famous rock-star manager had moved into the community in which I live. Eager to meet him, I started to walk my dogs down the street on which he had bought a home. After walking my dogs down the same route for over four weeks, I eventually bumped into him at the small lake which was the walk's turn-around point. As luck would have it, he too had a dog who loved to swim in the lake. As the dogs played in the water, I got the chance to meet this person and talk with him for twenty minutes. I can now count this powerful person among my friends, all because of a not-so-chance meeting while I walked my dogs.

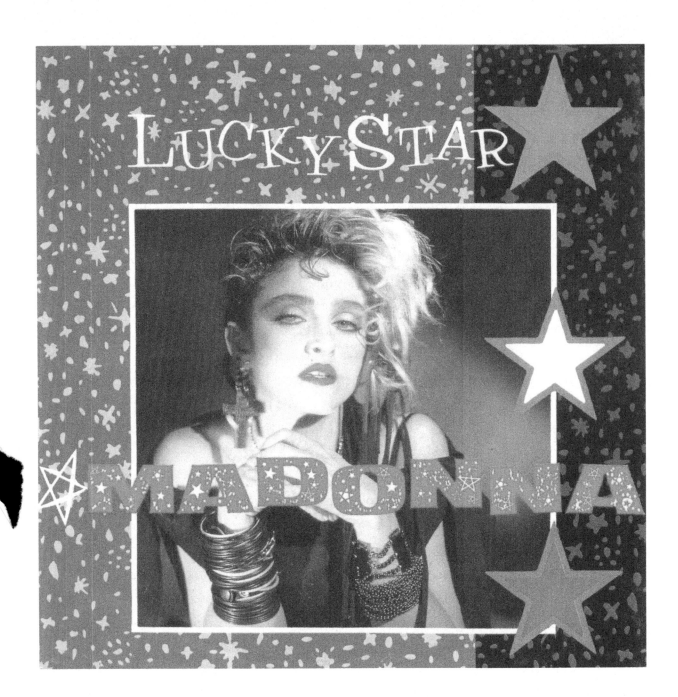

KEEP WORKING IT

On her way to stardom Madonna moved to New York city to dance and suffered through a series of low-paying jobs, including counter help at Dunkin' Donuts, coat-check at the Russian Tea Room and nude modeling. She once said of the move to NYC, "It was the first time I'd ever taken a plane, the first time I'd ever gotten a taxi cab. I came here with $35 in my pocket. It was the bravest thing I'd ever done."

After collaborating with bands, The Breakfast Club and Emmy, she eventually decided to go solo and sent demos to all the record labels in New York City. She was rejected by all, including

CHARITY WORK PAYS OFF TWICE

Another great way to mingle with the type of people you want to meet is by involving yourself in charitable work. The great thing about doing charity work is that it pays off twice. First, it gives you the great feeling of having helped a good cause, and second, it can help you further your own personal goals. I do not know of one famous or influential person who is not involved in doing some work for charity. Find out in which charities the people you need to meet are involved.

TALK TO STRANGERS, MAKE THEM YOUR FRIENDS

The average person knows approximately two hundred to two hundred and fifty people. Famous people know four or five times that amount. Research by Stanley Milgram showed that most of us are only six degrees of separation, on a friendly basis, with anyone.

Other research on Facebook and elsewhere suggests that the links may be less than four in the United States. This means that everyone you talk with could put you in touch with someone who knows someone who is the type of person you're looking for. This idea has been around long enough that they even made a movie with the name.

I always make a point of starting a conversation immediately when I come into direct contact with a new person. As they sit down next to me, I ask, "What is that book you have?" "Is that author good?" or some other question that will engage the person in conversation. "What a nice watch you have. What make is it?" Ask any question that is likely to get the person to begin speaking and interacting with you.

Whatever method you use to break the ice, make it your habit to break the ice first. Often people are shy or feel awkward with strangers. It is up to you to take the lead by making the first move and then making them feel comfortable with you. You will be amazed by the many interesting and potentially useful people you will meet in the most unlikely places -- if you only make the effort. Try to be outgoing. The worst thing that can happen is that someone may not want to talk. But the chances are they will talk and be glad you made the effort to break the ice.

You may be shy too, but if you really want to succeed you can overcome your own shyness in small ways. For instance, most people like to talk about themselves so you can learn to use a few simple openings to get the talk started. Every time you meet or engage in conversation you increase your chances of becoming lucky. Every time you go to a charity event, social function, business club, or simply talk to the person next to you in line at the post office, you are increasing your chances of meeting that person who can be a step in helping you reach your goals. Meeting new people and talking with them is also one of the main ways to discover new opportunities. Make it a point to start today and see how many new people you can meet this week, this month, and this year.

TAKE LUCKY ACTION

Americans spend over 200 million dollars a year on amulets and good luck charms. While that's great for the economy, it makes you wonder whether people think they can control their own destinies. The simplest part of improving your luck is to take care of the little things of everyday life over which you have control. These are the mundane tasks that build up and contribute to your **bad luck** over time if you do not take care of them. When they are taken care of, they are never mentioned as **good luck**. In fact, they are never mentioned at all.

One of the most prominent themes in the ads for state lotteries is, "You can't win if you don't play," and it's true. Opportunities in business and career advancement will not come if you do not take action to invite them. It is a simple fact that the more often your band plays, the more chance you have of being discovered. The more sales calls you make, the more chances you have to sell something. The more times you go up to bat, the more chances you have to hit a home run. The people who take the most action in life to move forward are the people who are designated by others as the **luckiest**. The odds, of course, are simply on their side. **Lucky** people are not afraid of failure because they know each time they fail, the odds are irrevocably increased in their favor.

Lucky people are persistent people, and persistent people are lucky.

CLAIMING YOUR POSITION

Now that you see that the element of luck can be used to your advantage, you must now state your claim. Exactly what do you want to be famous for and how famous do you want to be? What position do you want to hold in the minds of your fans, customers or clients? The clearer you are on what you want to be known as, the easier it will be to line up the tools behind that goal to make it happen. You may want to be the best lawyer, realtor, salesperson, accountant, investment advisor, doctor, instructor, band, expert, or specific business. How far must your fame reach to be effective in helping you reach your goals in your company, town, city, county, state, country or world? Whatever your answer, it all starts with claiming your position.

This position might be your dream, goal, vision, creed, unique selling proposition, or a combination all of these things. It has to be something you can believe in and convey your passion about to others.

THE GREATEST

There were lots of great fighters before Mohamed Ali and lots of famous champions. None came close to achieving the fame Ali did because none understood the elements of fame like he did. Asked in a 1975 Playboy interview why he chose "The Greatest," Ali replied: "I'm the most talked-about, most publicized, the most famous, and the most colorful fighter in history. I'm the fastest heavyweight-with feet and hands-who ever lived. Besides that, I'm the onliest poet laureate boxing's ever had. One other thing, too: If you look at pictures of all the former champions you know in a flash that I'm the best-looking champion in history. It all adds up to being The Greatest, don't it?"

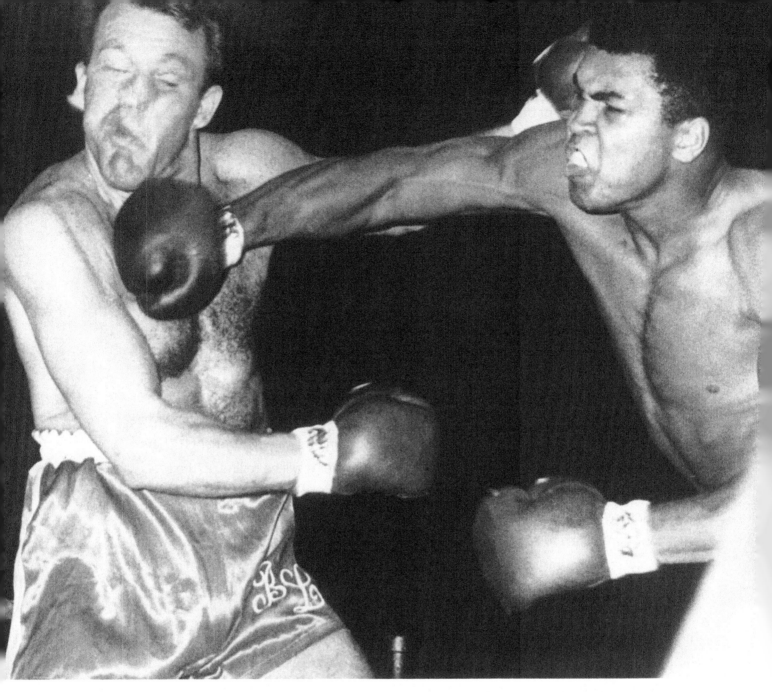

"It ain't bragging if it's true" - **Muhammad Ali**

THE FAMOUS ARE RARELY BASHFUL

In the seminars I do for golf teaching professionals, I always ask the question "Who's the best teacher in the room?" Everyone looks around the room nervously, there are a few giggles. Sometimes someone offers up a name of someone else, usually not someone in the room. Only once in twenty years has someone piped up and said, "I am" and it was a lady pro, Lucinda Davis, who said "I am the best lady teacher in here." Of course she was the only female in the room, but I still admired her chutzpah.

"A man has to have goals - for a day, for a lifetime. Mine was to have people say, 'There goes Ted Williams, the greatest hitter who ever lived.'" - **Ted Williams**

Which reminds me of a little ditty:

He with something good to sell
Who yells his message down the well
Is not as apt to get the dollars
As he who climbs the tree and hollers.

Fame is driven by a passion for a cause, a community, a political agenda, a belief system or a dream. A very big dream. Little dreams have no capacity to stir men's blood. That dream, goal, mission, belief -- whatever you want to call it -- must be encapsulated into your creed, a modus operandi that customers, clients, coworkers, fans and followers can quickly and easily grasp and buy into!

Baseball legend, Ted Williams had a creed, "A man has to have goals - for a day, for a lifetime. Mine was to have people say, "There goes Ted Williams, the greatest hitter who ever lived."

Henry Ford wanted everyone to be able to afford one of his cars.

When the Beatles ceased to exist in 1970, the title of "World's Greatest Rock 'n' Roll Band" fell with very little dispute to the Rolling Stones, who by then were at such a creative peak that they might have challenged the Fab Four for the title anyway. It's a title the one-time "anti-Beatles" haven't relinquished since. Not only have the Stones been the greatest rock band in the world for more than 40 years, but they have been a functioning rock 'n' roll unit for more than 50, the longest run in musical history.

Evel Knievel wanted to be the world's #1 daredevil.

Mega preacher, Joel Osteen, preaches a gospel of prosperity, of inclusion, love, health and positive thinking, not the old fire and brimstone sermons where most of us are destined for hell.
Bill Gates in his role as a philanthropic giant wants to eradicate common diseases from Third World countries.

Elon Musk wants to colonize Mars and save our planet (overachiever).

Churchill's creed was victory...."Victory at all costs!"

Orville and Wilbur Wright had a dream…"To fly."

Martin Luther King had a dream…"A dream that all men would be judged by their character…not their skin color."

Pat Parelli is the world's leading expert in natural horsemanship, a term he coined himself.

Anthony Robbins is the world's top life coach, or at least the highest paid!

Renee Grant-Williams is the #1 Best Vocal Coach in the World.

Laura Wasser, is Hollywood's celebrity divorce lawyer representing such stars as, Johnny Depp, Angelina Jolie, Britney Spears, multiple Kardashians, top athletes, and countless other high-profile clients.

Being the best hotel operator, cook, real estate agent, chiropractor, instructor, coach, preacher, band or attorney in your town, county or state may be just as motivating to you, at least for now…

Everyone wants to be part of something bigger

Steve Jobs wanted to change the world by giving everyone access to technology. When Jobs urged John Scully to leave Pepsi and take over a young company called Apple Computer, (a decision he famously came to regret) it is said that he offered one final argument. It was, "John, do you really want to sell sugared water the rest of your life or do you want to make a difference?" The creed is what makes the difference.

I'D LIKE TO BUY THE WORLD A COKE

One man's discard, however, can be another man's creed. Robert Woodruff, who became president of Coca-Cola in 1923, was perfectly happy selling "sugared water," and stated that before he died that he wanted every man, women and child on earth to have tasted Coca Cola. When they ran the classic 1970s ad, "I'd like to buy the world a Coke," it wasn't just some cute ad campaign dreamed up by the folks on Madison Avenue. They actually meant it and had been living the creed for fifty years or more.

The Secret to Becoming the Leading Expert in Your Market Whether that Market is Your Town, Industry or the World!

At the time I wrote my first book in 1990 I was oblivious to what anyone in the martial arts industry beyond my small circle of local schools was doing. All I knew was that I was making two or three times what they were. I didn't know there were huge schools on the East Coast, billing companies that offered advice, and numerous large and powerful sanctioning organizations. All I knew was that I was more financially successful at running a martial arts school than anyone I had ever met. So I decided to write a book about how to run a successful school.

A year later when I finally published it as a manual in a three-ring binder, I billed myself as the world's leading expert on how to run a martial arts school. People all across the country came out of the woodwork crying foul. They had been in business 20 years. They made more money than I did. They were more successful than I was. They knew Chuck Norris, Bruce Lee, or Jackie Chan. Who the hell did I think I was? But it didn't matter.

I had the only book ever published at that time on how to run a martial arts school. Two leading magazines ran feature articles on me and the book. A martial arts production company filmed 12 videos on how I ran my school. A major supply company started selling the book and videos, so within a matter of months I was the de facto leader in the martial arts business. Amazingly Chuck Norris eventually hired me to help him with a marketing project!

A decade later I did the very same thing in the golf industry with identical, successful results. I won by default just as in the martial arts business since no one in the golf industry was claiming the title. **"World's leading expert on golf marketing."**

Perhaps I was overbold at first, but over the next five years I made the claim a reality that would be hard for my most ardent critic to dispute.

You too can be the leader in your market in sixty seconds or less by simply announcing that fact to the world.

You do not gain fame by being meek, humble, quiet, bashful or modest!

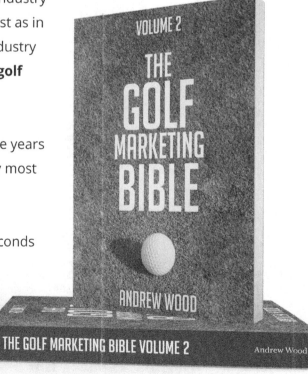

JOE GIRARD, WORLD'S GREATEST SALESMEN

Joe Girard decided early that if he was going to sell cars for a living he was going to be the world's greatest salesman, a status he quickly reached. His claim to fame was backed up for over forty years by The Guinness Book of World Records. Just how good a salesman was Girard?

In the period between 1963 and 1977:

- He sold more than 13,000 vehicles, an average of six cars per day.
- On his best day, he sold 18 vehicles.
- His best month, he sold 174.
- In his best year, he sold 1,425.
- By himself, Joe Girard has sold more cars than 95 percent of all dealers in North America.
- To make his feat even more incredible, he sold them at retail - one vehicle at a time.

Joe had the spark to overcome his humble beginnings in the Detroit's depression-era slums, the words of an abusive father, and the failure of a home construction business. "This is what made Joe Girard," said Girard. "Every day was a challenge. The more people can use things that aren't good as an advantage toward their life, they will do better."

The bankruptcy of Girard's construction business in 1962 led to his automotive career. He got a foreclosure notice for his house, and he had no car, no groceries and no money. Broke and out of work with a wife and two children to support, Girard got on a bus looking for work. When the bus doors opened, he stepped off in front of a big Chevrolet dealership. Girard begged the manager for a job. He spent that first day calling everyone he knew. At 8:30 that night, with all the other salesmen gone, a customer walked through the door. Ninety minutes later he had sold his first car.

He borrowed $10 from his manager to buy groceries and sold 18 cars during his second month on the job. But the owner fired him after complaints from other salesmen that there were not enough leads to go around. Girard ended up at Merollis Chevrolet in suburban Detroit and set sales records year after year.

The Funeral That Changed His Approach to Sales

It was around this time that he attended a funeral. It was a Catholic funeral and mass cards were given out to all those in attendance. Girard asked the funeral director how he knew how many mass cards to have printed up for each funeral. The funeral director told Girard that the number of people attending a funeral always seems to average out to 250. So that's how many he prints up each time. This became his ethos the Law of 250.

Girard never let go of being fired by the first dealership! Every year he mailed a copy of his W-2 to his old boss, with a note at the bottom telling him, "You fired the wrong guy." After his old boss died, Girard says he even took a W-2 to the cemetery and buried it atop the man's casket. The man could hold a grudge. But he also knew how to treat people well.

Long before computers or customer relationship management systems, Girard kept a file listing personal information about each customer - such as the names of their children, what they did for a living, their birthdays, their kids' birthdays, and so forth. He'd use that information to personalize his conversations with them. He also sent them non-sales notes or cards every month. He sincerely cared about people and made them feel so special they couldn't wait to recommend him to a friend or relative.

He took mechanics at the dealership out to an Italian dinner once a month so they always took good care of his customers and even paid for some parts on cars that were out of warranty. He paid fees to local bartenders, hairdressers, and waitresses for sales leads. But most of all he was famous for customer referrals.

Girard quit the car business in 1978 and went on to a successful career as an author and motivational speaker. "I never sold a car in my life," Girard said. "I sold a Girard."

Recently a salesman in Detroit claimed to have beat his single year record but he'll have a long way to go to keep up that pace for another decade as Joe did!

YOU MUST CLAIM YOUR POSITION

Being one of the top realtors, doctors, attorneys, instructors, salespeople, bands or mangers in town, is not nearly as strong a position as being the number one of any particular profession in town!

Can you claim to be the best at something in your town, county, or state? There are many specific ways that you can be the "best." You can take an original position that stands out because it is odd. Like the "happy mortician, dentist or lawyer" Something unexpectedly out of the norm.

Here are some possibilities:

- Can you claim to be the youngest, the most experienced, or have you performed the most operations, cases or claims?
- Can you claim the highest monetary volume of something?
- Best with a certain type of client/customer?
- The best network of contacts for your clients?
- Best with a specific problem?
- The way you provide services?
- Your image or style?
- The most booked acts?

- Or failing a current claim, make a future claim that you will be #1, a star or best-seller.
- Maybe you are a millionaire in training?

REPEAT, REPEAT, REPEAT

At the top of every profession in every town there is someone who has staked their claim.

If they haven't, someone else has. For better or worse they've created a position for which they are known. It is far better to decide on what your position will be early on and work towards putting everything in place to support it than to be usurped by someone else or stuck with an inferior label given to you by others.

Once you have decided on the position or creed you want, stick with it and repeat it consistently. Do not flip flop or allow others to change it; stick with it!

Although I do it tongue in cheek, when people introduce me as a "marketing guru or expert," I am always quick to correct them with the words...

"It's Marketing Legend not guru, I've got to keep my branding consistent."

Earlier in my career people would sometimes challenge me with comments like; "Marketing legend... a legend in your own mind?" I would smile and say, "Well, you've got to start somewhere." and they would always smile and agree.

Once a position has been claimed, we must now look at the blueprint you will need to back up this bold claim and turn it into a reality. There are 12 keys to the DNA of fame and we will cover each in detail.

But first, let's look at some practical examples of the entire road map.

HOW DID PAT PARELLI, A RETIRED RODEO COWBOY, BECOME THE WORLD'S MOST FAMOUS HORSE TRAINER?

In the first chapter we looked at the Parelli creation story. Now let's look at how Parelli's success fits neatly into our 12 key pieces of the fame DNA code.

1. Great Creation Story

Retired Rodeo cowboy, rodeo rookie of the year 1979, and in the Rodeo Hall of Fame. After a decade in rodeo he was getting too old for rodeo, what should he do next? Train horses of course but in a way that had never been done before.

2. Position - Passion for a Cause

Pat did not like the way horses were being trained; many techniques are abusive to the horse. Pat became an evangelist for the horse; his goal nothing short of changing the world, or at least how the world trains horses.

3. Sounds and Sacred Words

Picks a descriptive name for his mission. Natural Horsemanship - training horses without the use of mechanical aids in their mouth. Backs it up with a bunch of sayings known as Parelli - isms the most iconic of which is "keep it natural" or "Love, language and leadership."

4. Carefully Crafted Signature Cowboy Look

Pat is more cowboy than the Marlboro man with his cattleman's cowboy hat, Wrangler jeans, boots and mustache. He eats steak, drinks whiskey and of course has a big truck.

5. Fabulous Pictures and Videos

Professional photography and video throughout his career, often sparing no expense to make it perfect when good enough would have done!

6. Key Ritual and Icons

The Parelli logo. Parelli saddles, soft rope halters, carrot stick and in specific sizes 12,22,45, foot ropes that are indigenous to Parelli. The Savvy club connects Parelli fans across the globe while the annual Savvy summit attracts them to Pagosa Springs, Colorado. Parelli plays his guitar by the fire and tells stories at night during clinics.

7. Superb Communication

First with live seminars, then a newsletter, email and eventually his own magazine, Parelli's message travel far and wide. He was on Horse TV frequently and has a huge following on YouTube, Facebook and through his own creation, the Savvy Club.

8. Total Confidence and Competence

Pat displays world-class confidence and competence which he backs with an avowed commitment to lifelong learning. Pat is also quick to praise his early mentors including Ray Hunt and Tom Dorrance.

9. Legendary Charisma

Pat has charisma in spades; he's the Marlboro man on steroids because he has all the previous DNA making it natural to be charismatic.

10. Carefully Managed Story

He manages his own media, has professional photos, an in-house film crew and his own magazine. He has also authored three books, so you can be sure the stories he tells are good and consistent with his brand. He has been featured in over one thousand magazine articles, and has presented privately for the Queen of England, President Reagan, Tony Robbins, Gene Autry, and Tom Selleck.

11. Finding the Antagonist

Clinton Anderson and most other clinicians who use aggressive methods to train horses.

12. Perfected with Persistence

Built a grassroots movement of fans as he toured the country giving live seminars. Says Pat, "Just twenty people showed up for my first live event, but soon there were three hundred and then three thousand and eventually as many as fifteen thousand. By the time you count DVDs, YouTube, TV shows, and magazines, over twenty million people have been touched by the Natural Horsemanship movement."

As you will see as we progress through the book, these 12 key components can be found in just about every story of those who made it to the top, no matter what the industry.

SUMMARY

Luck plays a part in all success but, like most things, your luck can be improved. Few famous people get lucky entirely by accident. You must be proactive in making the right connections by hanging out in the right places. Join clubs, help charities and talk to people at every opportunity to expand your network. Then you must take action and go up to bat more often than your competitors. Never fear failure you must practice and out work them at every turn. Next, you must stake your claim to a bold position and define your territory. Protect your territory for all it's worth. Repeat your claim until you get all the tools in place to support it. Then look at the 12 parts of DNA that make up fame and start to formulate your plan.

Speilberg's back story is full of exaggeration and myth. But then again, he's the ultimate story teller!

ACTION PLAN

- How can you improve your luck?
- Are you meeting the right people?
- Are you hanging out in the right places?
- How can you put yourself in the right places more often?
- Are you constantly taking action towards your goals?
- What position will you state your claim for?
- How will you word craft it to create the right response in your audience?
- Are you the best, #1, new, different, prestigious, for this or anti that?
- What geography is important to you? Town, county, state, country, world, industry?
- How do you instill passion into your mission to motivate yourself and others to your cause?

"When you have confidence, you can have a lot of fun. And when you have fun, you can do amazing things." **- Joe Namath**

3

CONFIDENCE AND COMPETENCE: THE BEDROCK OF FAME!

Self-confidence is the foundation of all personal success. All iconic brands - such as Nike, Ferrari, Apple, and Virgin - ooze the confidence of their founders, as do superstar performers like Madonna, Beyoncé (pictured below), Patton, Cruise, Oprah, Tiger, Brady and Ronaldo.

With self-confidence, people will try new things, go to new places, and set larger and more ambitious goals. With self-confidence, you have a greater ability to be creative, to accept new challenges, and to bring opportunity into your life. When others observe your confidence in your abilities, opportunities will flow towards you as they recognize that you have the confidence to handle important or difficult situations. Self-confidence makes you become a more effective leader-of the band or the bandits-and is a prerequisite for peak performance in any field. Thus, you must be able to discern it, develop it, and inspire it in others.

In order to create the BIG opportunities needed for fame, you must take risks, sometimes huge risks. Only those armed with an ample supply of self-confidence have the capacity and intestinal fortitude for such decisions.

No one is born with confidence. Confidence-or the lack of it-it is a learned trait and, contrary to popular belief, not all famous people start out with great confidence in their abilities. Churchill, the greatest orator of the 20th century, stuttered badly as a child and took speech therapy even as an adult. During one of his early performances at the podium, he was so afraid of speaking to the crowd of people that he actually passed out.

John Wayne was also struck by stage fright and lack of confidence. As a young actor, he thought himself clumsy and could frequently be heard off camera behind a prop berating himself for his poor performance and lack of talent.

Most of his career Elvis too had crippling stage fright before a show. So did superstar singer Adele. Adele admits to being terrified of huge audiences and even vomiting on stage because she gets so nervous.

During a 1967 performance, singer Barbra Streisand forgot the lyrics to a song she was singing. She ended up taking a 30-year hiatus due to the stage fright she experienced during that performance.

Young Winston Churchill

Very often our confidence or lack of it is molded early in life. If, as a youngster you tried new things and succeeded, you gained in self-confidence. If your parents, teachers, peers or social network constantly praised your accomplishments and encouraged you to try new things, then there is little doubt you are endowed with self-confidence. If, however, your parents, coaches or peers constantly used negative motivation and told you things like:

- "That's not the way you do it."
- "Can't you do anything right?"
- "Why aren't you more like your brother or sister?"
- "You suck!"

Then this treatment most likely has had a negative effect on your self-confidence. Most parents, especially those of a few decades ago, had no idea of the power they had in shaping their children's futures based only on a few simple words. They certainly didn't mean to do a bad job. They simply treated their children the same way their parents had treated them.

CONFIDENCE AND COMPETENCE

Many a famous star has risen beyond the handicap of a negative upbringing. Winston Churchill had a very unhappy childhood, as did countless other famous people like Martin Luther King, Eminem, Rhianna and Shania Twain. Twain had a very difficult childhood. Her parents earned very little money and food was often scarce in their household. Twain did not confide her situation to school authorities, fearing they might break up the family. Her mother and stepfather's marriage was at times stormy, and from a young age, Twain witnessed violence between them. Her mother struggled with bouts of depression. In mid-1979, while her stepfather was at work, at Twain's insistence her mother drove the rest of the family 420 miles south to a Toronto homeless shelter for assistance.

Her mother returned to her husband with the children in 1981. In Timmins, Twain started singing at bars at the age of eight to try to help pay her family's bills; she often earned $20 between midnight and 1 a.m., performing for the remaining customers after the bar had finished serving. Although she expressed a dislike for singing in those bars, Twain believes that this was her own kind of performing arts school. She has said of the ordeal, "My deepest passion was music and it helped. There were moments when I thought, 'I hate this.' I hated going into bars and being with drunks. But I loved the music and so I survived." Twain wrote her first songs at the age of 10, "Is Love a Rose" and "Just Like the Storybooks", which were rhyming fairy tales. She states that the art of actually writing songs, "was very different from performing them and became progressively important" to her.

Albert Einstein was initially classified as mentally retarded, and Edison was thought to be "addled" (he was so described by one of his teachers). Even if your past experiences were negative, there is no need to despair. You can begin to recognize patterns of behavior that stem from your past and take the necessary steps to reassess your self-confidence about your personal competence levels.

THE FOUNDATION OF CONFIDENCE: COMPETENCE

The foundation of confidence in any field, from music to sports and business to science, from management to waging war, is competence. During World War II, the US Army gathered together 61 of the greatest authorities in the field of psychology and published a very special study. These authorities came from some of the most prestigious institutions in the country, including Harvard and Yale.

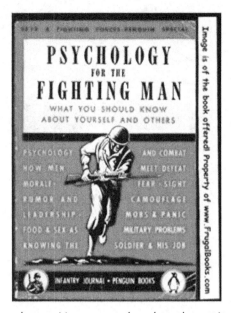

When they had finished their research, it was published under the title, *Psychology for the Fighting Man*. The study was especially unique in that it was the very first time in the history of the US Army that enlisted soldiers were asked their opinion about what factors constituted good leadership. Of the several thousand soldiers interviewed, the number one factor by frequency of response was competence. A good leader was expected to know his stuff.

While confidence stems from many areas, the first and foremost area is competence-knowing that you know as much or more about your chosen field anyone on the planet. You must develop the attitude the Japanese refer to as *Kaizen*. That means continued, never-ending improvement. You accomplish this by seeking knowledge about every facet of your industry, job, or career and anything else that might affect it. Once you have it all, you continue to seek more. As legendary basketball coach John Wooden said, "It's what you learn after you know it all that counts."

You must be committed to continued learning long after high school, college, and on-the-job training are over. Things change so fast in today's world that what you learn one week is often made redundant weeks later. Changes in laws, tax structures, robotics or Google's algorithms can wreak havoc on a business or career. Whatever your craft, seek out others with more knowledge than you. The real winners in life are those who never stop learning. They are not content to learn by osmosis; they constantly search for new information. They are not afraid to invest cash in search of knowledge, even if it's just to invite an expert in their field to join them for a cup of coffee-someone, perhaps, who can impart the essence of years and years of key experiences in just a couple of hours.

Those who have found fame know the power of imitating successful people. They seek out others who have gone before so they can learn from the mistakes of others. They also seek out and develop mentor relationships with others who can pass on to them valuable insights on a regular basis. They believe in the principle of continued improvement, not just for themselves but in all those who surround them. They take training seriously and know the value of role playing in their professions. They set aside time each day for reading and personal development. They encourage others to follow their lead and invest in the greatest asset they will ever possess-their minds!

BECOME THE EXPERT

Take it to the next level. Don't settle for competence.

As my friend Brain Tracy says, **"Get good, get better, be the best!"**

Demonstrate a measure of achievement in some field. Everyone is good at something.

In his book *Total Recall*, Arnold Schwarzenegger talks about how he excelled at sports as a child. The confidence he derived from being good at sports carried through to everything else he did in life, including body building, acting, directing and being governor of California.

Use the confidence you derive from things you do well to carry over to other aspects of your life.

Brian Tracy With Andrew Wood

As Marie Curie said, "Life is not easy for any of us. But what of that? We must above all have confidence in ourselves. We must believe that we are gifted for something, and that this thing, at whatever cost, must be attained."

READ YOUR WAY TO COMPETENCE AND FAME!

Nicknamed "Old Blood and Guts," General George S. Patton was the most famous and feared general of the twentieth century, but his life hardly started with much of a bang.

Having descended from a long line of warriors, from an early age Patton had one aim: to become a great combat commander. To him, this was not a goal but his destiny. However, there was a problem: The young Patton was a horrible student and struggled with what would today be diagnosed as dyslexia and ADHD. "I am either very lazy or very stupid or both," he said as a young man, "for it is beastly hard for me to learn and as a natural result I hate to study."

As a cadet at West Point, where he managed to finish only in the middle of his class, Patton continued to struggle with his studies, and was often be beset by an "overpowering sense of my own worthlessness." There was, he wrote, "no one in my class who so hates to be last or who tries so hard to be first and utterly fails."

Through a massive effort, Patton turned reading, and therefore learning, from a hated chore into a core passion. His library became very large and would ultimately become a key weapon in his quest for fame and fortune on the battlefield.

He dove into classics of history and was an ardent student of the Civil War, studying the lives of Lee, Grant and other famous generals. Hannibal, Caesar, Napoleon, Stonewall Jackson, Genghis Khan, Alexander, and Joan of Arc-these commanders who exhibited the qualities of self-confidence, enthusiasm, and bravery became his models, and he absorbed their genius.

Patton would also read books that offered insight into his potential enemies, or the mindsets of the people in countries in which he might end up fighting. Patton was one of the few Americans to read Lenin, Marx, the Koran, and Hitler's Mein Kampf. He also studied reports, memos, notes and the works of von Clausewitz, Churchill and other people of power and insight. Patton outread every general of his day many times over and even transported a small library with him on the battlefield. He was a studious note taker and often committed to memorizing entire chunks of text.

Patton's competence, confidence and even his image were derived from books. Said Patton, "I have read the memoirs of our enemy's generals and political leaders. I have even read his philosophers and listened to his music. I have studied in detail the accounts of every damned one of his battles. I know exactly how he will react under any given set of circumstances. He hasn't the slightest idea what I'm going to do. Therefore, when the day comes, I'm going to whip the hell out of him."

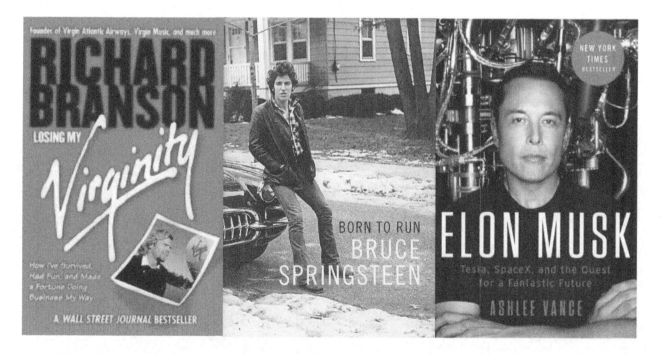

START WITH BIOGRAPHIES

Want to be a rock star, actor, golf pro or entrepreneur? Then start by reading or listening to the biographies of all those you admire who went before you.

The Stones, Beatles, Sex Pistols, Clash, Elvis, the Boss, Chill Peppers, Eminem, Drake, Beyoncé, Rhianna, Taylor Swift, Kobe and everyone in between. The business heroes, the great leaders or the sports stars. Don't skimp - only by reading in depth can you discover the magic that made them who they are. One or two key ideas gleamed from these books can make the difference to an entire career.

Although I never finished high school or college, I am one of the world's top marketing experts and the #1 expert in a couple of fields. The main way I accomplished this was simply reading. I have read over 2,000 marketing books, over 400 sales books and over 1,000 biographies. I read a book a week, every week. One easy way to help accomplish this is that I hardly ever listen to the radio in my car, 95% of the time I have an audio book playing, thanks to a life-changing bit of advice from motivational speaker Brian Tracy 30 years ago, "Go to college in your car," he said "Use your driving time to learn." I never go anywhere without a book in my hand, on my Kindle or iPhone. Every wait in line is turned into productive learning time.

Says world famous horse trainer Pat Parelli, "I did not stand out in school and was a C student at best, but when I got into business, I knew I had to be an A student to survive. I read books like *Think and Grow Rich*, *The Psychology of Winning*, and *The E Myth*, and in fact I studied personally with Michael Gerber. I developed the habit of lifelong learning later than I should have, but I never stopped once I did. I study other people's videos, webinars, and podcasts. I am friends with some amazing teachers like Tony Robbins and Cesar Millan, plus wherever I go there's always a book in my saddlebags!"

ONLINE COURSES AND VIDEOS

If you don't like reading you can watch videos or biographies on YouTube, although they never go into quite the same depth as a book. There are very few things you cannot learn on YouTube, albeit you have to be careful about your sources.

Recently I signed up for an online program called Master Class, an amazing resource where you can take direct classes from famous instructors including James Patterson, Ron Howard, Gordon Ramsey, Helen Mirren, Annie Leibovitz, and many others at the top of their crafts. What an amazing and cost-effective opportunity to learn from the best!

STAY ON TOP OF INDUSTRY HAPPENINGS

Top blogs, newsletters and thought leaders also offer timely insights into very specific niches from their fields. Subscribe to those that will be most helpful. Set up Google Alerts in your industry or niche so you start everyday with the most topical news in your field in your in box. Not only will it keep you up to date, but news can be reposted on social media to show others you are on the cutting edge of what happens in your industry. That helps build your reputation.

SET YOUR OWN SELF-GROWTH CURRICULUM

You must set aside time, money and resources for your education and continued self-growth-almost nothing is more important. My friend Pat Parelli says, "Most people spend more time and money worrying about what's on top of their head than what's in it." Brian Tracy's advice to "Invest 3-5% of your gross income on yourself." remains one of the most valuable pieces of advice I ever received. Set aside adequate time each day for learning. I start each day with a 45-minute walk and an audio book. After you have exhausted all the pertinent biographies in your field, study the topics most likely to aid in your fame: speaking, sales, marketing, leadership, presentation skills, and so on.

EVEN THE VERY BEST OFTEN LACK SOME CRITICAL SKILLS

Even the very competent, like the first president George Bush, perhaps the most highly trained person ever for the job, can fail because they lack secondary skills.

Despite being the youngest US Navy pilot in WW2, head of the CIA, ambassador to the UN, vice president and a self-made millionaire, he lacked basic presentation skills that hurt his effectiveness and cost him reelection. This was made all the worse by the amazing communication skills of the previous president, Ronald Reagan.

Often secondary skills may offer additional powerful traits for increasing your competence-for example, a lawyer might find humor of great use in putting a jury at ease or countering a claim. I find reading top fiction writers like Stephen King helps me discover storytelling tricks I can use in sales, marketing and in my own writing. Think outside the box when it comes to adding new skills to your repertoire.

CONFIDENCE AND COMPETENCE BORN OF EXPERIENCE

Experience is the second factor in building self-confidence. Through repeated and educated risk taking, you gain experience and your confidence in your own ability grows. Eventually, you are guided by the desire for achievement, rather than the avoidance of what you fear. This increase in confidence is the product of practice and experience. Lincoln, Churchill, Thatcher, Reagan, and just about anyone you can name in the corporate or entertainment world all had many years of practice in a host of positions-minor and major-before they reached their respective pinnacles of success and fame.

Opportunities to gain experience are all around you. All you have to do is pick one and take action. The experience you gain from open mic night, entering a sporting tournament or the politics, process, and problems of business leadership will form the groundwork for dealing with situations you will face on a grander scale. As famed Chrysler chairman, Lee Iacocca once said, "My overnight success, like most overnight success, was 20 years in the making." Indeed, there can be no long-term success without practice and experience. Once success is achieved on one level, it cannot be maintained or surpassed without more practice.

Unless you are a Kardashian, or the latest reality show contestant, you actually need to be good at something to be famous. According to Malcom Gladwell, author of the hugely popular book *Outliers*, it takes **10,000 hours of focused practice to master your art.** In the book Gladwell discusses the success of such famous people as Mozart, Bill Gates, Bill Joy, Bobby Fischer, and the Beatles.

According to him the Beatles had been playing together for over seven years before they become "overnight" sensations in the states. They weren't just hanging out together either. You see unlike your typical high school band, the Beatles actually practiced and played together. . . a lot! In fact, they used to take trips to Hamburg, Germany and play for eight hours a night, seven days a week! John Lennon said in an interview about their experience in Hamburg: "We got better and got more confidence. We couldn't help it with all the experience playing all night long. . . we had to play for eight hours, so we really had to find a new way of playing."

Gladwell then talks about the results of this experience and the resulting impact on their performance. "All told, they performed for 270 nights in just over a year

and a half. By the time they had their first burst of success in 1964, in fact, they had performed live an estimated twelve hundred times." That means the Beatles played over 1,200 live performances before they made it big, which as the author points out, is more shows than most bands play in their entire career. The Rolling Stones were no different, playing hundreds of live gigs a year.

"THE DUKE" PAID HIS DUES

Tom Cruise will never make as many movies in his career as John Wayne did before he was even a star. John Wayne was in eighty different B movies before finally getting a starring role in Stagecoach, which launched him to immortality. He was in some terrible movies and, by his own admission, was a very bad actor.

This was back in the days where they made a movie in six days on a budget of $28,000 and for which he was paid $450. Yet he never let that deter him from gaining the experience he needed to master his craft and match his acting skills with his natural good looks and easy manner. Wayne started out in the movie business working on props before he became a movie icon.

Yet when he did become a star, he never stopped helping out: holding scissors for a hairdresser making last-minute corrections on an extra, putting his back behind a wagon that was stuck in the sand, helping with lights, painting, or packing up at the end of the day. The Duke was never one to escape to his star trailer; he preferred hanging out and helping on the set.

THE VALUE OF MENTORS & COACHES

In Wyatt's Earp's later years, the legendary lawman, who survived the gunfight at the OK Corral, lived in Los Angeles. He was fascinated with movies and was a technical advisor on several silent cowboy films. There he befriended a young actor named Marion Morrison and regaled the young thespian with tales of the Old West. Enthralled, the young man used to fetch Wyatt cups of coffee. Later the actor who had gone from bad B movies to a king of the box office and changed his name to John Wayne claimed his portrayals of cowboys and western lawmen were based on these conversations with Earp.

Wayne also drew heavily from actor-turned-legendary-stuntman Yakima Canutt. In fact, much of the characterization associated with Wayne-the drawling, hesitant speech and the hip-rolling walk-were pure Canutt. Said Wayne, "I spent weeks studying the way Yakima Canutt walked and talked. He was a real cowhand and a world champion rodeo rider."

Unlike most actors especially of that era, Wayne studied all aspects of the movie business, from the building of sets, lighting, camera angles, and scripts, to directing and producing. This gave him unusual insights into his own performance and helping others improve theirs. He had a great eye for detail and would often suggest changes on the set. This thorough knowledge of the business eventfully lead to him directing and producing his own movies, something rarely done by actors at that time.

Oprah Winfrey was mentored by celebrated author and poet, the late Maya Angelou. "She was there for me always, guiding me through some of the most important years of my life," Winfrey said. "Mentors are important and I don't think anybody makes it in the world without some form of mentorship," she added.

Former Apple CEO, Steve Jobs served as a mentor to Facebook CEO Mark Zuckerberg. The two developed a relationship in the early days of Facebook and often met to discuss the best business and management practices for the company.

When Jobs passed away in the fall of 2011, Zuckerberg posted on his Facebook page, "Steve, thank you for being a mentor and a friend. Thanks for showing that what you build can change the world. I will miss you."

Musician Woody Guthrie, whose musical legacy includes hundreds of political, traditional and children's songs including "This Land is Your Land," mentored fellow singer-songwriter Bob Dylan.

As a high school student in the 1950s, Dylan listened to Guthrie's music, eventually moving to New York City and befriending the musician. Dylan played and wrote to his idol, which was often met with Guthrie's approval. In 1962, Dylan released "Song to Woody," an ode to Guthrie.

Virgin Airlines founder Richard Branson asked British airline entrepreneur Sir Freddie Laker for guidance during his struggle to get Virgin Atlantic off the ground. In his fight with giant British Airways "It's always good to have a helping hand at the start. I wouldn't have got anywhere in the airline industry without the mentorship of Sir Freddie Laker," Branson has been quoted as saying. Branson honored his mentor by naming his first plane Spirit of Sir Freddie!

I was mentored in the martial arts business by 10th degree black belt Fred Villari, and later in the marketing and consulting business by Brian Tracy, Jay Abraham, Dan Kennedy and others, sometimes in person but always through their books, audios and videos.

COACHES

Long before the TV show "The Voice," people with talent knew they needed coaches to help them become the best they could be and take their shot at immortality.

Golfer Jack Nicklaus had Jack Gout.

Tiger Woods had Butch, then Hank, then a host of others.

Tennis star Andy Murray had a multiple champion in Ivan Lendl as his coach.

Ali had legendary Angelo Dundee who also trained Sugar Ray Leonard and George Foreman.

Mike Tyson had the equally famous "Cus" D'Amato who had also coached Floyd Patterson before him.

Says Robert De Niro of his early coaching, "I went to the Dramatic Workshop when I was 16 for about a year and then I went to study with Stella Adler when I was about 18 until about 21. She had Brando as a client but I didn't know that until later.

I started getting involved at the Actor's Studio when I was 24 years old. Some friends were going there and I did a play there so I started going to the Studio after I left Stella's. It was just another approach. At the Studio, everything was more in the moment."

One of the best coaches in history was UCLA's John Wooden. His secret was mastering basics. Every practice, his team would train relentlessly in ball handling, footwork, conditioning, and hitting the high-percentage shots. Was it always fun? No. Exciting? No? Did it work? YES! It produced ten championships in twelve years (seven of them back-to-back) and four undefeated seasons. Ask his players if mastering the basics was the most exciting thing they had ever done and the answer would be no. Ask them if being a part of his legendary program was one of the most exciting things they had ever done and, the answer, a resounding yes!

Coaches bring out the very best in superstars, so surely a good coach could help you quickly enhance your key skills.

Back when I was starting out in the speaking business, in the early '90s, I paid a lady, the grand dame of speaking, Dottie Walters, $380 for a morning consultation. She gave me excellent advice!

The following year I paid a man, whose name eludes me, $900 just to have coffee with me for about an hour. He had been the top guy in Anthony Robbins's organization, and I wanted to know how he filled the room. Now bear in mind, at this time I was flat broke and had over $121,000 in debt on nine different credit cards. **I needed quick answers. I could not afford to wait!**

In 1995, I paid speaking consultant Burt Dubin, $1,595 for his three-manual Speaking Success System and some phone calls. Well, well worth the money!

Later, when I had moved up the ladder, I booked Brian Tracy to speak at my annual convention for martial-arts schools. One of my clients asked me what it cost to have Brian Tracy speak for an hour. When I informed him that Brian made $18,000, he was astonished.

Although the presentation was well worth the money, the real reason I hired Brian Tracy was not so he could enlighten my clients but so I could develop a personal relationship with him. Through hiring him, I went to his office in San Diego and met with him personally. I was able to pick his brain and develop a more personal relationship with him. Once I had done this, I approached him about coauthoring a book with me. Since I had written most of the book already, he found the idea appealing. I was able to leverage off his fame and credibility in the marketplace by teaming up with him.

When I wanted to franchise my martial-arts schools, I paid the guy who started Sylvan Learning Systems over $1,000 for a single phone call. Then I paid someone from Michael Gerber's organization $10,000 for showing up and another $60,000 over the next few years for phone advice.
Now as a marketing legend in my own right, I still pay people top dollar for specialized knowledge-knowledge that will get me the answers I want in minutes-not weeks, months, or years!

Several years ago, I paid a young man named Russell Brunson on his way up (Click Funnels) $500 for a five-minute phone consultation. The call lasted eight minutes, and he did follow up with a short PowerPoint! Money well spent again! Have I ever not received a hundred times the value from taking this approach? No!

- Who knows what you want to know?
- What one person can fast-forward your business or career?
- Who has the connections you need to tap into?

Whoever that is, find them and pay them whatever they ask. It will shorten your journey by years, not months!

INCREASE YOUR OPTIONS

The fourth factor in building confidence is creating options for yourself.

The control you have over events, and therefore the confidence you have in the successful outcome of any endeavor, is in direct proportion to your well-developed options. Stress and worry are caused by things that we perceive to be beyond our control. If the problems we face are easily within our sphere of control, we rarely feel insecure. We are, instead, brimming with confidence. Your confidence in any major decision, such as changing jobs, moving to another state, buying a business, or firing a key employee, will always rest on one factor- the quality of your well-developed options. It's much easier to yell, "Take this job and shove it," when you have six month's income in the bank in reserve. It's much easier to fire a key employee if you have two or three qualified people who you know can adequately replace him. Options increase your courage dramatically.

Always be on the lookout for options. You can both find them and create them. The more options you have, the less chance there is of you being boxed into a situation from which you feel you have no escape. Most Americans live from paycheck to paycheck, and I suspect that most Europeans do the same. It's hardly any wonder, then, that people are always worried about their job, their company, and their health. If any one of these things fails for more than a week, they will be in desperate trouble. Free yourself from this form of anxiety. Prepare for whatever problems could hurt you. Save more money, buy catastrophic health insurance, put extra canned food and water in storage, keep your job contacts active, earn an MBA at night, and so on.

Make whatever sacrifices are necessary to accomplish give yourself options. It's amazing the increase in confidence you enjoy when you know, no matter what happens, you have half a year to regroup and follow a different path.

PLAY TO WIN

The fifth factor in creating confidence is developing a play-to-win attitude. Unlike average people who play to maintain the status quo or, worse still, play specifically not to lose, you must play to win. The famous are never content themselves with maintaining their position in the marketplace. Instead, they are always on the lookout for new ways to increase brand, sales and market share. When starting out, playing to win often means the same thing as survival, but once you have established a solid foundation, people often find a comfort level and become complacent. Your motto should be, if you are not going forward, you are going backwards.

Seven-time Formula 1 champion Michael Schumacher always played to win.

Building an iconic business usually results from a making a series of play-to-win decisions. Such decisions are made faster, put into effect sooner, and carried out more precisely when they are made with confidence. People around you can sense the level of confidence with which you reach decisions and they will act accordingly. So, it's important to maintain an air of quiet confidence and make it plain that you play to win.

ACT AS IF IT'S IMPOSSIBLE TO FAIL

The sixth factor in developing confidence is to act as if it's impossible to fail.

Is there something deep in the back of your mind that you always wanted to do but never actually did?

Something fun, something exciting, something challenging?

Something scary, something at which you might fail, lose your money, and perhaps lose the respect of your peers?

Most people have just such dreams, and for most people they remain just that, dreams that end the moment they wake up and reality returns with the first smell of the morning coffee.

However, let's pretend for a moment that the dream lingers on-that it just won't go away. Would you go after it if you knew there was absolutely no chance of failure? If the only possible outcome was the complete and wonderful success of your dreams, what would you do? What would you try to accomplish?

When you act as if It's impossible to fail, others support you more, you move with more assurance, and things work out better. The only real failure is not taking an intelligent risk. If you experience setbacks, your self-confidence will help you take another route to your ultimate success.

Sometimes your confidence is symbolic.

At the height of World War II, many high officials were urging Winston Churchill to make plans to dispatch the British naval fleet to an American port in the event of a British defeat. Some members of Parliament called for the Royal family, priceless works of art, and women and children to be sent to Canada. Churchill, however, felt differently. He knew the adverse symbolic effect that sending the fleet or the King abroad would have had on the confidence of the man and woman in the street, who needed to dig in and fight as never before. He dismissed all such suggestions at once.

Churchill knew the value to public morale of acting as if you couldn't fail. He knew that acting with confidence was paramount to the successful outcome of the war, even if he had private doubts. At one point during his legendary "We will fight them on the beaches" speech, he covered the microphone, turned to his bodyguard and announced, "We will hit them on the head with beer bottles, for it's all we have left."

Nonetheless, the image he presented was one of complete confidence in ultimate victory.

NETWORK WITH OTHER WINNERS

The seventh factor in building confidence is to form your own "mastermind" or support group comprised entirely of winners: people who inspire you, make you laugh, and encourage your success. It's a fact of life that winners are more than happy to share their success and enthusiasm with others. Remember, birds of a feather flock together. Make it your habit to form relationships with winners.

The more confident and positive the people you network with, the more it will rub off on you. Nothing breeds optimism and confidence like the company of positive people, and nothing drains it faster than pessimists.

TURNING DEFEAT INTO VICTORY TO BOOST YOUR CONFIDENCE

The eighth factor in building confidence is positive self-talk. Do not get in the habit of beating yourself-up mentally when things go wrong or mistakes are made. There are plenty of other people in the world more than willing to do it for you. You must focus all of your energy on remaining positive and refocusing your efforts on the successful accomplishment of your vision.

It's an interesting fact that you will almost never hear famous people use the word failure.

The famous deliberately and consciously reinterpret their failures as mere delays or mistakes. They make the deliberate, conscious effort to judge themselves and their experiences in a positive way-a way that improves rather than undercuts their self-confidence.

Use positive self-talk when dealing with negative situations and reframe each loss or failure from the perspective of how you will learn from the experience to do better next time. Never allow your self- esteem or confidence to be adversely affected by short-term problems

VISUALIZATION OF A SUCCESSFUL OUTCOME

The ninth factor in building your confidence is visualization. Top stars have the ability to visualize the successful outcome of achieving their goals long before it actually happens. This skill is valuable in giving you the confidence to act and to help you reach goals quickly. It is also critical in helping you build reserves of determination and persistence. The sharper and more vivid your vision, the easier it will be to accept temporary defeat in one battle but still have the confidence and the courage to go on and win the war.

You must develop a picture of yourself as you will be when your vision comes to fruition See the respect, sense of achievement, and payoff you will enjoy when you reach your goals. This vision should be as vivid in your mind as the picture on the big screen TV. The sounds of victory should ring in your mind as loudly as the cheers for the fans. The more details you can picture in your mind, the clearer your mental image and the greater your confidence will be.

WHEN IN DOUBT, FAKE IT

We have covered a number of ways to inspire self-confidence and boost your competence. The final way, when all else fails, is to fake it. There may be those who feel that "fake it till you make it" is a breach of integrity, but if you look at the history of the famous, you will find that this tactic was very often used as a last resort for gaining the confidence they needed to break though. Psychology also tells us that causality is not a simple matter.

No one will follow anyone who appears to lack self-confidence. While confidence on the inside is a combination of the characteristics, confidence on the outside is largely measured by others' perceptions. If you stand tall, look confident, and act in a confident manner, people will perceive you to be a confident person, no matter how much churning is going on inside your stomach. No one will follow anyone who appears to lack self-confidence. While confidence on the inside is a combination of the characteristics, confidence on the outside is largely measured by others' perceptions. If you stand tall, look confident, and act in a confident manner, people will perceive you to be a confident person, no matter how much churning is going on inside your stomach.

In ancient Rome, there was a legend about a legion commander whose troops were holding a hill but surrounded by three or four times their number. Hopelessly outnumbered and with no escape, he told his soldiers to strip naked. Then, armed only with a short sword, he ordered them to advance in line down the hill towards the enemy. At first the waiting army laughed and jeered, but as the Romans came closer they began to have second thoughts. Why had the Romans removed their armor? What tricks were they up to? What secret weapon did they have? What did they know that the waiting army did not? Certain that the answer, whatever it was, couldn't be good, they fled. The power of confidence had won another victory.

All great athletes, entrepreneurs and entertainers have experienced a lack of confidence at some point in their careers, but they sucked it in, put on a brave face, and played through it. Now I know they looked cool as cucumbers in action. I know they look and acted as if self-doubt could not be found anywhere in their vicinity. But believe me, sometimes it's there. It's just well-concealed.

SUMMARY

Always be on the lookout for ways to build confidence in yourself and your team and avoid at all costs anything that undermines that confidence. Challenge yourself and others to become more knowledgeable in key areas. Never let anyone outlearn you. Competence will always be the foundation of confidence. Practice and encourage those you lead to gain experience in small ways to prepare them for future challenges. Become good at something and use that confidence to expand into other areas of excellence. Generate alternatives to every situation. Your confidence increases in direct proportion to your well-developed options. Play to win, and act as if it is impossible to fail. Network with other positive people. Use positive "self-talk" to reframe your challenges in a positive light. Combine that with visualization of the successful outcome of your goals. When all else fails, fake confidence until it catches up with you.

Super pitch man Billy Mays pitched every product with supreme confidence.

ACTION PLAN

- How specifically can you increase your aura of confidence?
- How specifically will you increase your competence?
- What does your reading list look like?
- Your video, courses and YouTube learning?
- Do you have a mentor?
- How can you can gain more experience?
- Do you have a coach for a specific subject?
- Do you mirror anyone?
- How can you increase your number of options?
- Are you playing to win?
- Are you acting like it's impossible to fail?
- Are you networking with other winners?
- Are you practicing positive self-talk?
- Do you visualize a successful outcome?
- Are you willing to fake it until you make it?

"Remember that a person's name is to that person the sweetest and most important sound in any language." - **Dale Carnegie**, *How to Win Friends and Influence People*

4

THE SOUNDS OF FAME

The sounds of fame encompass many factors, including your name, nickname, catch phrase, music and your quotable sayings. These are all things you and others will use and repeat often, so all must be given serious consideration.

Start with your given name. Did your parents bless you with a fame-worthy name?

What's in a name?

Your personal, company, or product name can make a huge difference when it comes to building your reputation and image in the marketplace. Names can make or break a business or career, and you certainly don't have to stick with the one you were given at birth.

In fact, few stars do! Many iconic brands start with one name and evolve into better ones. Those that don't change their names entirely often opt to use part of their names, rearrange their names, or in some cases use their nickname. Very often this move makes perfect sense.

For example: Would you buy a $500 pair of signature jeans from Ralph Lifshitz?

Most likely not, but you and the rest of the world might buy some Ralph Lauren jeans. A great name change, if ever there was one!

Edson Arantes do Nascimento was the only athlete in the world as famous in the 60s and 70s as Muhammad Ali (who had changed his name from Cassius Clay). You might know him better as

Chuck Connors as *The Rifleman*

Pele. He received the nickname "Pelé" during his school days, when it is claimed he was given it because of his pronunciation of the name of his favorite player, local Vasco da Gama goalkeeper Bilé, which he misspoke.

In his autobiography, Pelé stated he had no idea what the name means, nor did his old friends. Lucky for him, because Pele is a helluva lot more marketable than Edson Arantes do Nascimento.

Born Kevin Joseph Aloysius Connors, the actor and athlete (he is only one of 12 athletes to ever play in the NBA and MLB) tried out the names "Lefty" and "Stretch" before becoming known as Chuck. Connors ended up choosing the name "Chuck"

because when he played first base in baseball, he would yell to the pitcher, "Chuck it to me, baby, chuck it to me!" Connors was a huge star in the '60s and '70s but was most famous for his role in the TV series The Rifleman.

Imagine rocking to the sounds of iconic new wave tunes like "Rock the Casbah" and "London Calling" by the band The Weak Heartdrops. That sounds like the kind of band who you don't admit to your friends that you secretly like. Thankfully for all of us, they became the band Clash, which New Musical Express, the leading publication on the UK music scene, dubbed "the only band that matter

I think you'll agree that Marion Morrison doesn't quite sound as tough an American icon as John Wayne. Wayne was actually born Marion Robert Morrison on May 26, 1907. When Marion roamed the neighborhood, he never went anywhere without his Airedale terrier, Duke, at his side. The two were such constant companions that local firefighters began calling the boy "Little Duke." The nickname stuck for life. He certainly preferred it to the feminine "Marion." When the man began working in film, studio bigwigs were no more impressed with his name than he was. He appeared as "Duke Morrison" in 1929's Words and Music, and in 1930, director Raoul Walsh and Fox Studios executive Winfield Sheehan started billing him as "John Wayne."

Why do the vast majority of movie stars and pop stars change their names? Because some names just don't conjure up images of success, high status, rebellion or whatever word they want to own.

Elvis Costello sounds a lot more intriguing than Patrick MacManus.

Back in the mid-'70s, before going off on his own, the musician born Declan Patrick MacManus was playing in a pub band and decided to take on the name D.P. Costello, after his father -- also a musician -- Day Costello. Later, when he was signed to his first solo contract, he added Elvis (after the King) to the front of his name and became Elvis Costello.

Norma Jean sounds common, but Marilyn Monroe sounds alluring. Alluring enough to get President JFK and his brother Attorney General Bobby Kennedy fawning over her. And you thought Clinton and Trump were bad?

Madonna Louise Ciccone does not quite have the same ring as simply Madonna, one of the few stars to keep her original name!

Stefani Joanne Angelina Germanotta became Lady Gaga. The inspiration for her name came from the Queen song "Radio Ga Ga."

Alphonso D'Abruzzo was having a lot of trouble getting an acting job until he changed his name to Alan Alda, another great name. He became a TV legend playing "Hawkeye," in the long-running TV series MASH.

Shawn Corey Carter became Jay-Z. Known as "Jazzy" around the neighborhood, Carter later adopted the showbiz/stage name "Jay-Z" in homage to his mentor Jaz-O.

Alecia Beth Moore became Pink. She took her name from the movie Reservoir Dogs, a film she saw as a teenager and whose character Mr. Pink is someone her friends all agreed she resembled.

Before Marshall Bruce Mathers, III, became famous as Eminem he used to rap in clubs under the name M&M, which are his initials. Later on, to avoid issues with M&M's (the chocolate that he'd loved since a child), the name was changed to Eminem.

The U2 front man and humanitarian we all know as Bono wasn't actually born with just one name. Before he became world famous, the Irish musician was known by the name Paul David Hewson. The name Bono was originally a nickname, short for bono vox, meaning "good voice" in Latin, said to be given by his friend Gavin Friday.

Michael Caine was born Maurice Joseph Micklewhite. In a New Yorker article Caine explained re-naming himself after Humphrey Bogart's character in "The Caine Mutiny". "Bogart was my hero, and even though he came from a sort of snobby, aristocratic family-he was a distant relation of Princess Diana-when I was a kid I thought he was a tough guy," said Caine. "Any person with my working-class background would be a villain or a comic cipher, usually badly played, and with a rotten accent. There weren't a lot of guys in England for me to look up to."

Of course, it's not just actors and rock stars who change their names. Two decades before Tiger mania, a young, handsome, blonde California kid named John Miller turned pro and won everything. He was instantly a sports agent's dream, but manager Ed Barner had Miller change his name, from John to the more "apple pie" sounding Johnny. Although this was undoubtedly a good move in a promotional sense, Miller went along with it grudgingly. If you come across an early autograph, you will see he used to sign himself John "ny" Miller.

The trend of changing names goes way back in the golf industry. In the Thirties Gene Sarazen also changed his name, albeit a little more dramatically. He was born Eugene Saraceni but, when he saw his name in the paper after winning a local tournament, he decided it was a great name for a musician but a lousy name for a golfer! After picking the name Gene Sarazen from the list he had made out for himself, he went directly to the phone book. He wanted to make sure he would be the only one in there with that name. He was determined to be an "original."

Mark Twain's real name was Samuel Langhorne Clemens. Before Clemens became well known as a writer, he held a variety of odd jobs including piloting a steamboat up and down the Mississippi River. He was licensed as a steamboat pilot in 1859 and worked on the river until fighting there during the Civil War ended traffic traveling from north to south. His experiences along the river helped him come up with his pen name.

In 1863, when Clemens was 27, he wrote a humorous travel story and decided to sign his name "Mark Twain." This name comes from something shouted by crewmen on a boat. To test the depth of the water, a crewman shouts "mark twain!" The crewman is calling for two fathoms, or a depth of 12 feet, which is barely enough for a boat to navigate safely. "Twain" is an old-fashioned way of saying "two" and a fathom is six feet. "Mark Twain" is a "pen name" in the same way that many people in show business use a "stage name."

Motorcycle daredevil Robert Craig Knievel was world famous in the Seventies for his daring exploits jumping, buses, shark tanks and canyons. After a police chase in 1956 in which he crashed his motorcycle, Knievel was taken to jail on a charge of reckless driving. When the night jailer came around to check the roll, he noted Knievel in one cell and a man named William Knofel in the other. Knofel was a well-known local law breaker nicknamed "Awful Knofel" ("Awful" rhyming with Knofel), so the cop on duty making a joke said, "Well, look at this: Awful Knofel and Evil Knievel" ("Evil" rhyming with Knievel). Knievel liked the sound of it but chose a misspelling for his first name (Evel) because he didn't want to be considered evil.

CHANGING HIS NAME TO SOLVE A PROBLEM

When horror writer Stephen King started attaining success he was eager to write more books. Unfortunately, publishers at the time thought that one book a year was more than enough for an author and that publishing any more would oversaturate the brand.

Instead of accepting this limitation, King adopted the pen name Richard Bachman to write more than one book a year. A bookstore clerk eventually caught on to the fact that the writing style of King and Bachman were very similar and the ruse was uncovered. King confirmed the connection and promptly declared that Bachman had died of "cancer of the pseudonym."

Another prolific author, Dean Koontz, faced the same problem as Stephen King when he was told that writing more than one book a year, especially in different genres, was a bad idea. Undeterred he adopted at least ten different pen names and went on to publish up to eight books a year during the 1970s. Some of his pen names include Anthony North, Richard Paige, David Axton, Aaron Wolfe and a host of others. According to Koontz he only used ten pen names, but fans have long suspected that the author might be behind even more books written under different names.

Author Joanne Rowling adopted the more masculine sounding pen name, J.K Rowling, when writing the Harry Potter series of books. Her publishers were afraid that young boys would not want to read the books if they knew the author was a woman, so she used her initial and added the fabricated "K" for good measure. After concluding the Harry Potter series she once again adopted a pen name, Robert Galbraith, for her detective story The Cuckoo's Calling. However, much to the author's disappointment, it was soon discovered that she wrote the book and not a former member of the Royal Military Police as it was marketed. The book was the author's first aimed at adults and was supposed to be published without expectation or hype, but after the discovery of her pen name sales skyrocketed.

John le Carré doesn't just write about spies - he's been one. Le Carré was working for MI6 in Hamburg, Germany, when he wrote his first spy story, *The Spy Who Came in From the Cold*. The man who was born David John Moore Cornwell published as John le Carré because MI6 officers are not allowed to publish under their own names.

ELVIS SOLVES A MAJOR SALES PROBLEM

A couple of years ago I hired a young man with the first name Kemp. His unusual first name began to cause problems immediately.

He'd call a prospect and say, "Hi, this is Kemp from Legendary Marketing."

The prospect would pause and then say, "Did you say Kent?"

"No," he'd say, "it's Kemp." The prospect, unused to the name, would invariably say "Ken?"

"No," he'd say with rising irritation "Kemp. K-E-M-P. Kemp!"

By this point, the prospect was either feeling stupid or Kemp was so frustrated and distracted from the sale process that he couldn't sell anything. It seemed as if every conversation he had started out as an argument!

One day I walked in and he was practically yelling at the person on the other end of the phone, trying to get the person to say his name right! "That's the final straw," I said. "Every time I come in here you are arguing with someone about your name. Change it to something else-anything else!" "Like what?" he said as I walked out the door. "Like Elvis," I said. "No one will forget that!"

Despite his misgivings, the very next day he started introducing himself as Elvis Anderson. All of a sudden no one ever asked him to spell his name or asked him to repeat it!

And guess what?

People liked the name. They chatted with him; he built rapport; they put his calls through. People actually called him back, and sales went up!

Thank you. Thank you very much!

If your name is hard for people to pronounce, use a nickname or your initials. If you have a difficult or unusual name that will inhibit your sales, change it. It's not that hard to do!

Just this week I was talking to a friend in the credit card processing business in a Redneck area of central Florida, who knew of my Elvis story. He was training an Egyptian born rep whose name was Mustafa and every conversation started with him repeating his name multiple times. Kevin suggested he just tag on the like "You know like the Lion King!" Immediately the questions stopped, and rapport was instantly built!

Joseph Samuel Girardi, better known as Joe Girard, for decades called himself the world's best salesman, and recognized by the Guinness book of world records as such. In his book How to Sell Anything to Anybody, Girard describes how he decided early in his sales career to adopt the name "Girard" for business purposes as a way to avoid confrontations over his ethnicity or losing customers who might be prejudiced against Sicilians and Italians.

NAMES CREATE FEELINGS

Comedian Rodney Dangerfield, who was born Jacob Cohen, had a classic comedy routine where he said, "If I ever get in a bar fight, I'm going to stop and check out where the guy's from. If he's from Sparta or Troy, I'm outta there. What I really hope is that the guy's from Pleasantville, (New Jersey). After all, how tough can someone from Pleasantville be?"

People associate certain names with trust and leadership. Names like John, Jack, and Tom are good solid names that generally create a positive perception. People associate other names with slyness, wimpiness, or trickery. Slick Willie, Tricky Dicky, and other such nicknames are common in English-speaking countries. I use my middle name as my professional last name rather than my given last name because it just sounds better! Others use a nickname or initials to increase their visibility and build their reputations.

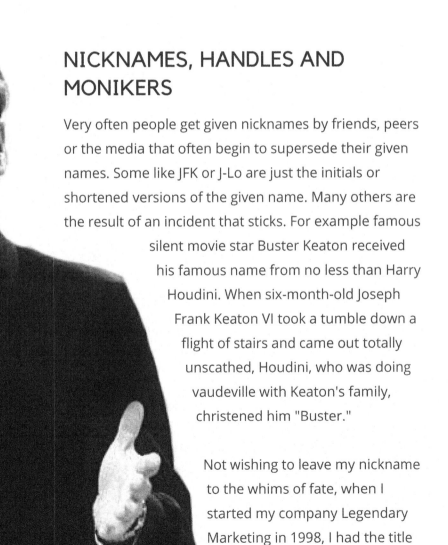

NICKNAMES, HANDLES AND MONIKERS

Very often people get given nicknames by friends, peers or the media that often begin to supersede their given names. Some like JFK or J-Lo are just the initials or shortened versions of the given name. Many others are the result of an incident that sticks. For example famous silent movie star Buster Keaton received his famous name from no less than Harry Houdini. When six-month-old Joseph Frank Keaton VI took a tumble down a flight of stairs and came out totally unscathed, Houdini, who was doing vaudeville with Keaton's family, christened him "Buster."

Not wishing to leave my nickname to the whims of fate, when I started my company Legendary Marketing in 1998, I had the title on my business cards not as CEO, owner or president but as Marketing Legend. Now, after repeated use, many people just call me Legend or Legendary, which is nice!

Bruce Springsteen acquired the nickname "The Boss" when he played club gigs with a band. He took on the task of collecting the band's nightly pay and distributing it amongst his bandmates.

"The Chairman of the Board," Frank Sinatra. In 1960, after over 20 years of recording, Sinatra wanted control. He founded Reprise Records and installed himself as CEO (hence "The Chairman of the Board" nickname). The Chairman gave his buddies, Dean Martin and Sammy Davis, Jr., recording contracts. He also gave all the artists on his label something rarely found in the music business: full creative control and ownership of their work.

Sinatra also recorded some of his most memorable recordings at Reprise, including perhaps his most iconic tune, "My Way." Apparently Sinatra did not like his Chairman nickname, which only goes to show why you should create your own before someone else does it for you!

Would Tiger Woods have been so appealing to NIKE's commercial success if everyone was calling him by his given name of Elderick? Tiger's father Earl Wood's nicknamed his son "Tiger" after an army buddy in South East Asia, replacing his more cumbersome given name.

Greg Norman had the good fortune to acquire a memorable nickname early in his career. After a fine performance in the second round of the Masters, he was being interviewed in the press tent and mentioned that he loved to fish for sharks in his native Australia. The press corps loved it! The next day the Augusta Chronicle ran a banner headline reading, "Great White Shark Near Masters Lead." Norman loved it, too, and the name stuck, so did an exciting shark logo adding to his image as a strong, aggressive man's man.

Many other famous golfers had nicknames:

Ben Hogan, The Hawk. Arnold Palmer, The King. Jack Nicklaus, The Golden Bear. Gary Player, The Black Knight. This list of golfers turned their nicknames into brand names that made millions in a variety of different business ventures.

William "The Refrigerator" Perry

William Perry, a 350+ lbs lineman and offensive back for the Chicago Bears was a fan favorite for the seven years he played. Unlike most backs, his fame lived on long after that, thanks to his catchy nickname. Perry was described as "a man in a white jersey resembling a refrigerator coming through the offensive line." When the Bears needed a short yardage gain, there was "The Fridge," banging through the line and stumbling into the end zone.

Earvin (Magic) Johnson

Basketball legend, Earvin Johnson was first dubbed "Magic" while playing at Everett High School as a 15-year-old sophomore. When he recorded 36 points, 18 rebounds and 16 assists, Fred Stabley Jr. of the Lansing State Journal, gave him the moniker, despite protest from Johnson's mother, a devout Christian, who claimed it was sacrilegious.

As it turned out there was a lot more money to be made as Magic than Earvin!

Sting

Gordon Sumner, was just a guy playing the bass with a band called The Phoenix Jazzmen when he wore a sweater onstage that would change his life. The sweater had black and yellow stripes, prompting the Jazzmen's bandleader, Gordon Solomon, to call him "Sting." It stuck.

George Herman Ruth

Over 80 years after Ruth's professional baseball career ended, he is still regarded as the best player to have ever lived. Equally important as his stats to his legacy are the monikers we have come to know and fondly use to remember him. "The Bambino," "The Sultan of Swat," and simply "The Babe" are all references to baseball's greatest legend. We even remember his name, as "Babe" Ruth, instead of George Herman Ruth. Truly the champion of nicknames, "Babe" is a symbol of how nicknames take on a life of their own.

Here's a few more:

Hulk Hogan
Real Name: Terry Gene Bollea

George Michael
Real Name: Georgios Panayiotou

Slash
Real Name: Saul Hudson

Elton John
Real Name: Reginald Kenneth Dwight

Whoopi Goldberg
Real Name: Caryn Johnson

Jane Seymour
Real Name: Joyce Penelope Wilhelmina Frankenberg

Snoop Dogg
Real Name: Calvin Broadus

Marilyn Manson
Real Name: Brian Warner

Vin Diesel
Real Name: Mark Vincent

Bruno Mars
Real Name: Peter Gene Hernandez

THE SONG MAY REMAIN THE SAME, BUT THE BAND NAME DOESN'T HAVE TO

In August 1968, Jimmy Page invited Robert Plant and John Bonham to join his band, the New Yardbirds, for a September tour in Scandinavia.

In October of that year they took the iconic step of changing the band's name to Led Zeppelin, which stemmed from a humorous conversation among several musicians about their chances of going down like a lead balloon.

Pink Floyd's original name was The Tea Set. Band member Syd Barrett created the name Pink Floyd on the spur of the moment when he discovered that another band, also called The Tea Set was to perform at one of their gigs. The name is derived from the given names of two blues musicians whose Piedmont blues records Barrett had in his collection: Pink Anderson and Floyd Council.

Both John Lennon and Paul McCartney liked Buddy Holly's rock & roll band The Crickets, so they named their own band after another insect, the beetle. During the first months of 1960 they were known as The Beetles but tried other names such as Johnny and the Moondogs, Long John and the Beetles. After a few gigs they stuck with The Silver Beatles, eventually shortening it to just Beatles!

The Stone Temple Pilots were originally named Mighty Joe Young until they realized a blues musician had already claimed that name. Then, they went through a period with the name Shirley Temple's Pussy before switching to Stone Temple Pilots by the time they signed with Atlantic.

Before they became the alt hip-hop group that made them famous, the Beastie Boys were a punk-rock group called the Young Aborigines.

Original member John Berry said in an interview with SPIN that he came up with the name Beastie Boys because he wanted a gang-like name.

Other Notable Band Name Changes:

KISS Original Name: Wicked Lester

VAN HALEN Original Name: Rat Salad

GREEN DAY Original Name: Sweet Children

NIRVANA Original Name: Pen Cap Chew

BLACK SABBATH Original Name: Polka Tulk Blues Band

COLDPLAY Original Name: Starfish

THE WHO Original Name: The High Numbers

U2 Original Name: The Hype

RED HOT CHILI PEPPERS Original Name: Tony Flow and the Miraculously Majestic Masters of Mayhem

QUEEN Original Name: Smile

DEF LEPPARD Original Name: Atomic Mass

THE BEE GEES Original Name: Rattlesnakes

THE SUPREMES Original Name: The Primettes

Many Iconic Companies Have Changed Their Names to Something More Strategic and Memorable

Playboy magazine is one of a host of iconic brands that almost bore a different name. Hugh Hefner has said that he wanted to call his magazine Stag Party -- a nod to a book of racy cartoons from the 1930s called Stag at Eve but changed it to Playboy as a last-minute decision.

Luckily for Hef, right before the first issue went to print, he received a cease-and-desist letter from Stag magazine, another publication for men. After briefly considering Gent, Bachelor, Pan and Satyr he eventually settled on the now iconic PLAYBOY!

Back in 1996, the world's number one search engine was created under the name "BackRub." The search engine's early name was actually meant to reference the way it analyzed the internet's "back links" to measure the importance and relevance of websites.

Creators Larry Page and Serge Brin renamed their business and technology Google in 1998. It's "a play on the word "googol," a mathematical term for the number represented by the numeral 1 followed by 100 zeros. The use of the term reflects their mission to organize a seemingly infinite amount of information on the web. They changed the spelling to Google because it was an easier spelling for people to remember.

Nike was founded in 1964 as Blue Ribbon Sports. At that time the company didn't actually produce shoes, it merely distributed them for Japanese manufacturer Onitsuka Tiger. When Blue Ribbon started making its own shoes in 1971, they also refreshed the brand name. Though "Dimension 6" was briefly in contention, founders Phil Knight and Bill Bowerman settled on "Nike" after the Greek goddess of victory, certainly more iconic than Blue Ribbon!

In 1893, a North Carolina druggist named, Caleb Davis Bradham invented a delicious concoction of sugar, water, caramel, lemon oil, nutmeg, kola nuts, and a few other secret ingredients. The creation, which he called Brad's Drink, was an overnight sensation. In 1898, Bradham rebranded it "Pepsi-Cola" because he believed it was a health drink that helped with indigestion, also known as dyspepsia.

In 1965, 17-year-old Fred DeLuca took a $1000 loan from family friend Dr. Peter Buck to open a sandwich shop in Bridgeport, Connecticut. He wanted it to help him pay for college. He named the shop in honor of his friend Pete's Super Submarines. "When people heard the name 'Pete's Submarines' over the radio, they often thought they heard the words 'pizza marine,'" DeLuca wrote in his autobiography. When customers showed up at his restaurant requesting seafood pizza, he knew they needed a simpler name. They changed it to "Pete's Subway," and eventually just "Subway" as the business grew. Today they have 45,000 stores!

Skype's name evolved from the description of its service. The original prototype of the company's phone product had the name "Sky-Peer-to-Peer," which was shrunk down to Skyper, then finally to Skype.

If you type "relentless.com" into your browser, you'll find yourself quickly redirected to Amazon. That's because founder Jeff Bezos was sold on Relentless for the name of his burgeoning business. Friends felt that the word seemed a bit sinister, so he floated a few other ideas, including Awake, Bookmail, Browse, and Cadabra. The latter name, which referenced "Abracadabra," was nixed when Bezos's lawyer misheard it as "cadaver."

"Amazon" was the winner because it suggested scale-the Amazon is the largest river in the world by volume-and because it started with "A," which was valuable in an era when websites were often listed alphabetically.

When Apple Computer started out, their name would not fit into any of the existing categories. They did, however, have two big advantages. First, their market, personal computers, was a brand-new market.

Second, their competition had terrible names. Which name would you remember: the MITS Altair 8800, The Commodore Pet, the IMSAI, or the Apple? It's not exactly rocket science to conclude that those other companies spent millions trying to build reputations for companies with faulty names!

WHAT DO YOU WANT YOUR BUSINESS NAME TO SAY?

Consider the name of your business and look at the perceptions it might create in the minds of a customer, client or fan. If those perceptions are not good, consider a change. It's really not that hard. In fact, thousands of corporations a year change their names, and the individuals who do so number in the tens of thousands.

Sometimes companies outgrow their names or move in completely different directions.

Minnesota Mining and Manufacturing Company was a mouthful to say and evolved far beyond its roots as a small mining company. A name change to 3M provided a general umbrella under which to market different products and services. International Harvester was once synonymous with agricultural equipment. After they sold off most of their agricultural products, the name no longer fit and they changed their name to Navistar.

While some of the examples I have given were pure chance, the majority are carefully thought-out decisions to align a look, feel, sound or concept with the brand. In fact, many well-funded start-up companies spend tens of thousands of dollars to hire a firm to develop a name for them.

My company, Legendary Marketing is a name that says success. My previous company Martial Arts America was also a very marketable name.

Engineer, Karsten Solheim scored when he named his first putter Ping. He won big with its name by keeping it simple and naming their product after the sound made when their early putters hit the ball squarely! Now that's genius: Every time a player used their product, it said their name - PING!

Die-Hard batteries has a great brand name that in effect describes what you want the product to do - last a long time and never let you down late at night in a dark parking lot! It needs no explanation and therefore no marketing money need be wasted on explaining the product. Instead marketing dollars can be spent on selling the product!

Given the choice of:

Bright Smile Dentistry
or
Dr. Milton R. Smothers, DDS

Which name are you likely to choose or remember?

What thoughts do you want your name to evoke?

Power
Security
Creativity

What feelings do you hope to elicit?

Trust
Excitement
Rebellion

What values are you trying to convey?

Speed
Size
Futuristic

Because you probably don't have the massive financial resources of the big players in your town or industry, you must take great care in deciding on your business name. Over time, it will be your most potent weapon in conquering your market. Your name should capitalize on your key strength, the one thing you have that others don't, or even if they do have it, the thing they are not claiming (your USP - unique sales proposition).

The most effective business or product names are the ones that connect instantly with your customers' needs.

THE PHRASES OF FAME

Take this quick test and see how many famous TV shows you can identify by just three or four words. These indelible words spoken by our favorite TV characters and personalities are forever etched in our brains.

1. "THIS TAPE WILL SELF-DESTRUCT IN FIVE SECONDS."

2. "YADA, YADA, YADA."

3. "YABBA DABBA DOO!"

4. "WHAT'CHOO TALKIN' 'BOUT?"

5. "JUST ONE MORE THING..."

6. "GOOD NIGHT, JOHN BOY."

7. "WHO LOVES YA, BABY?"

8. "BOOK 'EM, DANNO."

9. "THE TRUTH IS OUT THERE."

10. "WINTER IS COMING."

Answers at the end of the chapter.

Before the advent of cable and and digital news, revered newsman Walter Cronkite closed his nightly broadcast with these iconic words, **"And that's the way it is."** For three decades, long before "fake news" existed, all of America believed him.

Ed McMahon hailed the arrival of Johnny Carson from behind the *Tonight Show* curtain for 30 years with the words "Heeeere's...Johnny!"

This intro was so famous it even showed up in movies like *The Shining*. In it, homicidal maniac, Jack Torrance, played masterfully by Jack Nicholson, was driven insane by isolation and supernatural occurrences in the giant, empty hotel where he has been hired as the winter caretaker. He smashes an axe through the bathroom door where his terrified wife and child are hiding. Then he pokes his head through the gap saying, "Heeeere's...Johnny!"

Reality TV has spawned countless catch phrases but Jeff Probst's final words to the ousted *Survivor* competitors, "The tribe has spoken," remains one of the best.

Donald Trump built a successful reality TV career that gave him the national audience to launch a Presidential run on just two words, "You're fired!"

"Look! Up in the sky! It's a bird! It's a plane! It's Superman!" - *Adventures of Superman*

"Baby, you're the greatest." - Ralph, *The Honeymooners*

"The thrill of victory and the agony of defeat." - Jim McKay, *Wide World of Sports*

"Live long and prosper." - Spock, *Star Trek*

"De plane, de plane!" - Tattoo, *Fantasy Island*

"TO THE BATMOBILE!" - BATMAN, *BATMAN*

"Nanu-nanu." - Mork, Mork & Mindy

"Tenk you veddy much." - Latka, Taxi

"Let's be careful out there." - Esterhaus, Hill Street Blues

"Make it so." - Picard, Star Trek: The Next Generation

"Eat my shorts." - Bart, *The Simpsons*

"No soup for you!" - The Soup Nazi, *Seinfeld*

"Clear eyes, full hearts, can't lose." - *Friday Night Lights*

The Fonz, Henry Winkler on the popular 70's TV Show *Happy Days*, drove his audience wild with the single drawn out cry of, "AAAyy!"

Cartoon icon, Homer Simpson also only needs one word to define his personal brand. In fact it just a sound, "Doh!" It's so famous the *Oxford English Dictionary* even deemed it worthy of an entry.

The massive impact of an artist like John Lennon could also be summed up in just one word, "Imagine."

Steve Job's iconic ad campaign for Apple computers, had the pictures of historical giants like Einstein and Gandhi with just two words, "THINK DIFFERENT"!

Famous comedian Rodney Dangerfield built his entire career on a routine around the punch line, "I don't get no respect.,"

Although many actors have played the part no one said it better than Sean Connery: "Bond, James Bond."

The Lone Ranger cried, "Hi Ho Silver."

Sargent Shultz on Hogan's Heroes, "I know nothing!"

Legendary horse trainer Pat Parelli says, "Keep it natural."

Best-selling author and motivational speaker, Brian Tracy says, "Be good, be great, be the best!"

Bruce Forsyth said, "Nice to see you to see you nice."

"Make America Great Again," says Donald Trump.

Ronald Reagan: "I said it once and I'll say it again, America's best days are still ahead."

Almost every famous person has a catch phrase or key words that is attached to their brand.

MAKING YOUR PHRASE MEMORABLE

You walk into a bar, a hotel, an office or store and the person in front of you predictable says, "How are you today?"

You say what...?

Fine
OK
Not bad
Great
Pretty good
I'm hanging in there
I've been better
Excellent!
Good
So, so
Alright
Wonderful

Or any or all of the above depending on how the mood hits you.

When people ask me, "How are you?"

I always say, "Legendary."

They either say, "Wow, I love that answer; I have never heard that before," or ask me, "What?" at which point I explain that I am feeling "Legendary," and then they reply, "Oh, I like it!"

One simple unexpected word that never fails to get a response to a question asked 1,000 times a day.

Combining your signature phrase with a gesture, like opening your arms, clapping, pumping your fist or something subtle can enhance the impact of your words further.

Most charismatic personal brands have their own unique phrase. Many movie stars, rock bands, comedians and business leaders can be defined by a single phrase or sound.

Start thinking of how you can make your phrase memorable.

SIGNATURE SOUND

Music has a great capacity to zone us in to a place, a year, a feeling --that moment when we first heard the tune or the summer they played it every other song. This powerful tool can be used to your advantage if you can associate a sound to your brand. Think the theme from the movie, Rocky, 40 years old but as motivating as ever!

You might not know the name **Ennio Morricone** but he was a big part of Clint Eastwood's rise to stardom with his haunting soundtracks for the spaghetti western series. With just a few notes of its twangy tones, "wha wha wah," instantly Clint springs to mind, even fifty years later. Many movies are in fact defined by their sound. Think for example of the iconic theme from James Bond or listen to just a few bars of the Rocky theme and tell me you don't immediately feel stronger!

When I started out in the martial arts business, I used the Pet Shop Boys' "Opportunities" song as our theme song. We played it at the start of every day and at every business seminar I gave. *"You got the brains, I got the looks, let's make lots of money"* was perfect for a garage-based operation on the way to becoming the industry leader.

Legendary locomotive engineer Casey Jones was famous for his peculiar skill with the train whistle. His whistle was made of six thin tubes bound together, the shortest being half the length of the longest. Its unique sound involved a long-drawn-out note that began softly, rose and then died away to a whisper, a sound that became his trademark. The sound of it was described as "a sort of whippoorwill call," People living along the line upon hearing it would remark "There goes Casey Jones" as he roared by.

QUOTE YOUR WAY TO FAME

Coming up with your own quotes is another sure way to enhance the sound of your fame. New York Yankees baseball star Yogi Berra was more famous for his humorous quotes than his play with such gems as:

It's like déjà vu all over again.

You can observe a lot by just watching.

No one goes there nowadays, it's too crowded.

Baseball is ninety percent mental and the other half is physical.

When you come to a fork in the road, take it.

I never said half the things I said.

In 1998 Yogi published *The Yogi Book*. Yogi stated that he the following line when he was attending a ceremony in the '70s during which the mayor of New York City, John Lindsay, gave him the key to the city. The day of the event was hot and humid:

Mayor Lindsay's wife, Mary, commented on how cool I looked, and I replied: "You don't look so hot yourself." I guess I was a little nervous about the speech I had to make.

In my business dealings, my go-to quote is "speed is a strategy," and when I play golf my quote is "If I can find it, I can par it."

Come up with a couple of quotes that espouse your values, mission or talents, and repeat them often.

For those bold enough to go beyond mere quotes, there is always poetry to enhance your brand. No one did it better than Muhammad Ali, spouting out quick ditties faster than a modern-day rap star.

Float like a butterfly, sting like a bee.
The hands can't hit what the eyes can't see.

The two lines above are the most famous Muhammad Ali poem.

I've wrestled with alligators.
I've tussled with a whale.
I done handcuffed lightning.
And throw'd thunder in jail.

-Muhammad Ali

In the 1800s, California bandit Black Bart robbed stagecoaches alone, never shot anyone and wore socks over his boots, so he could not be tracked. His real name was Charles E. Boles, originally from London, England. He was known as a gentleman outlaw who enjoyed writing bits of poetry which he left in empty strongboxes for the pursuing posse.

I've labored long and hard for bread,
For honor, and for riches,
But on my corns too long you've tread,
You fine-haired sons of bitches.

- Black Bart, 1877

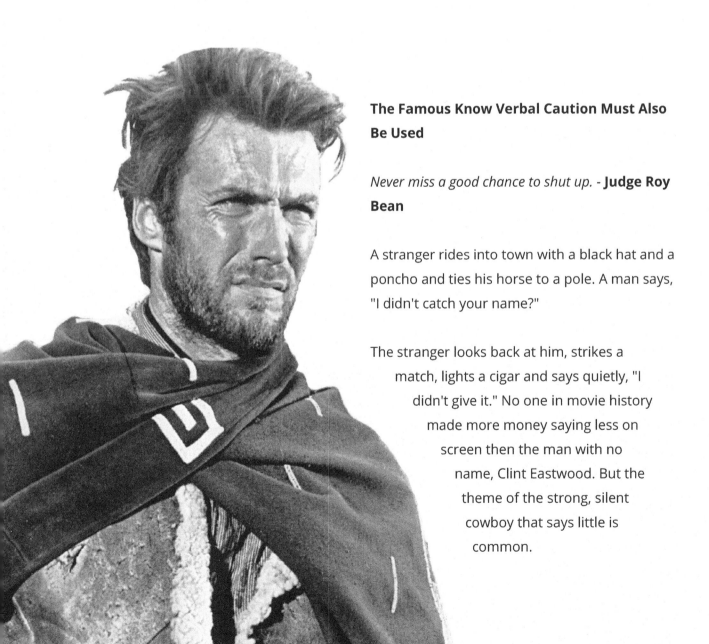

The Famous Know Verbal Caution Must Also Be Used

Never miss a good chance to shut up. - **Judge Roy Bean**

A stranger rides into town with a black hat and a poncho and ties his horse to a pole. A man says, "I didn't catch your name?"

The stranger looks back at him, strikes a match, lights a cigar and says quietly, "I didn't give it." No one in movie history made more money saying less on screen then the man with no name, Clint Eastwood. But the theme of the strong, silent cowboy that says little is common.

Greta Garbo, a goddess of the silver screen, was known for saying very little. From the early days of her career, Garbo avoided industry social functions, preferring to spend her time alone or with friends. She never signed autographs or answered fan mail, and rarely gave interviews. Nor did she ever appear at Oscar ceremonies, even when she was nominated.

Her aversion to publicity and the press was undeniably genuine, and exasperating to the studio at first. In an interview in 1928, she explained that her desire for privacy began when she was a child, stating, "As early as I can remember, I have wanted to be alone. I detest crowds, don't like many people."

Because Garbo was suspicious and mistrustful of the media, and often at odds with MGM executives, she spurned Hollywood's publicity rules. She was routinely referred to by the press as the "Swedish Sphinx." Her reticence and fear of strangers perpetuated the mystery and mystique that she projected both on screen and in real life. MGM eventually capitalized on it, for it bolstered the image of the silent and reclusive woman of mystery.

In spite of her strenuous efforts to avoid publicity, Garbo paradoxically became one of the twentieth century's most publicized women.

In these days of social media, Facebook, Twitter, YouTube, and so on, live video is in constant use. Sometimes it's better to heed the words of noted French writer Antonie De Rivarol, who said, "Silence never yet betrayed anyone!"

Often, especially in situations where you spend a lot of time with a particular client or friend, there is the temptation to cross the boundary and share personal information or problems. In the course of normal conversation, they may even ask questions or probe about your personal life.

You feel you should be open, but in reality they are not interested in your problems. Do not be conned into sharing them. Find out everything you can about your customers and friends while saying little or nothing about negative aspects of your own life.

This holds true for your political, religious and moral views (unless that's your business). These days, prospective customers or employers might well hit your Facebook page and dig deep to see who you "really are." Anything they deem inappropriate may well hurt your chances.

Upon running into a young Michael Caine in the lobby of the Beverly Hills Hotel in the mid-Sixties, John Wayne said, "You just did that movie...?"

"*Alfie*," said Caine.

"Yeah," said Wayne, "I liked it. You're gonna be a big star kid, but let me give you some advice." Putting his arm around the young man as he walked with him, he said, "Talk low, talk slow and don't say too fucking much!"

As the Chinese say, "Keep the tiger behind the bamboo." This will only add to your sense of mystery, control and power. Since you seem to be in complete control of everything, it will also help build your reputation faster. Just like it does Clint Eastwood as the man with no name.

SUMMARY

Iconic brands are rarely built on the power of one modality alone. Most combine powerful keys from each and sound is no exception. Even if that sound is silence.

Your name, nickname and company name will be repeated millions of times in your lifetime so better make sure they are good ones. You should also pay attention to the sounds, catch phrases and sayings associated with your rise to stardom. Destiny often hangs on just a few words.

Having a signature phrase and sound is a great way to increase your memorability, thus increasing your charisma, which in turn enhances your brand. Then again, depending on your situation the mysterious, thoughtful silent type may serve you better!

Gerald Ford was born Leslie Lynch King Jr., a name that might have lacked presidential appeal.

ACTION PLAN

- Is your name ready for stardom? Should you change it or perhaps lead with your middle name or nickname?

- What is your nickname?

- Is your business name the best one for success in a crowded market?

- Is it easy to say and remember? Does it project the desired outcome?

- What is your theme song or sound?

- Have you considered creating your own?

- What is your catch phrase?

- What are your key quotes on business, life, the arts and success?

- Are you thoughtful enough about the strategic use of silence to further your cause?

Phrases of Fame Answers:
1. Mission Impossible
2. Seinfeld
3. The Flintstones
4. Different Strokes,
5. Columbo
6. The Waltons
7. Kojak
8. Hawaii Five-O
9. The X-Files
10. Game of Thrones

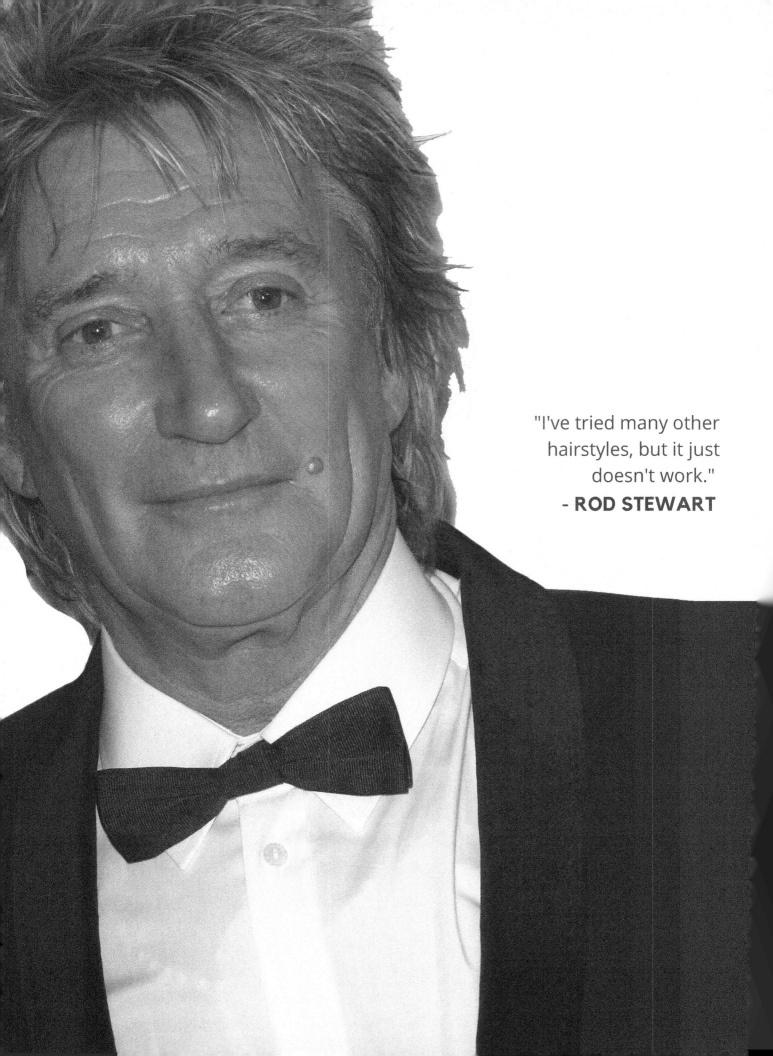

"I've tried many other hairstyles, but it just doesn't work."
- **ROD STEWART**

"Create your own visual style... let it be unique for yourself and yet identifiable for others." - **Orson Welles**

5

CREATING AN ICONIC LOOK
"YOUR LOOK!"

Personal branding starts with the "look" your look.

You don't have to be as handsome or beautiful as JFK, Tom Cruise, Elizabeth Taylor, Kim Kardashian or any other celebrity to pull it off. In fact, you don't have to be attractive at all. No one is going to confuse Lady Gaga with a supermodel, but many a supermodel would quickly trade places. What you need is "the look," your unique combination of fashion, style, colors, symbols and accessories.

What you need is "the look" your unique combination of fashion, style, colors, symbols and accessories. Traits that are uniquely associated with you, your power, talents, charisma, brand and fame!

Creating a "look" will make you stand out from the crowd, yet at the same time makes you more familiar. Think Steve Job's black crew-neck sweaters, Tiger Wood's red Nike shirt or Mark Zuckerberg's sweatshirts. It's how you expect to see them dressed and it makes a statement about their perspective on life.

It's as much a part of their brand as Lincoln's top hat and beard, Churchill's cigar or Donald Trump's hair. In fact, let's start at the top with hair -- or in some cases lack of it -- and see how famous people have used it as part of their brands.

"That is what fame is, isn't it? To get the world to fall in love with you."

LADY GAGA

LEGENDARY HAIR

—

Name some famous boxing promoters? Yep, that's right. You only know one, Don King, and you only know him because of that spiked-up, grey afro he sported for decades -- while he scammed millions from Muhammad Ali, Joe Frazier, George Foreman, Larry Holmes, Mike Tyson, Evander Holyfield and a host of others. Prior to his fame as a promoter, King was infamous for being convicted of second-degree murder. His crime? Stomping to death an employee named Sam Garrett, who owed him $600. Not the way you want to become famous; still, the hair worked!

The story of hairstyles that *matter* goes back as far as Cleopatra, but it was four lads from Liverpool, who put hair on the front page forever. While women were cutting their hair short with pixie cuts or the inverted bob, the Beatles made the mop-top style of long hair fashionable again for men. It defined the group's image and the term was often used in headlines describing them.

In the 1920s, Josephine Baker's jet black, slicked down, Eton crop haircut helped her achieve stardom as an entertainer in Paris. She used a thick pomade to flatten her short hair and created kiss curls on her forehead. Her look was so iconic it came to define the entire Jazz Age. Adding to her fame, during World War II she was also an agent for the French resistance.

Jean Harlow the original blonde bombshell captivated movie audiences with her platinum blonde look and was the childhood idol of one Norma Jean, who would later do pretty well with a blonde look of her own.

Rod Stewart's spikey hair is iconic as is Dolly Parton's massive hive. Bridgette Bardot's disheveled, just-out-of-bed look defines the 1960s. Buffalo Bill, General George Armstrong Custer, race-car driver James Hunt and entrepreneur Richard Branson, all sport flowing, long, blond locks as part of their signature styles.

Eminem bleached his close-cropped hair blonde for that perfect Slim Shady look. Bowie went for orange hair with his alter ego Ziggy Stardust. Tennis ace Bjorn Borg's long hair and Fila sweatband were in stark contrast to the big permed look of arch-rival John McEnroe.

The iconic Farrah Fawcett's long, voluminous, sun-kissed mane with a center part was the look that defined women's hair of the same era until the Princess Di look trumped it.

Australian motivational speaker and nutritionist Susan Powter was huge in the 1990s and early 2000s with her cry of, "Stop the insanity." An advocate of a whole-foods, organic, low-fat diet, and regular cardiovascular and strength-training exercise, Powter also condemned the diet industry for ripping off consumers. Her platinum-white, close-cropped haircut, aggressive manner of speaking, and being barefoot while speaking in public became all became elements of her fame.

Pink has often been seen as "adventurous" with her hair, and has had styles such as fluorescent spikes, pink-streaked dreadlocks and even a pitch-black skater cut. Regarding her style, she told InStyle, "I'm eclectic. I'm a tomboy, but I'm kind of a hippie and kind of a gangster. I don't know if that's a good thing, but it's my thing."

CREATING AN ICONIC LOOK

FOLLICLE CHALLENGED FAME

Having no hair is not necessarily a disadvantage to fame or so proved actor Telly Savalas long before the shaved head look was popularized. Savalas rose to superstardom playing the cuddly, 1970's New York detective, Kojack and a host of forgettable movies like the Dirty Dozen. He along with Yul Brynner, of King and I and Magnificent Seven fame became the first bald stars to flaunt their baldness as a symbol of their manhood rather than something to hide. Later Captain John Luke Picard of Star Trek the Next Generation made bald sexy. Suddenly bald was in and people who weren't bald started shaving their heads to look like Michael Jordan, Seal and the Rock. Even Brittney Spears did it although in retrospect that might not have been such a great idea for her career.

Perhaps your unique look is in somewhere between Farrah and Kojack like Mr. T's Mohawk. I mean who can remember the rest of the A-Team? But MR. T now there was a look that demanded attention.

Mr. T pioneered the look pop culturally in 1977 after reading National Geographic magazine. The Mohawk haircut was a look also adopted by several early punk rockers only they traded Mr. T's accompanying gold chains for safety pins.

Then again perhaps you just move on as your hair decides to leave you. Tennis star Andre Agassi had huge 80's, bleached blonde hair that would have fit in with any glam rock group, the only problem was it was a wig. During one match on a scorching day it started to come loose while he was playing. He played the entire match worrying more about the humiliation of it falling off on center court than where he hit the ball. That night after a pep talk from his them wife Brook Shield's he shaved it off and never looked back.

Sinatra, William Shatner, John Travolta, Chuck Norris, Charlie Sheen and Ben Affleck are just a few of the famous toupee wearer's.

Sean Connery wore a toupee in all his Bond movies and so did John Wayne but Wayne was never bashful about it he just saw it as another prop, another part of his costume but one the public expected to wear.

I never want to draw attention to myself, but that's all I do - **Slash**

ICONIC HEADWARE

Legendary golfer Ben Hogan always wore a flat, white hat pulled down low over his hawk-like eyes to keep him focused and it suited his steely persona perfectly. World-famous golf instructor David Leadbetter adopted a straw hat and sun glasses, a look that eventually became so recognized he made it his logo. Australian Greg Norman started a new trend on the PGA Tour by wearing a low-crowned, cowboy style hat.

Rock star Slash is instantly recognizable by his top hat although others like Slade's, Noddy Holder and Tom Petty had done it before, it became "his look." Meanwhile, Guns and Roses front-man, Axl Rose, had his red bandana, a look he may have copied from Springsteen who was sporting one in the 1980s on his "Born in the USA" tour.

Not content to wear what anyone had worn before, rock group Devo designed their own hats. Immortalized on the cover of Devo's third album, Freedom of Choice, these nutty, energy dome hats were inspired by both the Bauhaus movement and Aztec temples. Band members Mark Mothersbaugh and Gerald Casale designed them "according to ancient ziggurat mound proportions used in votive worship.

Whatever...but would anyone remember the band without them?

French emperor Napoleon had a keen understanding of the importance of branding and throughout his life used imagery and clothing to convey his power and status. The hat featured in all his popular images was his black-felted beaver fur bicorne. Traditionally, the bicorne, with its distinctive deep gutter and two pointed corners, was worn with the corners facing to the front and back, but so as to be distinct on the battlefield, Napoleon wore the hat sideways so that anyone scanning the crowds would instantly know him by his jauntily angled hat. A cunningly simple but clever move to stamp his personal brand.

Winston Churchill was renowned for his hats and sported many, including bowlers and top hats. But he is most often associated with a Homburg: which, oddly enough, was German. Churchill himself once wrote a humorous essay on the subject of hats, remarking that since he did not have a distinctive hairstyle, spectacles, or facial hair like other famous statesmen, cartoonists and photographers of the day focused instead on his love of headgear.

Marlene Dietrich is someone anyone interested in timeless style should study. In a silk evening gown or a tailored tux, Dietrich's looks, capped off with top hats, epitomized sexual prowess and radiant confidence. The cabaret singer's androgyny figured into her charm, worldliness, and Weimar-era act, which she later exported successfully to Hollywood. This power look helped her to become the first ever female star to earn a percentage of the film's gross.

Jackie Kennedy was one of America's greatest style icons. Her most memorable look was the classic pillbox hat perched on the back of her head rather than the top. She had many

Jamaican Reggae Legend, Bob Marley was almost as famous for his dreadlocks as his music. Marley was also known to put it all under a roomy knit, multi-colored beanie or Rasta hat.

versions of the pillbox, which she first wore at the inauguration of her husband. The most famous is the watermelon pink one she wore with matching pink Chanel suit on November 22, 1963, the day President John F. Kennedy was assassinated. Jackie, who had been at his side in her pink suit, was covered in her husband's blood.

The options for the perfect headgear are many and varied:

Hulk Hogan's skull caps.

Picasso's classic French beret.

A black Cuban-style military beret with embroidered communist red star was also adopted by guerilla fighter Che Guevara and still adorns the posters and T-shirt of young men around the world. He achieved lasting fame, which is astonishing given how little he accomplished.

Charlie Chaplin's bowler hat.

Oddjob's killer bowler hat in the movie Goldfinger. The hat was weaponized with a chakram (a circular Indian throwing weapon) added to the brim which in the movie he throws like a boomerang, decapitating a statue's head.

Other endearing hats from movies include Indian Jones's fedora, Sherlock Holmes' deerstalker or the Sorting Hat in Harry Potter.

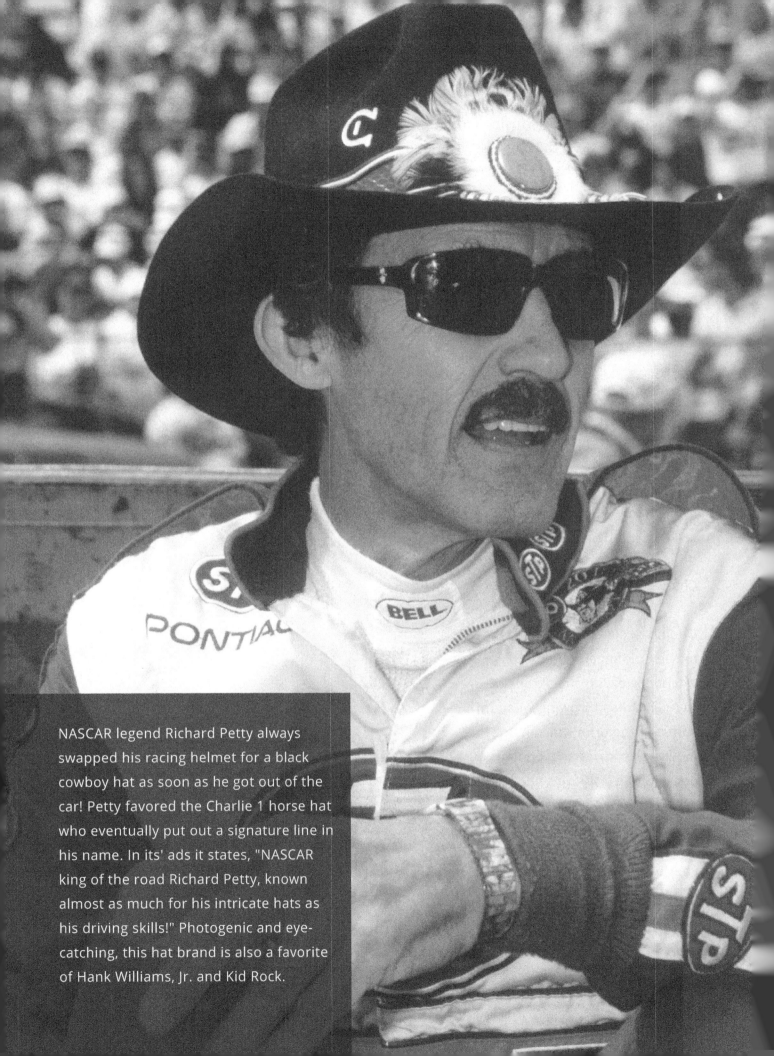

NASCAR legend Richard Petty always swapped his racing helmet for a black cowboy hat as soon as he got out of the car! Petty favored the Charlie 1 horse hat who eventually put out a signature line in his name. In its' ads it states, "NASCAR king of the road Richard Petty, known almost as much for his intricate hats as his driving skills!" Photogenic and eye-catching, this hat brand is also a favorite of Hank Williams, Jr. and Kid Rock.

A black Cuban-style military beret with embroidered communist red star was also adopted by guerilla fighter Che Guevara and still adorns the posters and T-shirt of young men around the world. He achieved lasting fame, which is astonishing given how little he accomplished.

Abraham Lincoln, at 6 foot 4 inches, was very tall, especially for those times. The addition of his famous stovepipe top hat accentuated his height even further. Lincoln used to keep papers and speeches tucked inside his hat and would fish them out when needed, making his hat not just a natty bit of headgear but also a mobile briefcase.

Davey Crockett had his coonskin hat, while the Cisco Kid sported a sombrero, and Tom Mix had his ten-gallon hat. Indian Chief Crazy Horse would either tie the body of a hawk against the side of his head or wear a war bonnet with buffalo horns and a dozen eagle feathers. He often wore a red blanket like a cape.

For others like Cher, Lady Gaga and the English Queen there was no particular hat but there sure were lots of them.

Since her ascension to the throne at age 25, Queen Elizabeth II has worn over 5,000 different kinds of headwear - floral caps, turbans, cloches, fur Cossack hats - until she finally found her signature hat, variations of which she's been wearing for the past few years. They tend to have an asymmetrical top.

For each of these famous people a signature hat became an integral part of their personal brand.

Who do you think of when you see these glasses?

FAMOUS EYEWARE

—

Elton John's zany eye wear, like massive sunglasses that spelled ZOOM, heart shaped lens, square ones, triangular ones, even lens with a garden gnome, become one of his endearing symbols.

John Lennon's simple round glasses, were similar to those worn by Gandhi. Given both men's commitment to non-violence, one would have to think this was not an accidental choice on Lennon's part.

Later John Denver also projecting a wholesome, down-to-earth country image adopted the same look with his glasses.

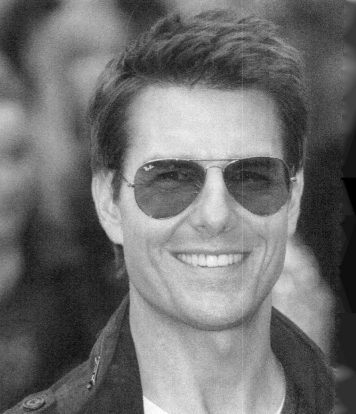

The Futures So Bright You've Got to Wear Shades

Wayfarer sunglasses emerged as a staple of Hollywood glamour in the 1950s, notably adorning James Dean in *Rebel without a Cause*. By the end of the 1960s, sales declined. Though Wayfarers' cultural popularity was aided in 1980 by the film *The Blues Brothers*, only 18,000 pairs were sold in 1981. Then in 1983 a young actor named Tom Cruise, stared in the movie *Risky Business*. Throughout the movie, Cruise is seen wearing the square-shaped Wayfarer glasses. Sales for Wayfarer sunglasses shot up 50% thanks to Cruise sliding around in his underwear.

Wayfarers were also worn around this time in performances by musicians, including Michael Jackson, Billy Joel, Blondie's Debbie Harry, Madonna, Depeche Mode, Elvis Costello, and members of U2 and Queen, as well as many movie stars such as Jack Nicholson. The glasses become so famous they even wrote songs about them. Don Henley's 1984 song "The Boys of Sumer" contained the lyric "You got that hair slicked back and those Wayfarers on, baby." Corey Hart's music video "Sunglasses at Night" shows the artists wearing Wayfarers in darkness.

CREATING AN ICONIC LOOK

Wayfarers was not the only model of shade Cruise would single-handedly lift back to iconic status. Three years later he stared as Pete "Maverick" Mitchell in the 1986 action movie *Top Gun* wearing Ray-Ban's Aviator Classics, gold frame with green lens. Sales again sky-rocketed by 40% and the shades are universally recognized today as *Top Gun* sunglasses.

In the 2017 movie *American Made,* Cruise got yet another prime opportunity to make some frames famous. This time Tom sports square-framed aviators by Randolph Engineering, which enjoyed a Cruise inspired bump to their sales!

When you are "The King," though, a mere Iconic brand will not do, which is why Elvis customized his famous Neostyle Nautic, 14-carat gold, aviators, with his initial "EP" custom fitted to the double-bridge and "TCB" (Taking Care of Business), his "phrase," on the temples. These babies have swagger written all over them.

Said his wife Priscilla, "We were shopping on Sunset Boulevard in 1979 and we walked into a store that sold sunglasses. He was trying on different shapes and Dennis, the owner, showed him the pair that would look right for his face. He told Elvis the shape was good because it covered his eyebrows and that when picking out sunglasses that should be considered. Elvis always wore that same shape, he never varied. Unless, of course, maybe in a film."

Get the right shades for your face because your future is so bright you are going to need them.

CRITICAL GROOMING

It's astonishing how many famous men are defined solely by their facial hair: Dali, Clark Gable, Errol Flynn, Buffalo Bill, Sean Connery (after Bond) Charlie Chaplin, Groucho Marks, Tom Selleck, Burt Reynolds, Rollie Fingers, Sam Elliot and many more.

Tom Selleck's, "Magnum PI," "Blue Bloods" mustache is the epitome of the perfect chevron mustache (chevron refers to the area between the nose and the upper lip, out to the edges of the upper lip but no further). It's a mustache masterpiece; it's thick, it's luxuriant, it's well shaped and groomed-it's basically everything you could ever look for in a mustache. A close rival was actor, Burt Reynolds, whose mustache was, both commanding and debonair, bushy yet streamlined and the perfect match to his often-seen hairy chest. Queen's lead singer, Freddie Mercury, was another Chevron wearer as was long-running British TV host Bruce Forsyth.

Athletes, too, love the chevron. Steve Prefontaine, one of the few middle-distance runners to ever gain fame, was a chevron man as is NASCAR "King" Richard Petty. Olympic swimmer Michael Phelps may now have more medals, but Mark Spitz's mustache could beat Phelp's any day of the week.

Anytime Hollywood needs a cowboy mustache, also called a horseshoe they call Sam Elliot's and he comes with it. My good friend and Legendary horse trainer Pat Parelli, is another fine example of this style as was Wyatt Earp and Hulk Hogan. Another friend, Master Bill Clark, is an icon in the martial arts industry, both as a fighter and as a businessman. For over 40 years his Fu Manchu mustache went with him.

The Van Dyke is a style of facial hair named after 17th-century Flemish painter Anthony Van Dyke. A Van Dyke specifically consists of any growth of both a mustache and goatee with all hair on the cheeks shaven. It was sported two centuries later by Buffalo Bill and later shared by Colonel Sanders of fried chicken fame.

Members of rock group ZZ Top were define by their long beards. Guitarists Billy Gibbons and Dusty Hill have been wearing the signature look since the late 1970s, while the group's drummer, whose name is ironically Frank Beard, prefers to maintain a clean shave. At the height of their fame, Gibbons and Hill were once offered $1 million to cut off their facial hair, but they declined.

The Walrus, a bushy style often covering the mouth, was sported by such notables as writer Mark Twain, German philosopher, Friedrich Nietzsche and actor Wilford Brimley.

Spanish surrealist painter Salvador Dali's legendary mustache mirrored his artistic nature. Then there's the toothbrush-style mustache worn by Oliver Hardy and Charlie Chaplin -- and while I hate to even give Hitler the courtesy of a mention, his mustache was pretty famous.

Clark Gable's pencil mustache doesn't give a damn, which is probably why actor Sean Penn also adopted it.

Australian film star Errol Flynn had a swashbuckling mustache that could make even tights look manly.

World Famous horse trainer Pat Parelli has a macho cowboy look that would make the Marlboro man jealous. Blue jeans, leather chaps, Cattleman's hat, flannel shirt and a mustache most real cowboys other than Wyatt Earp can only dream of.

THE MUSTACHE GANG

Rollie Finger, was a pitcher for the Oakland A's and in his day the most recognized player in the league thanks to his waxed handlebar mustache, which he originally grew to get a $300 bonus from Athletics owner Charles O. Finley.

On the first day of spring training for the 1972 season, Reggie Jackson showed up with a beard which was against club policy. In protest, Fingers and a few other players started going without shaving to force Jackson to shave off his beard in the belief that management would also want Jackson to shave. Instead, Finley, ever the showman who would do anything to sell tickets, offered prize-money to the player who could best grow and maintain their facial hair until opening day.

Fingers went all out for the monetary incentive offered by Finley and patterned his mustache after the images of the players of the late 19th century.

By the time "Mustache Day" rolled around, all 25 members of the Oakland Athletics were sporting mustaches. Even Dick Williams, the As manager, decided to grow one.

To further promote his team's new look, every fan that showed up to the Oakland Stadium wearing a mustache gained admittance for free. The players would become known as the "Mustache Gang."

Most players shaved their mustaches off after leaving the team, but Fingers maintained his after signing with the San Diego Padres as a free agent in 1977, and still has his mustache today.

The 70's Kicked the Cult of Fame into to High Gear

In the 1970s, for the first-time, actors became more famous for the parts they played than for whom they actually were, and their costume clothing actually mattered. Sean Connery and the black tuxedo he amply filled became James Bond. Detective Lt. Colombo, played by Peter Falk, had his famous raincoat. John Travolta in a white suit danced his way to stardom as Tony Manero in *Saturday Night Fever*.

Body Parts

Some people are naturally beautiful like Sophia Loren, Pierce Brosnan, Ronaldo, Anna Kournikova or Hallie Berry. For those less fortunate, their best option may be to go with just a part of their body.

Arnold's muscles, Bruce Lee's abs, Mick Jagger's lips, Gene Simmons' tongue, Spock's ears (even if they were fake), Gerard Depardieu's or Bob Hope's nose. Seal's facial scars. 50 Cent's gold teeth. Prince Charles's big ears. Van Gogh's missing ear (NOT recommended). Sinatra's blue eyes, Elvis's or Shakira's hips, John Holmes's penis or Dolly Parton's breasts. All those features played major roles in their brands reaching iconic status.

Fake it Until You Make it!

Porn star Long Dong Silver, famed for the size of his penis, reputedly 24 inches (61 cm), appeared in many pornographic movies during the late 1980s. Later photographer Jay Myrdal revealed that although Silver "was very well endowed... a good nine or ten inches," the penis featured in his porn shoots was faked.

After at first using "complicated multi-exposure techniques" to enhance Silver's natural endowments for still photography, Myrdal later persuaded the makeup artist for the film the Elephant Man to create the prosthetic which greatly contributed to the notoriety of Long Dong Silver. Myrdal comments that, "It was very light, a very delicate foam latex sleeve that fit on over the cock, carefully glued down underneath by the pubes and then made up." Apparently no one ever caught on to it and a generation of men was left feeling more inadequate than ever!

The Fonz, played by Henry Winkler, in the long running TV series "Happy Days," had his black leather jacket -- a jacket so famous it resides in the Smithsonian Museum alongside Ali's boxing gloves, Dorothy's red slippers and Captain Kirk's communicator. Meanwhile back in the UK, Richard Branson became the first celebrity CEO to opt for blue jeans over a traditional Saville Row suit (at least when he wasn't dressed as a woman for charity, as a pirate for publicity or as a spaceman simply because he can).

Marilyn Chambers, **what you didn't recognize her with her clothes on?**

CLOTHES MAKE THE MAN OR WOMAN

"Clothes make a man. Naked people have little or no influence on society." - Mark Twain

Twain was right, unless you are Linda Lovelace, Marilyn Chambers, Ginger Lynn, Jenna Jameson, Traci Lords, Ron Jeremy or John Holmes, who all became superstars in the 1970's video porn era, wearing nothing at all. (I looked all the names up --honest!) Just imagine how much they saved on clothes! But for most of us clothing is a critical part of our look. The closest thing to nothing in the real world, if you could call the Playboy Mansion the real world would be Playboy founder Hugh Hefner.

Hef managed to live his entire adult life in his pajamas, a silk dressing gown, slippers, a white captain's cap that looked like it came from the set of Gilligan's Island and, of course, his ever-present pipe.

President John F. Kennedy had many subtle ways of asserting his image, power, charisma, and style. Breaking with the tradition of the day, he was the first president to wear European-style suits with two buttons, rather than the traditional three-button American suits.

This fashion statement added to the existing public perception that the Kennedy White House had style, pizzazz, and energy. Within months, thousands of top executives across the country had followed his lead.

There was a practical reason for the suits as well, they hid the back brace he wore constantly to alleviate debilitating back pain.

The Armani or Boroni designer suits of the 1980s and 1990s were a trend started by the film "American Gigolo" starring Richard Gere. This film not only epitomized the masculine style of the day but also drew attention to men's fashion in a way no other had before. The Armani suits Gere wore put the fashion house on the map. Later movies like "Wall Street" with Michael Douglas played a big part in setting the fashion trends of "power suits and ties."

Brioni suits had been worn by celebrities since the 1950s, including by stars such as Clark Gable, John Wayne, Gary Cooper and Henry Fonda. But Brioni only became famous when their suits were worn impeccably by the classically handsome Pierce Brosnan in all of his Bond movies and by Daniel Craig in "Casino Royale."

The Black Knight

Legendary golfer Gary Player stood out from the crowd by being "The Black Knight." Player originally wore white outfits to reflect the sun and keep cooler. When he changed to all black, he told reporters he did it to absorb the sun's energy, but the truth of the matter was that it made him easily identifiable, even at a distance. Eventually it became his trademark. A similar style also worked for Johnny Cash, so much so that he became known as "the man in black."

Steve Jobs of Apple fame had his black crewneck shirt and jeans in stark contrast to the conservative suits of IBM and other rivals.

Tiger Woods wore his "victory red" Nike shirts on Sundays for the final round in all of his big wins!

Trump used his red power tie to great effect throughout his career as a property developer.

Elvis wore leather jump suits, while Prince was associated with the color purple (as were Roman emperors). Gandhi made the white toga famous again two thousand years after Greece and Rome.

Clint Eastwood as the man with no name had his brown poncho and ever-present cigar.

Before his tragic death in a plane crash, golf superstar Payne Stewart's colorful, 1920s-style cap and kickers made him stand out among an army of PGA clones. He adopted the style in the early 1980s after walking onto the practice tee one morning and finding six other players all dressed exactly as he was, in white shoes, red golf slacks and white shirts. Stewart's father, a furniture salesman, gave him this advice:

"Always stand out from the crowd. That way people will remember you."

With that in mind, Stewart switched to cap and knickers, sometimes called plus-twos. He was quickly rewarded with a lucrative contract from the National Football League, the terms of which

required him to wear the colors of the NFL team most popular in the area currently being visited by the Tour. More lucrative opportunities came his way because he stood out from the other players.

Stewart ignored jibes from his fellow pros and maintained that the outfits were cooler and more comfortable to wear than regular golf slacks.

They certainly were "cool" for him and for the legion of fans that will always remember him as much for the way he dressed as for his outstanding play, humor and competitive personality.

Let's look at some possible professional applications

A Swedish realtor in Delray Beach, where a lot of Swedish x-pats reside might dress in the blue and yellows colors associated with her national flag as a subtle way of gaining instant rapport with clients and standing out from the hordes of other realtors.

A lawyer might dress in a light-colored Panama suit to stand out from the crowd of dark suits in the court room. An accountant in San Francisco might go with jeans and t-shirt to bond with millennials. Perhaps T-shirts with different humorous accountant slogans.

A dentist providing "happy smiles" might opt for a Hawaiian shirt instead of the traditional white or light blue overalls or have something fun printed on the overalls these days you can print on anything!

The fishing charter captain who wears a bowler hat rather than a captains hat?

EVOLUTION OF MADONNA'S LOOK

—

While most of the examples I have given focus on core elements of style, no pop diva has reinvented her fashion image with the consistency and creativity of Madonna.

She emerged on the scene in the early '80s as a street-smart "boy toy." Over the course of her long career, she evolved into a fashion-forward icon whose sense of style became as influential as her chart-topping tunes. "Mostly what Madonna wears is an evolution of what is relevant at the time," said her stylist of over 20 years, Arianne Phillips, "The visuals reflect the music in a kind of seamless marriage of her point of view." she said in an interview with billboard magazine. Somehow Madonna carries off the cowgirl, medieval princess, virgin bride and cheerleader looks, and cone-shaped bras, without missing a breath. But keeping up with her might leave you and your credit card breathless.

When I started in the martial arts business in the late 80's, everyone wore either white or black "karate" uniforms, nothing else. I wore a grey one and later switched to a blue. I always stood out. When I started my company, Legendary Marketing, in 1998, I decided to use orange as our signature color. It was bright, it stood out, and at that time I couldn't find one major company using orange. It worked. Soon partners and prospects alike were calling our bright orange polo shirts "Legendary Orange"!

As I grew into a "Marketing Legend" I opted for a bright blue pinstripe suit, bright yellow shirt and starry night tie for my more professional engagements.

As my brand grew I eventually opted for blue jeans, a bright custom shirt, blue gator shoes and a colorful sports jacket.

Together with longish hair, a Union Jack faced BRM watch and blue Oakley sunglass, my look is in stark contrast to the rest of the conservative golf industry.

There must be something to it though because often complete strangers ask me if I'm famous?

To which I reply, *"I'm a legend in my own mind but you've got to start somewhere."*

Ali's Everlast, shorts and gloves were almost as famous as he was.

YOU ARE WHAT BRANDS YOU USE

—

Many stars are so attached to brands as to become one with them. Golfer Jack Nicklaus played his entire career with a giant green-and-white MacGregor golf bag, signaling to the world the clubs he swung. Tom Watson spent his glory days with a similar-sized white bag emblazoned with a giant Ram's head in red holding his weapons of choice, Golden Ram irons. Golfer Jordan Spieth became the first mega star for the upstart brand Under Armor. Tiger and Nike were as joined at the hip. Basketball star Michael Jordan and Jordan's air shoes are still flying high long after he retired.

Roger Federer plays with a Wilson racket. Novak Djokovic and Andy Murray play Head, Rafael Nadal a Babolat, and then there was Borg.

Bruce Springsteen has his Fender Telecaster guitar, while Gibson was the choice of Bob Marley, Jimmy Page of Led Zeppelin, Slash of Guns & Roses.

1970s tennis star, Bjorn Borg, played with a Donnay racket and seemingly had it all. Long blond hair, a headband, facial hair and a series of outfits that became as famous as he was. When it comes to sportswear logos, Fila's rounded "F" is only slightly less iconic than the triple stripes of Adidas were long before Nike and Under Armour even existed. Fila CEO Enrico Franchey spotted a young Bjorn playing at a tournament in Monte Carlo and was impressed by what he saw. Franchey wanted to make him Fila's poster boy and in 1975 the Bjorn Borg and Fila collaboration became a reality. Franchey let Pierluigi Rolando design a completely new, charismatic look for the aspiring youngster. The outcome was the legendary Fila pinstripe polo shirt Borg started wearing in 1976. It soon became the defining look of the '70s.

It did not hurt that Borg grand-slammed his way into sports history wearing the Fila crest on his chest, capturing five Wimbledon titles in a row. Less than a decade later the logo resurfaced as an urban status symbol for New York's burgeoning hip-hop scene. There was even a group called the Fila Fresh Crew. Forty years later the vintage styles remain the company's best-selling items. In an odd twist of fate, Borg now runs his own clothing line, which started as an underwear brand.

"A gentleman's choice of timepiece says as much about him as does his Saville Row suit."
- **Ian Fleming**

Time Precious Time

Golfers Arnold Palmer and Jack Nicklaus both wore Rolex watches and had long-term affiliations with the company, as did many iconic sportsmen from Jackie Stewart to Roger Federer. It was actor Paul Newman, who like Cruise with sunglasses, took a dying watch model and made it iconic by simply putting it on his wrist. In 2018 his 1968 Rolex Daytona (a gift from his wife, Joanne Woodward, who bought it for around $200), sold for $17,752,500.

Steve McQueen's personal watch of choice was a Rolex Submariner, always worn on his right wrist, but the watch he's most closely associated with is the Heuer Monaco 1133.

Jack Heuer launched the square-cased, water-resistant Monaco at Basel in 1969. Always ahead of the pack, Heuer forged a strong partnership with racecar driver Jo Siffert to promote the brand within Formula One. On hearing that his friend McQueen wanted an authentic wardrobe for his new film *Le Mans*, Siffert naturally suggested he wear a Heuer.

Jack was invited to the set to display several models, and you'd think the producers would go with an Autavia, Siffert's favored model. But they needed three the same, and the only model Heuer had three of on that day was the Monaco. Thus, film (and watch) history was made.

Ian Fleming, author and originator of the world's most-beloved spy, wore a Rolex Explorer 1016-as did Bond when he made his novel debut. When Sean Connery debuted Bond on screen in Dr. No, he had a Submariner on his wrist that stayed there for most of his Bond movies.

By the time product placement had taken over from personal choice Pierce Brosnan, as James Bond sported an Omega Seamaster and Daniel Craig continued the relationship.

Before he discovered Hublot Jay-Z rapped about Rolex and Audemars Piguet.

Putting the Pieces Together

All of these examples are a part of the DNA code for creating an iconic personal brand. Symbols of power, mystery, action, beauty, adventure traits others aspire to emulate.

These various symbols and icons are often copied, amended or reborn by others to enhance their image and increase their fame.

Is it a Bird, Is it a Plane? No, It's Evel Knievel

Lots of young men do daring or stupid things on motor bikes but there was a time when only Ali and Elvis were as famous as daredevil Evel Knievel. With his stars-and-stripes leather jumpsuit, large EK-initialed cowboy belt, superhero's cape and diamond-studded walking stick (which had a hidden liquor compartment), Knievel's look was part Elvis, part Liberace and part Superman. Crowds loved it and Knievel crafted his brand into an iconic status with the self-promotions skills of P.T Barnum and Houdini combined. To get ahead of other motorcycle stunt people who were jumping animals or pools of water, Knievel started jumping cars, first with a Norton bike but more famously with a Harley Davidson XR-750. He began adding more and more cars to his jumps. Then he would return to the same venue to get people to come out and see him again. Testament to his lasting fame came in 2017 when the jumpsuit (and cane) that Knievel wore to jump over 50 cars in Los Angeles fetched $200,000 at auction.

A Horse of a Different Color

My good friend and business partner Linda Parelli (married to Pat Parelli mentioned earlier) has her own unique brand in the equestrian world. While Pat is the iconic western cowboy, Linda's focus is on English and dressage. Her natural beauty and blonde hair is enhanced with her ever-present visor and pony tail. Her preferred colors are turquoise or black. Her belts are large with a little bling, and when not in designer blue jeans, she has colored jodhpurs that make her stand out from other riders.

Her philosophy of kindness to her animals is magnified by a saddle wider than the norm so as to be more comfortable to the animal. And her bridle is elastic rather than steel so as to be gentler on her horse's mouth. As a former cosmetics professional, her make-up is always perfect. This is helped by a careful diet and lots of riding to keep her in shape. The result is a look of radiance, charisma, confidence and vitality which has the added benefit of giving her the look of a woman far younger than her physical age.

While one or two of these elements might be the key to your look, the subtle use of many of them will make more impact since different fans will be attracted to different elements.

Summary

From rock stars to Realtors, entrepreneurs to athletes, having a personal style, color, signature, gesture or accessory can help build your personal brand quickly, bringing the additional opportunities and income along with it. Einstein was defined by his cloud of gray hair, Dolly Parton by her beehive hairdo and bust. What hair style makes you rock? Then there is your all-important face, or in Sam Elliot's case the thing that's attached -- his moustache. Many famous people like Charlie Chaplin, Tom Selleck and Burt Reynolds were defined by their moustaches. In stars, often one part of their face becomes their signature, like Streisand's nose, Jagger's lips or Prince Charles's ears.

Gandhi had his simple white garment. Elvis, Evel and Liberace had their bling jumpsuits while Tiger wore red on Sundays. What colors and clothing styles look best on you? What brands resonate with your audience?

Care should be taken with glasses, hats and shoes to maximize your appeal. Accessories like watches and jewelry are also an important statement that does not go unnoticed by fans. Famous people at the top of their game understand the effect of these seemingly insignificant styles, symbols, colors and gestures as a way to increase their power, charisma, and personal brand. You must do likewise by coordinating all of these elements into creating a look that is uniquely YOU!

So what's Your Unique Signature Look Going to be?

David Beckham, always an icon of style.

ACTION PLAN

- What's your hairstyle shape?

- Your Color?

- Your preferred headwear?

- Glasses/shades, what colors, what shapes what styles are yours?

- Grooming?

- Any unique body features you might be known for?

- Make up?

- Clothes Type - stylish, casual, punk, sophisticated, conservative, playful?

- What brands do you favor?

- What colors look best on you?

- Shoes?

- What watch is your watch?

- What accessories will tie your look together perfectly?

"The best thing about a picture is that it never changes, even when the people in it do." - **Andy Warhol**

6

IS A PICTURE WORTH A THOUSAND WORDS?

The famous go to great lengths to get the right photo and to avoid the wrong one. Let's take a world-class example of this from a master of the game. In various photos we've seen he's bare chested riding a horse across the steppes. In another he's in a judo suit on the mat. Next we see him playing ice hockey in a charity match, followed by a shot of him in a frogman suit. In other shots, he's hunting with a rifle, spearfishing from a speed boat or peering from the window of a mini sub.

Cleaned up, he's now in a dark designer suit with designer shades to match. Yes, Vladimir Putin is the ultimate action man. If his pictures are to be believed, he makes James Bond look like an amateur. They reinforce his multiple skills, his health, strength and vitality. Like GI Joe or Action Man he does it all, and has the kit for every occasion!

Obama played hoops in city neighborhoods for photo ops when he ran for office, showing he was just "one of the guys." He continued while he was president, often photographed playing with aides, congressmen and military personnel.

Churchill to was a master of fame-building photos, and he used props to masterful effect. He wore a boiler suit like "everyman" wore (most likely for the only time in his life) when he inspected the bomb damage among the people of London.

The famous photo of Winston Churchill with a Thompson submachine gun in hand was taken during his visit to the coastal defense positions in the North of England on July 31st, 1940. Britain's prospects for success in the war were looking very grim for her new prime minister. Governments in exile were arriving in London daily from the continent overrun by the Nazi war machine. The Home Guard, made up of men too old to join the army, was ill-prepared. For a month, Hitler had been preparing to invade Britain, and the Luftwaffe had been commencing what would eventually be known as the Battle of Britain. Britain had lost the Channel Islands barely a month before, and for a while it looked as if Russia might join the war from the German side.

The Churchill photograph was timely. It was used to convey Churchill as a war leader. Both sides of the war tried to use this picture for propaganda purposes. The British, long before the term existed, "photoshopped out" two soldiers standing next to Churchill, making him look statesmanlike, determined and menacing.

On the other hand, the Germans got hold of the photo, and compared it to those of American gangsters like Al Capone. The Nazis used this photo in their propaganda leaflets airdropped onto Britain during the Battle of Britain.

No writer was ever as famous as Hemingway, in part because no writer in history ever had better pictures. If Putin had a role model, Hemingway could have been it. When he wasn't writing, Hemingway spent much of the 1930s chasing adventure: big-game hunting in Africa, bullfighting in Spain, deep-sea fishing in Florida. While reporting on the Spanish Civil War in 1937, Hemingway met a fellow war correspondent named Martha Gellhorn, soon to become wife number three, and gathered material for his next novel, *For Whom the Bell Tolls*, which would eventually be nominated for the Pulitzer Prize. When the United States entered World War II in 1941, Hemingway served as a correspondent and was present at several of the war's key moments, including the D-Day landing. He was not just writing about action, he was the action, and he made damn sure someone was there to take a picture of him!

Hemingway saw the world, and his place in it, in grand, almost-mystical terms. He said, *"From ...all things that you know and all those you cannot know, you make something through your invention that is not a representation but a whole new thing truer than anything true and alive... You make it alive, and if you make it well enough you give it immortality."*

His personality and constant pursuit of adventure loomed almost larger than his creative talent. He even went out with a bang. Suffering from acute depression, he killed himself with his favorite shotgun in 1961.

No one felt better about Hemingway's death in 1961, than the entire animal population of Africa!

Formal photography sessions scheduled by the White House staff date back to the 1930s, when President Franklin Delano Roosevelt's press secretary instructed photographers to avoid showing the polio-afflicted President in a wheelchair. He didn't want the American people to perceive him as weak.

Under the Reagan Administration, photographic access to the president was controlled and orchestrated to virtually guarantee that no unflattering or negative pictures would be recorded.

Believing that the "look" was more important than the meaning of an event, White House staff dictated the time, place and even the angle-of-vision of "photo-ops." Reagan, an actor for most of his life, understood the need for the perfect picture. He was often photographed at his ranch on horseback in a cowboy hat, mending *fence*s or drinking coffee on the porch, thus reinforcing his image of frontier Americ*an spiri*t.

Can anyone old enough to remember not shed a tear of joy as Reagan, framed by the *Brandenburg Gate, p*oints at the *camera and utters th*e ic*o*nic words, "Mr. Gorbachev, tear down that wall!"

Would the moment have been so memorable and special had he said it in a hotel ballroom? Of course not, Reagan knew the value of props like no other.

The iconic train wreck picture depicting the **Montparnasse derailment** occurred at 4PM on October 22, 1895

The Granville–Paris Express overran the buffer stop at its Gare Montparnasse terminus. With the train several minutes late and the driver trying to make up for lost time, it entered the station too fast and the air brake failed to stop it. After running through the buffer stop, the train crossed the station concourse and crashed through the station wall. The locomotive fell onto the Place de Rennes below, where it stood on its nose. A woman in the street below was killed by falling masonry.

A train wreck is exactly what happened to the careers of many famous people who allowed themselves to be photographed in the wrong place, at the wrong time, with the wrong people, and the wrong backdrops in place.

THE CRITICAL IMPORTANCE OF NOT BEING PHOTOGRAPHED THE WRONG WAY

Take no bad pictures. Reagan was keenly aware that one bad photograph of a public figure can have a devastating effect on public confidence. Just as a well-placed story can stick in the public memory, a single photographic impression of a leader can be viewed as representative of his entire persona. Reagan was always very conscious of his presence on camera. His staff were carefully trained to watch for any items in the vicinity of the President that might be caught on camera. For example, Reagan took great pains to avoid situations where military weaponry might creep into the picture, enabling opponents to foster perceptions of Reagan as a warmonger. This care and attention resulted in pictures that helped shape a positive, upbeat image of Reagan for the public. Other presidents and pretenders were not so careful or so lucky.

President Jimmy Carter, photographed collapsing during a run, became symbolic of the burned-out Carter administration.

It signaled to the world the general weakness of the Carter administration in the face of the oil crisis, hostage crisis and other maladies of the time. In the third mile of a tough 6.2-mile race through the Catoctin Mountains in Maryland, the president began to wobble. "Without the Secret Service, he would have fallen," says Paul Liebler, a CBS producer who was running close by. Carter was given smelling salts and rushed to Camp David where it was feared he might have suffered a heart attack. White House physicians

diagnosed heat exhaustion and declared him to be "perfectly normal." Ninety minutes later, Carter handed out trophies at the finish line. Despite his speedy recovery, the image damage was done and irreparable. The next day that picture made the front page of just about every newspaper in the world.

Before Carter, the same faux pas were also prevalent in the Ford administration. Despite the fact that Ford was probably one of the most accomplished athletes ever to hold the office, the media published repeated images of President Ford appearing to stumble down the steps of Air Force One or playing combat golf by hitting spectators with his errant shots.

While visiting the Alamo for a bicentennial celebration in 1976, Ford committed what would later be known as the "Great Tamale Incident" when he grabbed the Mexican delicacy from a plate and began eating—without first removing the husk. The pictures of beaned spectators, wrapped tamales and a stumbling President, tended to encourage the view that his entire administration might be prone to serious error.

THE PHOTO THAT SANK A PRESIDENCY

Matt Bennett was a 23-year-old political rookie in 1988. He was sent to a General Dynamics facility in Sterling Heights, Michigan on September 13th, 1988 to organize a campaign stop for Democratic presidential nominee Michael Dukakis and a ride in a 68-ton M1A1 Abrams Main Battle Tank. But Dukakis was booed and heckled the whole time about his "antimilitary" attitudes.

A photo was taken of a smiling Dukakis sticking his head out of a tank and wearing a helmet that looked several sizes too large for him. Despite having served in the Army, the photo made him look small and a bit loony.

The visit, meant to bolster the candidate's credibility as a future commander-in-chief, would go down as one of the worst campaign backfires in history. Following the event, after all the reporters' laughter had subsided and Dukakis's entourage was preparing to leave, one of the candidate's traveling aides approached Bennett. "Nice event, Matt," he deadpanned. "It may have cost us the election. But beside that, it was great."

John Wayne, in later life, was in constant pain from a variety of medical problems including battling cancer. He was too sore to get on his horse, so a saddle was built on a wooden structure. A reporter on set that day made the mistake of taking pictures of Wayne on the contraption. Forgetting his pain Wayne leapt from the wooden horse at the photographer, grabbing the camera from the astonish man's hands. He berated him loudly as he tore the film from the camera and threw it to the ground.

Although Wayne had a temper, friends said they never saw him quite that mad. But he knew the damage that photo would have done to his macho image.

In 1972, actress Jane Fonda went on a controversial tour to North Vietnam. The trip would come to be the most infamous part of her activist career, and lead to her nickname "Hanoi Jane." While in Vietnam, Fonda appeared on 10 radio programs to speak out against the U.S. military's policy in Vietnam and beg pilots to cease bombing nonmilitary targets. It was during that trip that a photograph was taken of her seated on an anti-aircraft gun in Hanoi, making it look like she would shoot down American planes.

She addressed the photo in her 2005 memoir My Life So Far:

"Here is my best, honest recollection of what took place. Someone, I don't remember who, leads me toward the gun, and I sit down, still laughing, still applauding. It all has nothing to do with where I am sitting. I hardly even think about where I am sitting. The cameras flash. I get up, and as I start to walk back to the car with the translator, the implication of what has just happened hits me. Oh, my God. It's going to look like I was trying to shoot down U.S. planes! I plead with him, 'You have to be sure those photographs are not published. Please, you can't let them be published.' I am assured it will be taken care of. I don't know what else to do. It is possible that the Vietnamese had it all planned. I will never know. If they did, can I really blame them? The buck stops here. If I was used, I allowed it to happen. It was my mistake, and I have paid and continue to pay a heavy price for it."

At the time the photo caused a massive backlash that still haunts her to this day. Some lawmakers at the time saw her protests as treasonous, and the Veterans of Foreign Wars called for Fonda to be tried as a traitor.

August Landmesser was a worker at the Blohm+Voss shipyard in Hamburg, Germany. He is best known for his appearance in a photograph, refusing to perform the Nazi salute at the launch of the naval training vessel Horst Wessel on June 13, 1936. An amazing act of defiance that took real courage, it ended in him being sent to the frontlines and his wife to a concentration camp; both died. Still I salute, August Landmesser for not saluting, may his name live on in the fight against oppression and tyranny everywhere!

I SAW IT IN A MAGAZINE, IT MUST BE TRUE

Back in 1993 I managed to get on a Martial Arts Business Information Magazine cover. There's a picture of me, standing with a red Ferrari Testarossa, outside a huge Spanish-style house. Although I had a nice home and an older Porsche, it was nothing compared to this look; car and house borrowed from my friend Doc McGhee, who was Bon Jovi's manager at the time.

After struggling for 18 months, I finally hit pay dirt in late 1994 and bought my own Ferrari, a white one.

I was having dinner shortly afterwards with one of the big players in the industry when he mentioned my red Ferrari. "It's white, I corrected him."

"I am sure it was red," he said, "I saw a picture of it in a magazine."

"Oh," I quickly said, "that one, I have a new one!"

In talking with many others, there is no doubt that as cheesy as seems, this type of branding does work to enhance your status and fame even if it's a little ahead of reality. Thirty years later the house and cars are really mine!

GET YOURSELF PHOTOGRAPHED WITH PEOPLE MORE POWERFUL AND FAMOUS THAN YOU!

A good policy to instantly enhance your fame is to get yourself photographed with people more powerful and famous than you are. This creates the illusion that you must be someone of great importance if these people spend time with you.

When I taught martial arts back in the 1990s, pop star Donny Osmond, a super nice guy, enrolled his son in my school. I decided to do a parent-child night, so I could get him in the dojo. Then of course we took pictures for all the parents including a really nice one of me teaching Donny Osmond! Before he took "lessons" from me, it was a well-known fact that he and his famous brothers flew Chuck Norris to Utah quite frequently to train them. With the photo, it appeared he was taking lessons from me :)

Travolta and who?

Back in the 1970's, Master Ed Parker's well-deserved reputation as the founder of Americanized Karate sky rocketed to fame when Elvis became a student.

Once you start your program of association with famous people, you need to keep it up. Don't for a minute think that once fame has been attained, your favorite celebrities stop doing this. Fame attracts fame and the more famous people you are pictured with, the more famous you must be - as evidenced by my photos below with some of the famous!

THE FIRST AT BEING FAMOUS FOR BEING FAMOUS

Long before Paris Hilton and Kim Kardashian became famous, largely from being famous, there was Angelyne. Angelyne's larger-than-life image was originally used to promote her first band, Baby Blue, which wasn't getting much attention in LA's punk music scene. They decided to promote it by posting her picture around town with posters and flyers. Things were going to get bigger, much bigger.

According to Angelyne, she met wealthy adhesive-free-tape entrepreneur Hugo Maisnilk in 1982. Maisnik owned a display-printing business in Los Angeles. Described as "very eccentric" and a "bored prankster," Maisnik reportedly saw potential in using Angelyne's image and understood the "intricacies of the outdoor-advertising game."

In February 1984, Angelyne's first billboard proclaiming "Angelyne Rocks" went up on Sunset Boulevard. The billboards quickly took on a life of their own as Angelyne signs were erected all over LA. Nobody really knew who Angelyne was or what she actually did. Her billboards only added to the mystery featuring only her image, name, and telephone number. The billboards seemed to be everywhere you looked, and at one point a decade later there were 200 all over LA.

These quickly caught the attention of local media outlets, and soon she received a number of offers for film roles, magazine interviews, and television show appearances as an unapologetic female sex icon. She quickly became the most recognized face in Hollywood, prompting countless appearances on television and in cinema, music videos, etc (Her biggest movie was *Earth Girls Are Easy*, starring Geena Davis.) .

Her billboards have been featured in a number of movies and television series, including the opening credits of Moonlighting, and spoofed in shows such as *The Simpsons*, *Futurama* and *BoJack Horseman*.

Angelyne may well have been the first person who became famous just for being famous, although by all accounts she had a good voice. The main trademark of her celebrity persona other than the billboards is her omnipresent pink corvette. Adding to the allure was her impulse of hiding her face in public so she was only seen as she wanted to be seen. She continue with a diverse career as a singer, actress and celebrity, and ran for Hollywood city council in 2002. She even entered the California governor's race in 2003, finishing a respectable 28th from a list of 135 candidates.

PUT YOURSELF IN YOUR ADS!

David Ogilvy, great British ad man and author, Created the "Hathaway man" to advertise Hathaway shirts. Then in the mid-1950s he made Commander Edwin Whitehead, manager of the British beverage company Schweppes, into a worldwide star. His print ads, featuring this distinguished, very British looking gentleman, were perfect for the American market. Sales increased over 500% in less than a decade after the introduction of the campaign.

Starting in the 1980s saw a new breed of CEO, the celebrity CEO who used their company's fame and money to create iconic brands of their own. CEOs appeared constantly in prints ads and on TV:

- Dave Thomas, founder of Wendy's
- Donald Trump
- Lee Iacocca
- Richard Branson
- Steve Jobs
- Victor Kiam
- Karsten Solhiem
- Papa John (including Peyton Manning)
- Colonel Sanders (even when the real one died)

We are all familiar with the local Realtor, attorney or car dealer who uses this strategy, but why not everyone? Repetition and familiarity are two of the key ingredients to fame; the more times they see your mug, the more famous you must be!

Find creative ways to work your picture into as many ads, emails, videos and promotions as you can.

If that chick only knew what he was getting into... Frank Perdue the original "Chicken man" and CEO, TV star.

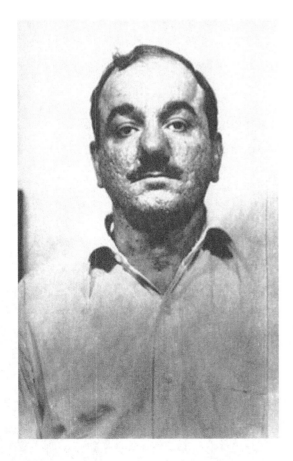

"The Chicken Man," also known as the Julius Caesar of the Philadelphia Mob, was blown up on his doorstep in 1981. Bruce Springsteen made this death more famous by including it in his song "Atlantic City." But another chicken man, one who confined his murderous activity to chickens was more famous. Frank Perdue was one of the first CEOs to appear in TV commercials, starring in over 200 beginning in the early 1970s.

Perdue became the face, voice and name of the chicken industry, pioneering the idea of branding for a previously generic product like chicken. His TV appearances created astonishing name recognition for his company, Perdue Farms, and allowed them to dominate the industry while starting a new trend of CEOs hawking their own products!

Dave Thomas Ruled the '90s in CEO Airtime and a 90% Name Recognition Rating!

After resigning in 1992 from the day-to-day operations at Wendy's, the company he founded, Dave Thomas was asked back several years later after a series of missteps had sent the company's sales plummeting. In 1989, he took on the role as the TV spokesperson in a series of commercials for the brand. Thomas was not a natural actor and initially his performances were criticized as stiff and ineffective by advertising critics. After some coaching and a change of direction to get humor into the campaign, a decision was made to portray Thomas in a more self-deprecating and folksy manner. This proved an instant hit and consumer brand awareness of Wendy's eventually regained levels it had not achieved since octogenarian Clara Peller's wildly popular "Where's the beef?" campaign of 1984. With his self-effacing style, his relaxed manner, and the help of over 800 TV spots, Thomas quickly became a household name. During the 1990s, a decade in which Thomas starred in every Wendy's commercial, 90% of Americans knew who Thomas was. Thomas became so famous that he made a cameo appearance as himself in *Bionic Ever After*, a reunion TV movie based upon *The Six Million Dollar Man* and *The Bionic Woman*.

Orville Redenbacher

Instantly recognizable as the eponymous popcorn brand image, Redenbacher appeared in many commercials--some alongside his grandson. Usually the format was to compare his product directly with a generic competitor. He appeared as the company's official spokesman, wearing a trademark outfit in public that included horn-rimmed glasses and a bow tie. Some customers wrote letters asking if Redenbacher was a real person, and not an actor. He responded to this by appearing on various talk shows, professing his identity. Redenbacher, in his book, states, "I want to make it clear that I am real."

Victor Kiam

Victor Kiam made a bigger fortune as the president and CEO of Remington Products, which he famously purchased in 1979 after his wife bought him his first electric shaver. Remington, which had lost $30 million in the previous three years, made a profit in his first year as owner. Kiam became famous as the spokesman for the Remington shaver. His catchphrase, "I liked the shaver so much, I bought the company," made him a household name. He recorded each commercial in the native language of the country in which it was broadcast. In the United Kingdom he became a celebrity, appearing on such television shows as *Wogan*, *The Tube*, and *Through the Keyhole*.

Charles Schwab

The head of the eponymous discount brokerage appeared in ads to identify with his clients' needs and successes. Making the connection between the image of "the man" with the image of "the company" helped develop the "Talk to Chuck" theme that runs through even the most recent ad campaigns

Lee Iacocca

In the 1980s, as American car companies faced an existential threat from overseas automakers, tough-talking Chrysler CEO Lee Iacocca became a symbol of pride in U.S. craftsmanship, captured in his tagline, "If you can find a better car, buy it." His on-screen presence was credited with helping the automaker turn a corner in a difficult market. He retired in 1992 but returned to the screen at age 80 in 2005 to make new TV spots for the company.

THE TREND CONTINUES

From the 1990s through today, inventor James Dyson revolutionized the vacuum cleaner industry before creating a wide range of other household gadgets. He brought a tone of sophistication and expertise to his company's ads, helping justify his products' higher price points in categories crowded with legacy brands. He also looked cool with a muscular body, jeans and T-shirt. Michael Dubin, CEO of Dollar Shave Club, is another modern example of an iconic leader and spokesperson, one whose mainstream appeal likely stems from the fact he began as a content creator before becoming a successful entrepreneur. For the last decade Papa John was hawking pizzas with his war cry "better ingredients better pizza" on every NFL broadcast up to 2018. Being on TV can rocket you to fame even if it's only to star in ads. That's just as true today for ads that run on YouTube or Facebook. Creativity and repetition can quickly build a brand!

PAPARAZZI

Rock stars like Jagger, Bowie, and Madonna developed relationships with the world's top photographers, as do many movie stars.

They know the value of a great picture and the image-wrecking potential of a bad one. Many of these photographers become famous in their own right like Helmut Newton, the fashion photographer, whose provocative, erotically-charged, black-and-white photos were a mainstay of *Vogue*. Philippe Halsman also contributed to fashion magazines, eventually stumbling into *Vogue* where he built his reputation as the best portrait photographer in France. He was known for iconic pictures of Ali, Dali and Brando.

Dorothea Lange had a long career but will forever be known for a single photo of Florence Owens Thompson, mother of seven, taken at the height of the Great Depression, with Thompson in the center of the frame. Our eyes go directly to her expression before we notice she's surrounded by three of her kids. The focal point of the image is her hands, which marked Lange's fascination with hands and their embodiment of hard, rural work.

Arguably the most famous photographer working today is Annie Leibovitz who has photographed almost all of the world's major celebrities in her illustrious career, often in elaborate and imaginative set-ups. She started her career in 1970 as staff photographer

working for the just-launched Rolling Stone magazine. In 1973, publisher Jann Wenner named Leibovitz chief photographer of Rolling Stone, a job she would hold for 10 years. Leibovitz worked for the magazine until 1983, and her stylistic photographs of celebrities helped define the Rolling Stone look. She sought intimate moments with her subjects, who "open their hearts and souls and lives to you."

She has a way of fine tuning the lighting in her shots to conjure a precise mood.

She also uses really bold compositions to make strong statements about her subjects.

INVESTING IN PHOTOGRAPHY TO BUILD YOUR BRAND

You probably don't have access to famous photographers like Lange and Leibovitz, but you can borrow ideas from them and clip pictures with looks that you'd like to duplicate. The most important asset you have for building your fame on social media is your images. In today's digital age there is an exponential increase in the power of images. Consumers have become more sophisticated in their consumption of photographs and images. A recent study shows that **posts that include an image receive 120-180% more engagement than posts containing text alone**. Major social media outlets like Instagram and Pinterest center solely on your visual content.

You can buy "stock" photos from special companies. These can relate to your business or activities, but won't include you in them. While I make daily use of stock photography, you are going to need a wide variety of custom photos to build your fame. Custom photography is an ASSET, therefore having a library of image files to pull from saves you time and money over the long term. That's why it's so important to begin thinking about photographs as ASSETS! You can MAXIMIZE your photograph investment by using them throughout all of your marketing strategies! Here's how to get started:

1. Find a good photographer.

A good photographer will make you money because they will save you time and get you the perfect shots you need to build your fame. A good photo shoot (creating multiple pictures) will last you several years so when you amortize the cost it's really not that much.

2. Think carefully about your various markets; you must be authentic.

You might use your photos in multiple vertical markets, so will need different props that resonate with each market. Accountants are not attorneys, doctors are not dentists, and rap audiences are not country audiences. The more each of your photos connects with your specific niche, the more effective it will be. For example, in the martial arts business every school teaches "martial arts," but there are subtle and not so subtle differences in styles of Karate, Taekwondo and Kung Fu uniforms. They will not accept the wrong uniform for their style. Even though the future customer has no clue, the instructors want their ads to be 100% authentic, so we had to develop ads in each specific style, not just generic "martial arts" or "karate."

I have seen the same disconnect in the golf industry where a big development hires an agency that knows nothing about golf to market them. You'll see models on the putting green in high heel shoes, a left-handed player's image reversed to be right handed (the golf glove is on the wrong hand), a player walking onto a green with a driver instead of a putter, and other such faux pas which destroy all credibility.

3. Think about the multiple ways these photos might be used to tell your story.

Consider your current marketing first: social media, brochures, websites and ads. There are also your blog posts and articles about you. Then think about new niches you would like to work in. What about future press releases? What about other media such as videos? You might even start thinking of your future biography. Take a look at your favorite pictures of yourself and try to spot a pattern. Do you like the way you look from a certain angle? When you smile a specific way? Try to replicate your best poses next time you have your photo taken.

Photographs of a product alone don't create emotional connections. Photograph your products or services being used by different people (for example, men, women, doctors, truck drivers) in different ways (at home, at work, in the car – whatever situations are appropriate).

Create a list of shots you want and provide it to the photographer in advance, so the photographer can consider the location, timing and the lighting and make the most efficient use of your allotted time.

Ask customers to post or send in their photos of them using your product or service. You might get some ideas from customers that you hadn't thought of.

Have photos of various staff members with your products. A photo of an executive with your product might be used in situations where you want to convey reliability. A photo of a smiling service rep helping a customer can provide reassurance.

A good studio portrait can do wonders for your fame!

4. Cover the basics first.

Start with the head shot, the close up, half shot and full-length photos. Get some pictures where you are professionally dressed and some casually dressed. Some head on and some from the side or various other angles. Some static and some with you in action, doing that thing you do best! Take some shots of you pointing in each direction. These can be very handy for a variety of situations like directing people to your opt-in box or phone number. Check the shots as you go to make sure all the bases are being covered.

5. Take some conceptual shots.

The more you can portray your emotion and passion for what you do, the more powerful the images will be. Show them who you are at work: the love, the joy or intensity of you in action as the master of your craft. This may take some stagecraft. When Annie Leibovitz shot the comedian Whoopi Goldberg, she photographed her in a bathtub full of warm milk. Goldberg's dark limbs and face emerge from a white sea. It was a startling image based on Goldberg's heartrending, politically charged impersonations of a little black girl scrubbing her skin in the hope that she will become white. Says Leibovitz, "Conceptual portraits are driven by an idea. Somewhere in the raw material of information about who the subject is and what he does is the nucleus of what the picture will become."

6. Take shots with props.

Props are a great way to add interest to your story. Big or small, they can make your photo stand out from the crowd. A few years ago, we were pitching a large account with a Western-themed resort. I found one of those period photographers you find in tourist places and had him come to my office. The staff had a blast, and all got to have a couple of personal portraits.

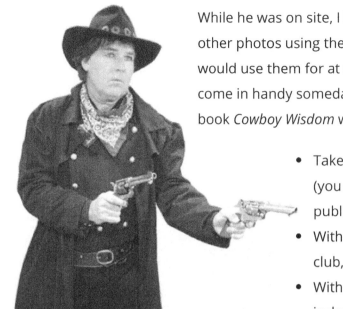

While he was on site, I had him take a whole bunch of other photos using the props. I didn't know what I would use them for at the time but knew they would come in handy someday. Four years later I wrote the book *Cowboy Wisdom* where they came in very handy!

- Take shots of you holding up a book (you can change the cover when you publish yours)
- With sports equipment like a golf club, football, baseball or cricket bat
- With different hats, shoes or sport jackets
- With cars, planes or boats as backdrops
- In action playing tennis, golf, riding
- With a microphone in your hand or signing a copy of your book
- Show your success with people, happy clients, customers and fans.
- Show success with a sold sign, car keys, money or whatever the successful outcome of your service is
- At home with pictures by the pool, in the garden or with family

Be creative in getting a wide range of shots that will work for you now and in the future. That way, you can go two or three of years before you need another big shoot.

7. Have some style guidelines.

Decide in advance on some style guidelines. What fits you, your story and your goals for the shoot? (By the way, a style guide can alse apply to your advertising and other marketing output.)

- What colors will you use, bright action colors or soft pastels?
- What look do you want?
- What lighting is best: bright, dark, mood?

- Vintage
- Corporate
- Urban
- Clean
- Grunge
- Sporty
- Punk
- Classic

8. Have some candid shots taken.

Just go about your normal day and have the photographer shoot you in your natural environment without posing. Very often you'll get some great shots where you least expect it!

9. Red carpet tricks to looking your best on film.

Most people, including top models, have to work at it to look their best. Here are a few tips straight from the dressing room to make your look red carpet ready!

- Put your tongue behind your teeth when you smile to avoid a goofy, too-wide grin.
- To avoid a double chin, elongate your neck and push your face forward a bit. Think of sticking out your forehead and tipping your chin slightly down. It might feel awkward as hell but it will look great—promise.
- Look toward a light right before someone snaps your photo doing so shrinks your pupils and help to avoid red eye.
- For a classic, no-fail pose, turn your body three quarters of the way toward the camera, with one foot in front of the other and one shoulder closer to the photographer. When you face the camera head on, your body tends to look wider. This pose ensures the camera catches you at your best angle with your belly in, buttocks tight, shoulders back, and spine straight.
- Aim your eyes to the side to show more white.
- A drop or two of Visine makes your eyes sparkle.
- Shiny hair looks best; use some spray.
- Bright lipstick looks better than dark unless you're shooting vamp stuff!
- Show your "good" side. Chances are, one side really is better, says Peter Hurley, a Los Angeles–based portrait photographer. To find yours, hold a piece of paper vertically over one side of your face, then the other, says Ian Spanier, a photographer in New York City. Your better side is the one with

more upturned features—for example, the corners of your eyes and lips. While not always the case, in one Wake Forest University study, researchers found that the left side of the human face is generally more appealing to others than the right side. For the study, participants were asked to rate photos of 10 male and 10 female faces, in both their original and mirror image form. Photos showing the left side were rated more "pleasant" than those of the right sides. Researchers said their results suggest that individuals' left cheeks tend to exhibit a greater intensity of emotion, which others find more aesthetically pleasing.

- While it should be obvious, make sure your clothes fit great, are pressed and are the best colors for your hair, eyes and skin tone.
- One Miss America advised to not be photographed eating. Few of us look good while eating.

10. Have all shots available on your website for media use in different formats.

You are going to use these photos in many different ways and so are the people who will be writing about you. You need large format, small format, vertical and horizontal images. You will also want them in different resolutions for everything from email, to a headshot, to a Hollywood billboard. Once you have decided on your best shots, upload a handful of them to the media page on your website in a variety of different files sizes so others who want to spread your fame can do it easily when they want to write about you!

Moving Pictures

Some photographers go on to even bigger things. Like the small, shy Jewish boy who in 1958 became a Boy Scout and fulfilled a requirement for the photography merit badge by making a nine-minute 8 mm film entitled The Last Gunfight. Years later, Steven Spielberg recalled to a magazine interviewer, "My dad's still-camera was broken, so I asked the scoutmaster if I could tell a story with my father's movie camera. He said yes, and I got an idea to do a western. I made it and got my merit badge. That was how it all started."

Video is now very important to fame, and not just for those discovered on YouTube or making a living from their antics and ad revenue. Professionals in every field should be using videos to enhance their fame. Intro videos for your Facebook page, LinkedIn, company page, and YouTube channel are among the first you are going to want to produce. You should also produce short videos for your products and services. It's nice to do a professional production, but while you are waiting for that to happen, turn on your computers video cam and start with a simple talking head promoting your services.

Your images don't have to be photos or videos. Some people get famous just by painting graffiti on walls. The key to their success, as with any fame, is an iconic look and a message that connects with your adoring fans.

In the case of English-born graffiti artist Banksy, his satirical, often dark and controversial art conveyed messages on politics, consumerism and philosophy. The messages were usually anti-war, anti-capitalist or anti-establishment. Adding to his fame is the fact that his identity remains unknown, even after over 30 years of being involved with the graffiti scene.

By the age of 18, Banksy began to develop his unique style after nearly being caught vandalizing public spaces by police. As his crew fled from the scene, Banksy was stuck hiding beneath a garbage truck. Banksy saw stencil letters on the truck. Looking for a faster way to paint, Banksy decided stenciling would be his new graffiti type.

Banksy began his graffiti art lifestyle by admiring the works of Blek Le Rat and often recycling his old ideas. He has been very active in the graffiti scene since the early 1990s. Initially, he hung around a graffiti crew in Bristol by the name of DryBreadZ crew or DBZ. Soon after, he began to partner with Inkie, another notable graffiti street artist. By the early 2000s, Banksy relocated to London, where he began to gain notoriety and worked on a series of international exhibits. Eventually, he decided to travel to Palestine and the West Bank, where he stenciled nine images on the Bethlehem Wall. These images were an instant hit and virally exploded on the Internet.

By 2007 Banksy's work was selling routinely at auction for between $75,000 and $150,000. After a big day at Sotheby, Banksy updated his website with a new image of an auction house scene showing people bidding on a picture that said, in typical iconoclastic style "I Can't Believe You Morons Actually Buy This Shit."

While painting brings fame to some, a lot of famous people then turn to painting. Some have real talent like Ronnie Wood, Bob Dylan, and Johnny Cash. Sylvester Stallone, Lucy Lui, Anthony Hopkins, Paul McCartney, Johnny Depp and Bowie are just a few of the celebrities who are/were prolific painters. Even if it's not what made them famous, their paintings keep them in the news in an entirely new way and bring in a nice second income. Ah, the rewards of fame!

SUMMARY

We live in a visual world. Getting great photos has never been more important. Take care where your picture is taken. Being in the wrong place at the wrong time can be fatal to your image, if not your entire career. Fortunately, the reverse is also true. Encourage photographs of yourself at charity events, with visiting customers, or working side by side with employees. Schedule a professional photo shoot every couple of years. There is nothing worse than meeting someone in person whose online photo is so old you don't recognize them. It instantly makes them seem vain and dated. Before the shoot, review the tips on how to look your best on camera.

Get multiple shots, in different clothes and settings using different icons to create the image you want. Once you have great picture of you, make it a point to get your picture taken with people even more famous than you, thus benefiting your career with the halo effect. Pictures should be authentic to your knowledge and goals, but that doesn't mean you can't use a few props to make your brand look as it's a little further down the line. Put your picture in your ads and commercials to maximize your fame from your ad spend. Use videos of yourself in action. While professional production is best, even talking into a simple web cam will do if the message is good. While it's not for everyone, art is another way to get famous visually or to capitalize on your fame!

Iconic pictures can make a career.

ACTION PLAN

Get Professional Photos

- Invest in professional photography.
- Study the tips for looking great in photos.
- Get head shots.
- Action shots.
- Playing sports, singing, dancing, working.
- Casual shots reading, writing, signing books, thinking.
- Shots with customers or fans.
- Shots with your products.
- Shots at home and at work.
- Think carefully what you want your photos to say.

Be aware of where photos are being taken

- What is the event?
- What are you wearing?
- What is in the background?
- Who else is in the picture?
- What do you want people to think when they see this picture?
- Be very careful and strategic on what photos you post on social media. Make sure everything enhances you brand.
- Use your picture in creative ways in your marketing.
- Put yourself in your ads and appear on video.
- Make intro videos for your products or services.
- Have high and low-resolution pictures in various sizes available for the media to access on your website.
- Perhaps your painting or drawing can add to your fame?

If a picture can replace a thousand words, make sure the picture says the words you want!

"The best leaders... almost without exception and at every level, are master users of stories and symbols." - **Tom Peters**

7

SYMBOLS, ICONS, RITUALS AND COMMUNITIES THAT TURBO CHARGE YOUR FAME!

Since time began man has heightened the experience and memorability of any meeting or gathering by the use of symbols, icons and rituals. The repetition of these create communities of like-minded people and build a strong bond among both the audience and those participating in the event. You too can use these ancient bonding techniques to build your personal brand more quickly and make the effect of your presence linger longer!

Legendary ad man David Ogilvy, was a firm believer in creating icons and symbols that defined a brand. Early in his career he won the account of a small Maine-based shirt maker called Hathaway. His task was to give national visibility to this practically unknown company. But in contrast to the two million dollars that competitor Arrow Shirts was spending at the time, he was given a budget of just $30,000. Ogilvy, never one to shy away from a challenge, went to work. Knowing that a unique photograph would grab the attention of magazine readers, Ogilvy was looking for some sort of symbol that would make his ads stand out from those of the competition.

Acting on impulse, on his way to the shoot, he stopped at a drug store and bought an eye patch he saw in the window for $1.50. At the shoot he put it on his model. Cast in a wide range of activities, from driving a tractor to purchasing a Renoir painting, and always wearing the black eye patch, he labeled his handsome, mustachioed model The Man in the Hathaway Shirt. The campaign attracted a great deal of attention worldwide and was widely copied overseas. It also served its purpose. The Hathaway Man campaign became a classic in the annals of advertising and helped establish both Hathaway shirts and Ogilvy's ad agency.

The man in the Hathaway shirt

AMERICAN MEN are beginning to realize that it is ridiculous to buy good suits and then spoil the effect by wearing an ordinary, mass-produced shirt. Hence the growing popularity of HATHAWAY shirts, which are in a class by themselves.

HATHAWAY shirts *wear* infinitely longer—a matter of years. They make you look younger and more distinguished, because of the subtle way HATHAWAY cut collars. The whole shirt is tailored more *generously*, and is therefore more *comfortable*. The tails are longer, and stay in your trousers. The buttons are mother-of-pearl. Even the stitching has an ante-bellum elegance about it.

Above all, HATHAWAY make their shirts of remarkable *fabrics*, collected from the four corners of the earth—Viyella and Aertex from England, woolen taffeta from Scotland, Sea Island cotton from the West Indies, hand-woven madras from India, broadcloth from Manchester, linen batiste from Paris, hand-blocked silks from England, exclusive cottons from the best weavers in America. You will get a great deal of quiet satisfaction out wearing shirts which are in such impe cable taste.

HATHAWAY shirts are made by a sma company of dedicated craftsmen in t little town of Waterville, Maine. Th have been at it, man and boy, for one hu dred and fifteen years.

At better stores everywhere, or wr C. F. HATHAWAY, Waterville, Main for the name of your nearest store. New York, telephone MU 9-4157. Pric from $5.50 to $25.00.

Ogilvy also worked very hard to build a brand image for himself. Blessed with the ability to toss off quotes from literary and historical figures at will, he was very much the Renaissance man. He described himself as conservatively flamboyant. In 1958, The New York Times noted, "The 47-year-old Mr. Ogilvy's dress and manner cause him to stand out, particularly amongst ad men, many of whom follow a pattern in their getup." In an industry known for dark suits and red ties, Ogilvy sported tweed jackets, light-colored suits, and an ever-present pipe. Better than most Legendary Leaders, Ogilvy knew the power of creating a brand image for himself, not just his clients, and become the first real rock star of advertising.

John Wayne, as US Marshal Rooster J. Cogburn in the movie True Grit, figured the eye patch finally won him the Oscar!

BUILDING YOUR PERSONAL BRAND WITH SYMBOLS

John Wayne, the most iconic American actor of the 20th century, made almost 200 movies. Near the end of that run, without a single Oscar to his name, he played an aging, drunk, US marshal named Rooster J. Cogburn in the movie True Grit. The script called for him to wear an eye patch, but Wayne refused to do it. Each day when he came in to the dressing room for rehearsals the eye patch was sitting there on the top of the pile. Finally, after a few days he tried it on and found it was rigged so although black to the audience he could see out of it perfectly. He decided to give it a try. In his Oscar speech a year later, having just won Best Actor, as he took the stand and tried to maintain his composure, the first words out of his mouth were, "If I'd have known that would have got me this, (looking at the Oscar) I'd have put that patch on 35 years ago!"

Churchill's V for VICTORY sign. Despite a long career in Hollywood in plenty of A movies, Telly Savalas became more famous as Lt. Detective Kojak than as Telly Savalas, in part thanks to his ever-present lollipop. Despite a long career in Hollywood in plenty of A movies, Telly Savalas became more famous as Lt. Detective Kojak than as Telly Savalas, in part thanks to his ever-present lollipop. Michael Jordan's diamond earring and red Air Nike sneakers. Doc Holiday had his guns backwards for a cross draw. The Lone Ranger had his mask and his white horse, Silver. Soccer superstar, and iconic personal brand, David Beckham has made his tattooed body art part of his unique look, as did boxer Mike Tyson and the whole Maori tribe before them. Chuck Connors, as "The Rifleman," had his Winchester. Sean Connery, and for that matter every other James Bond, had a Walther PPK and their martinis shaken, not stirred.

Long before rock group Kiss took the stage, famous Indians like Crazy Horse had several battle rituals, including painting face and body. Crazy Horse used lightning bolts and white spots to denote hailstones. General Patton wore a shiny steel helmet and pearl-handled six-shooters on both hips, while MacArthur sported a flat cap, sunglasses and a clay pipe. Both generals stood out a mile and used their head gear and accessories as trademark symbols for their personalities.

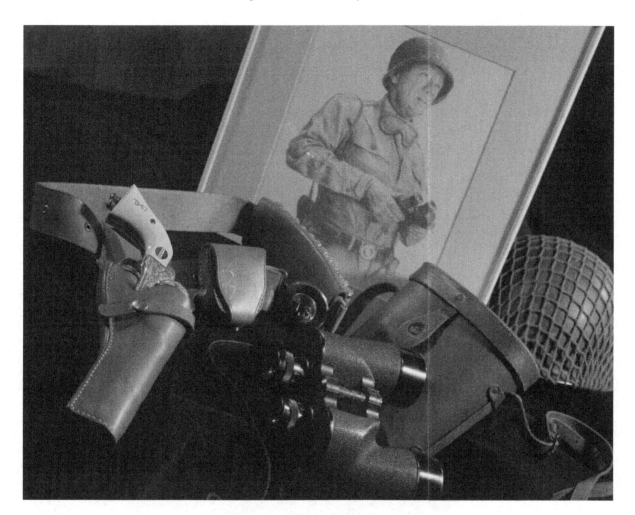

SYMBOLIC POWER RETURNING THE SALUTE

Ronald Reagan also studied and made important use of symbolic gestures. For example, he was the first president to break traditional protocol and routinely return salutes to military personnel in public settings.

The salute symbolized the President's unstinting support for the military, which at that time was still languishing in the aftermath of the Vietnam War. It was also a clear and constant reminder of the president's position as commander-in-chief and his belief, during the Cold War era, in a strong deterrent force.

Gregg Patterson, legendary manager of the Beach Club in Santa Monica, California, was famous for his potatoes and French fries greeting.

Of the greeting, Patterson says, "Every tribe has a special greeting. Mine was to give everyone---young people and old---the Club Tribal Signal. The signal---potatoes, which was a fist bump, followed by French fries which was a spread fingers. Everyone laughs and we've connected."

YOU ARE WHAT YOU DRIVE -- OR DON'T DRIVE

For 35 years Patterson rode his bike to work. Says Patterson "A mood and a focus adjustment is needed before arriving at the club. I biked to work (13 miles, about an hour), which allowed me a chance to think about the day, to enjoy a "stretch" before arrival, to get in a great mood. When I arrived, still clad in my spandex bike outfit, I'd gather all the senior staff in my office for a quick "energy transfer" and a review of the day. Then I showered, shaved, dressed and was BUZZED and ready for the day's adventure.

James Bond's Aston Martin DB5 and later models of the same marque became the most famous cars in movie history. . Steve McQueen's Mustang chase in the movie *Bullet* tripled that model's resale value. George Best's Jaguar XKE roadster was perfect for his playboy image. Rod Stewart's Lamborghini, Wayne Rooney's Range Rover, Tiger Wood's Porsche Turbo or Kim Kardashian Ferrari -- fast cars have always been a symbol of fame, wealth, success and power.

John Lennon's 1965 Phantom V Rolls Royce. It contains a telephone, television, refrigerator and the rear seat has been converted into a bed. Engine is a 6.2l V8 Top Speed 110mph.

While a luxurious Rolls or Bentley is the car of choice for rap stars of today, none has one quite so iconic as or controversial as John Lennon's. "You swine! How dare you do that to a Rolls Royce!" So screamed an outraged Englishwoman as Lennon cruised down a posh London street. The Rolls was sprayed an electric yellow and decorated with colorful floral tendrils, Romany scrolls and zodiac symbols, like a hallucinatory gypsy caravan. It so offended her sensibilities that she briefly attacked it with an umbrella – or at least that's the way Lennon always recounted the event.

Mary Kay had her Pink Cadillac, which not only became synonymous with her, but with her entire company. The much-coveted pink Cadillac prize is awarded to a Mary Kay Cosmetics consultant when she and her team reach $100,000 in sales within a year. As the story goes, Mary Kay Ash herself arrived at a Lincoln dealership in the late 1960s and asked them to create a custom car to help promote her burgeoning business. "The guy in so many words said, 'Little lady, go home and get your husband. And when you come back, we'll get you into that Lincoln,'" said Clayton Webb, Mary Kay's vice president of corporate communications. Ash turned to a different dealer—a Cadillac dealer—instead. And when she whipped out a compact and asked them to take a cue from the color of blush inside, they didn't bat an eyelash. Ash's custom job matched their archived "Mountain Laurel" tone.

Some of Mary Kay's sales directors fell in love with their boss's new ride, and ordered themselves cars to match. That's when Ash realized the eye-catching car could be powerful, both as a company symbol and as motivation for her growing network of consultants. In 1969, she rewarded her top five sellers with a brand new, blush-colored Cadillac Coupe de Ville. The tradition continues to this day. GM has painted over 100,000 custom cars for Mary Kay. The specific shade has varied over the years from bubble-gum to near-white pearlescent effects. GM had an exclusive agreement to sell cars of the specific shade only through Mary Kay. The cars are offered to distributors as two-year leases, and distributors who choose to buy the cars are only allowed to resell them to authorized dealers. After the lease expires, the cars are repainted before being resold.

Perhaps Mary got the idea of a pink Caddy from another icon of the era. In early 1955, Elvis bought his first Cadillac, a 1954 Fleetwood Series 60 that was painted pink. The car provided transport for Elvis and the Blue Moon Boys but, after the failure of a brake lining, was destroyed in a roadside fire between Hope and Texarkana, Arkansas, on June 5, 1955. On July 5, 1955, Elvis purchased a new Cadillac Fleetwood Series 60 in blue with a black roof. The first song recorded by Elvis to appear on a national chart, "Baby, Let's Play House," mentioned a pink Cadillac. So Elvis had the car repainted by Art, a neighbor on Lamar Street. Art designed a customized pink color for Elvis which he named "Elvis Rose," but the car kept its black roof. Once the car was finished Elvis gave it to his mother Gladys as a gift. Mrs. Gladys Presley never had a driver's license, and Elvis drove the car with the members of his band for most of 1955–1956.

These days you will find a good number of celebrities driving electric cars. Cameron Diaz drives a Toyota Prius while George Clooney dives a Tesla roadster. Even car aficionado Jay Leno has a Chevy Volt in his collection.

It all depends on how you want the world to view your choice of vehicle!

Sam Walton's Frugal '79 Pickup

The symbols of fame are not always the flamboyant trappings of wealth. As founder of Walmart, and at one time the world's richest man, Sam Walton could have driven any vehicle in the world. Yet he chose a 1979, Ford F-150 for its practicality, dependability and value. "Why do I drive a truck?" Walton is quoted as saying. "What am I supposed to haul my dogs around in, a Rolls-Royce?" The quote speaks to Walton's modesty and also fits Walmart's image as a low-price store.

"Sam was a practical man and liked the utility and versatility he got out of his Ford truck," said Alan Dranow, senior director at Walmart Heritage Group. "He loved that thing, and it embodied the practicality and frugality that was part of his business and personal life."

Urban legend has it that touching the door handle will bring you the gift of frugality, a legend he would have loved. Of course he also had a private jet, but he kept that well-hidden.

UNDERCOVER CEO

Legendary Apple CEO Steve Jobs never put a license plate on his cars. He got away with it legally thanks to a California loophole. Anyone with a brand-new car had a maximum of six months to affix the issued number plate to the vehicle. So Jobs would simply trade his silver Mercedes SL55 AMG for a similar one on the sixth month of his lease. Problem solved. No plate needed. While some speculate this was for privacy, it's far more likely Job's symbol of one-upmanship on the government.

Wraps and Decals

You can make your car stand out with a wrap or decals. You can use the wraps or decals to market your products or services, or simply as a means to stand out. The owner of a small dog-walking service had her car wrapped with the images of happy dogs and, of course, the company name and phone number. Full car wraps aren't cheap (often $2,000-$5,000), but the increased business from new customers paid for the wrap within a few months.

THE POWER OF RITUALS

According to the *Harvard Business Review*, All organizations have rituals — from the mundane everyday routines like coffee breaks or tea time to major, less frequent events like annual meetings. In Silicon Valley, even all-night programming marathons (hackathons) are part of the culture. . Smart leaders recognize that rituals like these and others are levers for improving the organization's performance and cohesiveness and they take the creation and nurturing of such rituals very seriously."

Most sports teams have rituals before and after games. These rituals build teamwork and social bonds between players and have existed throughout history. For instance, the legendary haka is a traditional war or challenge dance in the Maori culture of New Zealand. It is a powerful posture dance performed by a group, with vigorous movements, stamping of the feet with rhythmically and a shouted accompaniment. War haka were originally performed by warriors before a battle, proclaiming their strength and prowess in order to intimidate the opposition. Now you see it performed before international sporting events like rugby matches to psyche up one team and psyche out the other! Neuroscientific research shows that rituals like the haka trigger feelings of connectivity, timelessness, and meaning, which stimulate mental flow states. These, in turn, reduce anxiety and increase energy and focus. Incorporating such rituals, with their power to connect people in a community, into your quest for fame will not only increase your performance but will also attract others!

As Gianluca Vialli, former player and head soccer coach of Premier League's Chelsea, told the Harvard Business Review: "At Chelsea we had an 'initiation ritual' for newcomers. During the training camp at the beginning of the season, the new players had to get up on a table, in front of all their teammates, and sing a song that represented their country. It was a way to get players who came from different cultures to come together. After getting over the natural initial sense of embarrassment, we felt accepted, and truly became a part of the group." The book and movie Paper Lion talk about a similar ritual in the Detroit Lions American football training camp.

On March 25, 1983, dressed in his signature black trousers, silver socks, silver shirt, black-sequined jacket, sequined glove, and black fedora, Michael Jackson spun around, posed,

and began moonwalking for the first time. This was during a performance on *Motown 25: Yesterday, Today, Forever.* Through a series of intricate dance steps Jackson created the illusion that he was being pulled backwards by an unseen force while trying to walk forward. The audience went insane. Others had done something similar before, but the moonwalk became Jackson's signature dance, adding to his already legendary status, before an equally legendary fall.

When Starbucks founder and CEO Howard Schultz returned to the company in 2008 after an 8-year hiatus, he made it his mission to focus on improving the quality of the company's coffee. To do this required a large investment from every single employee at the company to learn the product and see it in a whole new light. In his 2012 book, Pour Your Heart into It, Schultz writes, "It's our partners who pass on to customers their knowledge and passion about Starbucks." As a way to ignite this in every partner, every new hire takes part in a ritual tasting of his or her store manager's favorite coffees. The manager tells the story of where the coffee is from, how it's grown, and how it's brewed. It's a ceremonial experience that reinforces Starbucks' values—for the new partners and managers alike.

At the Beach Club the ritual was Drink and Frostie Tickets: "People need an excuse to stop and talk and have a good laugh. I always carried drink tickets and frostie tickets (soft ice cream) in my pockets. The first kid each day who said "You the Man!" got a free frostie ticket and the first member who said "Nice tie" (whether I had one on or not!) got a free drink ticket. Although people knew later in the day that the tickets were gone, they still said the words, laughed and started talking."

Most events have specific rituals:

- The pre-event and post-event press conferences on the PGA tour or boxing matches.
- The National Anthem before sporting events.
- The boxing weigh in.
- Daredevil Evel Knievel would always ride up to the top of the ramp several times and stop, looking at the jump. This built up tension in the audience and re-enforced the length of the jump and the potential penalty for failure.
- The music acts that save their most popular song for the encore or end by smashing their guitars on stage.

Many organizations showcase their rituals at annual conventions or events. In the martial arts business, my annual Mastermind Weekend in Las Vegas grew from 200, 600, 900 to 1500 in just four years. It was the event to see and be seen at in the industry and was the showcase for our Top 200 Schools awards. Parelli's Annual Savvy Club Summit attracts thousands of horse lovers from around the world to Pagosa Springs, Colorado, every September. Others like Apple turn their product launches into carefully orchestrated rituals.

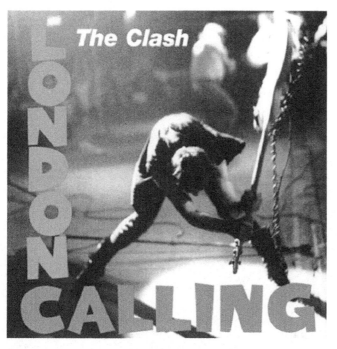

Paul Simonon of the Clash performs one of the most iconic guitar smashes in history.

The standard rock ritual of smashing a guitar on stage can be traced back to The Who's Pete Townshend who accidentally bumped his Rickenbacker onto a low ceiling during a gig in 1964, snapping the neck in the process. Not wanting to look clumsy in front of the crowd (and apparently legitimately upset about the loss of his guitar), he decided to finish the job...and thus, guitar smashing was born.

Pennie Smith was snapping photos of the Clash at New York's Palladium in September of 1979 when she captured one of the most iconic images in rock history.

Paul Simonon was annoyed by the relatively quiet audience, so he began smashing his bass against the floor. "The Palladium had fixed seating, so the audience was frozen in place," Simonon has said. "We weren't getting any response from them, no matter what we did. I'm generally good-natured, but I do bottle things up and then I'm like a light switch, off and on. It can be quite scary, even for me, when I switch, because it's very sudden. Onstage that night I just got so frustrated with that crowd and when it got to the breaking point I started to chop the stage up with the guitar."

In 1915, PR guru Ivy Lee became publicity counsel to John D. Rockefeller. Lee advised Rockefeller to hand out dimes to poor children as a way of showing his philanthropic impulses (which actually were few!). He also invented the Betty Crocker symbol and the "Breakfast of Champions" slogan for Wheaties.

Stretching and taking practice shots are acts of exercise performed by every athlete and therefore mundane. A King needs to warm up in style. LeBron James, known to fans as King James, has an elaborate pre-game routine known as "the Ritual." Although his full routine involves a complex sequence of actions ranging from putting on his mouthguard to giving out handshakes, the most visually prominent part of the Ritual is when James tosses moisture-absorbing chalk into the air, giving himself an almost magical air as if emerging from the white powder.

Athletes are often superstitious about their pregame rituals.

They wear the same socks, eat the same breakfast, and so on. For instance, the English football great, Bobby Moore, would always be the last one in the dressing room to put on his shorts. He claimed that it made sure that the shorts stayed ironed and kept the smart crease.

Gary Lineker is England's third highest goal scorer of all time with 48 goals, but unlike all the other players on the pitch, he never used to shoot towards the net when he was out warming up before a game. He said the reason behind it was because he didn't want to waste scoring any goals in the warm up, instead saving them for the match.

In his native Jamaica, they call the move "To Di World" but elsewhere across the planet it is known as Usain Bolt's signature move, the "Lighting Bolt," or just plain "Bolting." When the legendary sprint superstar bends one elbow and straightens the other at an angle toward the skies, crowds rise in appreciation and copy the move in numbers.

Watch any team sporting event from the NFL to the Premier league and you'll see it at work: the "secret handshake." Generally, a complex combination of subtle moves known only to teammates. The ritual handshakes of Free Masons go back hundreds of years. Now one can find such inside connections commonly on display from rap stars, athletes and even politicians.

Celebration rituals are not just for the players, many involve the fans. For example, the band member diving off the stage and crowd surfing across the heads of the audience. Or the wave in a football stadium or the chanting of Tampa Bay fans from the east and west sides of the Buccaneer's Raymond James Stadium.

Other rituals include the national anthem before a major sporting event, the jet fly over, the warm up laps, strawberries and cream at Wimbledon, and hats at the Derby. Consider the music you choose at a start of your seminar. For example, Anthony Robbins started many of his motivational events with Tina Turner's "Simply the Best." These are all are part of creating an iconic brand.

Instead of having our staff meetings on Monday mornings with coffee, we held ours at 5pm in the TGI Friday's bar and drank beers and ate nachos. Many a great idea happened after the 5th or 6th Heineken.

Your goal is to cre*ate* rituals that resonate with your audience, both in building your own unique status and in meeting their needs.

Salespeople should develop a specific way to hand over the keys to a new home or car buyer and the celebration you build around the event. Every time I made a big purchase of either has been totally anti-climactic. All missed opportunities to build my loyalty and garner referrals!

What about the pen you hand customers to sign a new contract? Perhaps give them a custom fountain pen in a nice box as a memento of the event?

Build a ritual celebration of new members or employees, or the fond farewell you give them when they leave. Rituals can increase our perception of value. In other words, if employees perform rituals as part of their jobs, they are likely to find their jobs more rewarding. And if consumers use a ritual to experience your product or service, they are likely to enjoy it more and be willing to pay more for it.

RITUALS INCREASE PERSONAL PERFORMANCE

Rituals can not only help you bond with employees or fans but can also help your personal performance. Composer Ludwig van Beethoven had several rituals he performed each day, like getting up early and making his own coffee, where he meticulously counted exactly sixty beans for each cup. After dinner each day he would go for a long walk but always carried a pencil and some music sheets in case genius hit him while out. I start each day with a 5k walk (listening to an audio book, usually a biography or business book) so I get a big jump on my 10,000 steps a day before breakfast and learn something while I'm at it!

In Harvard Professor Ben-Shahar's highly popular course in Positive Psychology, he teaches students how to be happy. One of his eleven happiness tips is to create rituals. He notes that "The most creative individuals, whether artists, businesspeople or parents have rituals that they follow. This routine frees them up to be creative and spontaneous."

Some rituals seem more like superstitions, but they create the same focus or reminder for the player. Nadal is tennis's most superstitious professional. In his autobiography, the Spanish great revealed how he has a cold shower 45 minutes before he heads out onto the court. "Freezing cold water. I do this before every match. It's the point before the point of no return. Under the cold shower I enter a new space in which I feel my power and resilience grow." This grand slam winner is clearly a very philosophical person, as he explains when talking about his water bottle habit. "I put the two bottles down at my feet, in front of my chair to my left, one neatly behind the other, diagonally aimed at the court. If it were superstition, why would I keep doing the same thing over and over whether I win or lose? It's a way of placing myself in a match, ordering my surroundings to match the order I seek in my head."

Bjorn Borg always started to grow a beard before Wimbledon each year and would not shave it off until the event was finished. A similar ritual is taken up by many NFL, FHL and NBA player on the road to the championship game. Basketball superstar Michael Jordan wore his North Carolina shorts underneath his Chicago Bulls shorts in every game. Curtis Martin of the New York Jets reads Psalm 91 before every game. And Wade Boggs, former third baseman for the Boston Red Sox, woke up at the same time each day, ate chicken before each game, took exactly 117 ground balls in practice, took batting practice at 5:17, and ran sprints at 7:17. Although Boggs was not Jewish, he also wrote the Hebrew word Chai ("living") in the dirt before each at bat.

What's in a Number

Number 42 Jackie Robinson
Number 7 Ronaldo
Number 16 Joe Montana
Number 10 Bobby Charlton, Pele
Number 13 Dan Marino
Number 23 Michael Jordan
Number 43 NASCAR, 1125 starts, 192 wins, 526 top fives, 676 top tens, 48,125 laps led. Not only the greatest of the 43s, but probably the greatest of them all, Richard Petty made the 43 famous. To this day, even though he hasn't raced in 25 years, ask any fan about number 43, and they know who you mean.

Sport psychology studies show that athletes who feel confident, comfortable, and ready to go because they take the field wearing their unique number may actually play with more mental toughness as a result. When athletes take pride in their number, they often create a self-fulfilling prophecy that allows them to "play up to" the identity they have created. The number they wear on their uniform is of great significance. The number, in essence, becomes their athletic identity. While the number itself may not do anything, the idea that when an athlete puts on his or her uniform a new identity takes over - one that is tougher, more focused, and motivated to succeed - can be a very powerful force!

LUCKY 13

I was born on the 13th so for me it was always a lucky number. Number 13 worked out pretty well for Hall of Fame Quarterback Dan Marino too. Other notable #13 wearers include basketball legend Wilt Chamberlin, German soccer star Michael Ballack, and baseball star Alex Rodriguez. If you take something that looks "negative" like 13 and turn it into a positive for you, it gets you extra attention from others.

While Friday the 13th gets a bad rap, Taylor Swift is one pop star who's not at all superstitious about it. Born on December 13th, she considers it great luck that she turned 13 on Friday the 13th, and attributes almost every big moment in her career to the number 13. Her first album went gold in 13 weeks, her first #1 song had a 13-second intro, and when she's up for awards, and she sees 13 all over the place that day—usually in her seat or row number—she wins. If she doesn't, she loses. She won her first MTV VMA on September 13, 2009, although that was also the year her acceptance speech was rudely and famously interrupted by Kanye West, which worked out in her favor anyway. Her company is called 13 Management; her Twitter handle is @taylorswift13. She even used to paint the number 13 on her hand before every live show.

LEGENDARY LOGOS ENHANCE YOUR BRAND

The legendary Ferrari prancing horse logo as a history as rich as its storied racing history. The horse was painted on the fuselage of the fighter plane of Italian ace Francesco Baracca — a heroic airman of the first world war. Baracca notched up for a total of 34 kills, before failing to return from a mission on June 19, 1918.

Said Enzo Ferrari, then an aspiring race car driver, "In '23, I met count Enrico Baracca, the hero's father, and then his mother, countess Paulina, who said to me one day, 'Ferrari, put my son's prancing horse on your cars. It will bring you good luck.' The horse was, and still is, black, and I added the canary yellow background which is the color of Modena [Enzo Ferrari's birthplace]."

In 1932, the Ferrari shield appeared for the first time on the Alfa Romeo cars of the Scuderia racing team at the Grand Prix of Spain. In 1947, on the 125S — the first car produced at Maranello, the prancing horse appeared on a yellow background, and always with the Italian flag at the top. However, no longer within a shield, with the letters S and F (Scuderia Ferrari) replaced by the word Ferrari. Thus the Ferrari brand was born, and in 2014 it ranked as the most famous brand in the world by Brand Finance.

The logo suggests speed, power, grace and sex appeal. In other words, exactly what you'd expect to get from a Ferrari. Far too many symbols mean nothing when you look at them and explaining what your symbol means when the audience doesn't get it right away, gets expensive fast!

While many corporations spend millions on logo design like Enzo Ferrari, Phil Knight did not. In fact, Knight paid just $35 for the iconic swoosh. Carolyn Davidson remembers she was sitting in a hall at the school, when Knight, then an assistant accounting professor, happened to walk by.

He had overheard her mention that she couldn't afford to take oil painting. Knight said he'd pay her so much an hour to letter some signs. It started from there. Knight remembers that he had offered her $2 an hour, though he joked in 1983 that "I never thought she'd spend 17.5 hours on the project!"

The logo is simple yet powerful. Nike is the Greek goddess of victory. The logo is derived from her wing, 'Swoosh'. Greek mythology says that Swoosh is the giver of immense power and motivation to the warriors. This makes it the perfect logo for an apparel and accessories brand for sportspersons as they swoosh by their opponents on the way to victory.

In 1983, Nike was a growing company and the founders had wanted to do something special to recognize Davidson's earlier contribution. They invited her to their office for lunch, then surprised her with a party where they presented her with a gold ring in the shape of her swoosh, complete with a small diamond. They also gave her a certificate of appreciation and 500 shares of stock now worth around a million dollars.

Nike's arch rival Adidas a name taken from the name of the founder, Adolf Dassler, who after the war had the good sense to adopt "Adi" as his name. The originally, logo had no real meaning. The "Three Stripe Company" as they called themselves, simply put three stripes on everything. Even their second logo design, didn't have much meaning, but they got it right with the third iteration. The iconic version we all know today has a three-striped mountain on top of the word Adidas to inspire athletes to achieve great heights. This is symbolic for the challenges that people must overcome in both exercise and life. It also represents how Adidas products are up to the challenge. The kicker is, it does all this while remaining true to the original three lines.

The simpler and clearer your logo is at visually conveying the promise behind the brand the better. The logo for my marketing company says "success."

And since many of my clients are in the golf industry the shape of the trophy (The Claret Jug awarded to the winner of the British Open) also says, "these people get golf" and it gives away a little of my heritage being from Britain.

Perhaps it's time to create a new logo for your company or, if you work for a company like a large real-estate franchise, perhaps create a personal logo in addition to the company one. A logo that's uniquely yours!

CREATING YOUR OWN FANDOM

Creating an identity for your staff and fans beyond that of mere workers or customers is another powerful way to bond with your group. "Fandom" is defined as a subculture composed of fans, characterized by a feeling of empathy and camaraderie with others who share a common interest.

Ferrari's fans are known as the Tifosi, which literally means "those infected by typhus," in the sense of someone acting in a fevered manner-- which if you ever witness the sea of red flags at a Formula One event is a pretty good description. No wonder Ferrari is one of the most recognizable brand names in the world.

Golfer Arnold Palmer's fans where called "Arnie's Army," Here's how it happened in the Kings' own words. "I was the defending champion at the Masters that year, and, as he always did in those days, Clifford Roberts – Augusta National's co-founder along with Bob Jones, used GIs from nearby Fort Gordon, the military installation where Cliff spent two years as a young soldier, to work the scoreboards.

"Many people don't realize that the Masters was not a sellout in those early years. Anybody with five dollars could walk up to the gates and buy a ticket for the day. Elementary school teachers had boxes of tickets on their desks with signs reading, 'Masters Tickets: Please Help Support Our Town.' Cliff wanted as large a gallery as he could get that year since the Masters was being televised for the second time, so he gave free passes to any soldier who showed up in uniform.

"A lot of the soldiers did not necessarily know a lot about golf, but when they found out that I was defending champion they joined my gallery. That prompted one of the GIs working a back-nine scoreboard to announce the arrival of 'Arnie's Army,' which is what it looked like. I can't remember another time, other than my stint in the Coast Guard, when so many uniformed soldiers surrounded me. A year later, when I won my second Masters title, I thanked the 'army' of supporters who came out to follow me.

"Johnny Hendricks, a reporter from The Augusta Chronicle, picked up on the phrase and ran the headline 'Arnie's Army' for the first time. Boy, did it ever stick! Before I finished my playing career I think every newspaper, magazine, or television station that covered golf used the phrase at least once."

Of course, it is generally better to take a proactive approach in case you don't like the name someone else comes up with...

T.C.B

The initials T.C.B. stand for Taking Care of Business, which is what Elvis Presley called his band. Elvis' wife Priscilla helped with the creation of this logo on a flight through stormy conditions. A lightning bolt flashed across the sky in front of them, and Elvis took inspiration from it. Priscilla sketched out the design on note paper, positioning the letters and lightning bolt in various ways before they found what they liked.

This emblem was used in several pieces of Elvis' custom jewelry including his famous T.C.B. ring, sunglasses and necklace. Taking Care of Business was a mantra and a point of pride for Elvis Presley and his entourage, known as the Memphis Mafia. The T.C.B. logo often is placed over a lightning bolt, which signifies Taking Care of Business in a Flash.

The Memphis Mafia was what some people might call Elvis's "yes men." Many of them were friends from his high school days growing up in the Memphis projects as well as his days in the U.S. Army. The media came up with the name "Memphis Mafia," known to cruise the city wearing black suits and dark sunglasses. Some reports say Elvis liked the name, while others have said he wasn't fond of the connection to the mafia. Either way, the group adopted T.C.B. as their symbol, something that was even painted on the tails of his jet, the Lisa Marie.

MONSTERS IN THE MAKING

While working on her second album, Lady Gaga developed the theme of monster, both in physical form, and to describe her inner fears (monster of death, alcohol, drugs, etc.). During the summer of 2009, she first started to use the name during her live performances to refer to her fans. The name fit them well because her fans crawl and scream during her show like monsters would do. The term Mother Monster was used by a fan who met her in Chicago and she quickly adopted it and started using it herself. Gaga later added it to her Twitter-bio. Other variations include Mommy Monster, Mama Monster, and/or Momma Monster.

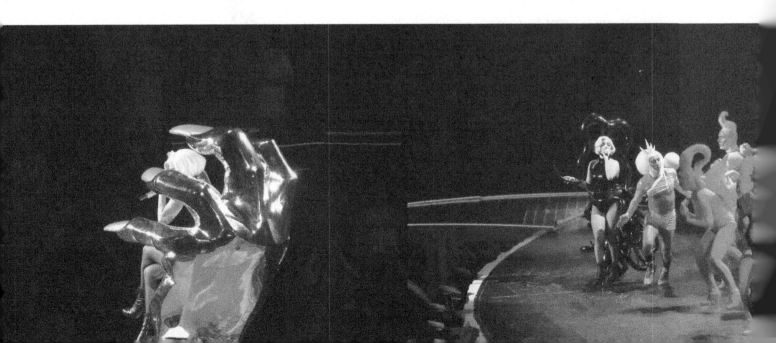

Gaga used the monster imagery repeatedly:

- Little Monsters hands on the dual piano during the Grammy in 2010.
- The international symbol is a claw made with the hand, like in the music video of "Bad Romance."
- During The Monster Ball, Gaga saw a fan in Boston greet another fan with the claw hand, and that's when she knew that was the "Little Monsters" symbol. "
- The Monster Claw" is also known as the Monster Paw. Both Gaga and her Little Monsters will use the term "Monsterpaws Up" or "Paws Up" to show they agree with something or to show how, like Gaga, they are inspired by art, music and fashion and have an undying passion for art as she does.

A Green Bay Packers Cheesehead

Cheesehead is a nickname in the United States for a person from Wisconsin or for a fan of the Green Bay Packers NFL football franchise. The use of the term "cheesehead" as a derogatory word for Wisconsinites originated with Illinois football and baseball fans to refer to opposing Wisconsin sports fans.

The term, however, was quickly embraced by Wisconsinites and is now a point of pride.

Parrothead is a commonly used nickname for fans of singer Jimmy Buffett "Parakeets" or "Keets" is the term used for younger fans of Buffett, or children of Parrotheads.

The term "Parrot Head" was coined in 1985 at a Jimmy Buffett concert at the Timberwolf Amphitheater in Cincinnati, Ohio. Buffett has said numerous times that he attributes much of his fame to this area.At the show, Buffett commented about everyone wearing Hawaiian shirts and parrot hats and how they kept coming back to see his shows, just like Deadheads. Timothy B. Schmit, then a member of the Coral Reefer Band, coined the term "Parrothead" to describe them.

In 1989, the first Parrot Head club was founded in Atlanta. Events range from single act concerts or happy hours to the annual Meeting of the Minds in Key West, Florida, which attracts approximately 3,500 Parrotheads each year.

A recent count suggested there were 239 Parrothead Club chapters in the United States, Canada and Australia, spanning 3 different countries, 47 states and 3 Canadian provinces. The total membership was almost 30,000 members.

DEADHEADS

Long before Cheeseheads or Parrotheads, Beatlemania once swept the U.S., where the demand to see the Fab Four live created stadium rock. The Rolling Stones still have audiences under their thumbs despite their combined age of almost 300.

The Boss has a formidable base, but in terms of unbridled loyalty and devotion to the late Jerry Garcia and his bandmates, Deadheads are without peer.

Even though the Dead only had one Top 10 album in its entire career, the group had enough of a following to tour for 30 years and build an army of loyal fans that followed them from show to show. It's a group that counts such famous devotees as Al Gore, Whoopi Goldberg, Game of Thrones author George R. R. Martin, Carlos Santana, Nancy Pelosi, Mario Batali, and Ann Coulter to name but a few.

The "Deadhead" phenomenon was first touched on in print by Village Voice music critic Robert Christgau at a show in 1971, noting "how many 'regulars' seemed to be in attendance, and how, from the way they compared notes, they'd obviously made a determined effort to see as many shows as possible. This was driven in part by the fact that the band had such a large catalog of songs. The varied song selection allowed the band to create a "rotation" of songs that was roughly repeated every 3 to 5 performances ("shows"). The rotation created two phenomena. The first was that the desire of Deadheads to hear their favorite song or attend a good show led many of them to begin following the band on its tour. The second was that the large number of traveling fans empowered the band to perform multiple shows in each venue with the assurance that the performances would be mostly sold out!

By the late 1970s, some Deadheads began to sell tie-dye t-shirts, veggie burritos, or other items at Grateful Dead concerts. This gave many Deadheads a way to monetize their following the band on its tours. During the early 1980s, the number of Deadheads taping shows increased, and the band created a special section for fans who wished to record the show. In the earlier days of the Grateful Dead, there were questions as to whether or not it was in the best interest of the band for fans to tape concerts. In 1982, Garcia himself was asked what he thought about it, and he replied, "When we are done with it [the concerts], they can have it." The practice of taping has evolved with the digital age, and the rise of the Internet has made it extremely easy to share concerts through unofficial channels.

The Dead's model was so successful, it's taught in business schools and codified in books like *Marketing Lessons from the Grateful Dead* and *Everything I Know About Business I Learned from the Grateful Dead*. In *Garcia: An American Life,* the biography of Jerry Garcia, the Dead's guitar player, songwriter and figurehead, a clear picture emerges of the tenets Garcia upheld from the very beginning of the band:

The most important thing is playing and creating. Everything else is secondary. Work is a family affair. It's important to shelter, support and share with a larger community. Money is second fiddle to living the kind of life you want to live. You can build your own economy. There are pitfalls to being a renegade but they come with the territory. Accept the hazards and finger-pointing as a small hindrance to living differently. Push the envelope whenever possible. These personal beliefs happened to add up to a worldview that aligned very nicely with the values of flower children of the '60s who were intent on reshaping the world in their image. Now it's up to you to shape your world in the image that works for you.

SUMMARY

The use of symbols, rituals, closed *community* groups *a*nd icons come from the powerful, primal urge to "belong" in every culture. You must learn from this and create the tools to make adopting your creed natural and fulfilling for your fans. This might include a special prop, a handshake or a unique gesture. The car you drive, a lucky number or morning ritual. A logo that speaks to your audience and creates a loyal group of fans eager to show their appreciation of your efforts.

Make them remember your number.

ACTION PLAN

- What kind of ritual can you add to your repertoire to increase the emotional connection with your fans?
- What symbols or icons are important to your brand?
- How do they add to your power, prestige, charisma or memorability?
- Is your car making the right statement for you?
- Do you have a special number?
- Does your logo connect and convey your brand's underlying promise to your fans?
- What special name can you create for your fandom?
- What secret handshakes, dances, walks, moves or gestures are unique to your fans and create a sense of belong to an elite group of insiders?
- How can you think like a fan, customer or client to foster a greater feeling of community?
- What rituals can you build into your conventions, sales meetings, staff trainings or performances?

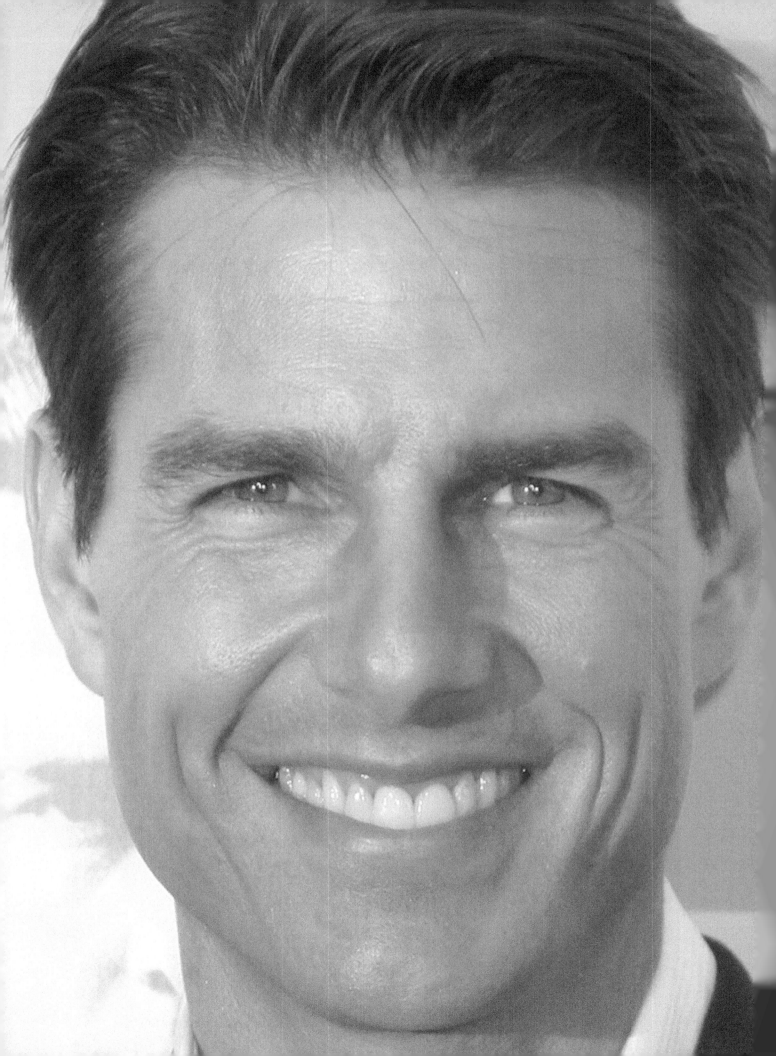

"Good actors aren't enough. You need charisma. Can you imagine 'Casablanca' without Bogart and Bergman?" - **Sydney Pollack**

8

CREATING LEGENDARY CHARISMA

One trait almost all famous people have is charisma -- that magical "something" that makes you stand out from the crowd and increases your chances for every opportunity. It's a trait that will attract people to your cause, and increase the number of friends, clients and fans available to help and support your efforts. Many people have described charisma and said how to develop it. But at the heart of it, charisma is something you project to others, so you must feel it.

Professor Antonakis and others writing in the Harvard Business Review discussed 12 ways to be charismatic, focusing on communication patterns. In addition to integrity, authority and passion, they included nonverbal cues, like you showing animation in your features. Focus on attainable goals and tell stories to engage, entertain, and motivate others. Ask rhetorical questions to stimulate responses in others. All these cues and techniques are ways of projecting enthusiasm and passion about something to others and engaging them.

Charismatic people motivate and build commitment in any organization where they are involved, be it a band, office or army. Whether you are a teacher, preacher, coach, entrepreneur or corporate CEO, charisma amplifies your fame. While some people seem to develop charisma effortlessly from the day they are born, this invaluable trait can also be acquired. This is because the key ingredient of charisma is perception rather than reality. As somebody once said, beauty is in the eye of the beholder.

But how does one acquire charisma, that elusive essence of personal magic that is so evident in such famous personalities as Richard Branson, Tom Cruise, and Oprah Winfrey, to name but a few?

CAN ANYONE CREATE CHARISMA?

Can anyone create charisma and build an iconic personal brand?

Imagine you are a short, fat, bald, chauvinistic senior citizen, who drinks like a fish, smokes heavily and speaks in a mumbling tone with lengthy pauses between sentences.

What are your chances for being thought of as an icon of charismatic leadership? Pretty low you might think, but they'd be pretty good if your name was Winston Churchill!

Churchill's charisma was certainly not natural. He stuttered badly as a child, fainted with fright during his first speech in front of an audience and fought his weight all his life. Churchill is a shining example of how charisma can be manufactured. Many other now charismatic people didn't start out that way: people as diverse as Lady Gaga, Steve Jobs, General Patton, Buffalo Bill, Prince and Arnold Palmer.

All were from humble beginnings with none of the obvious shine of charisma at the start of their careers. Yet all reached the status of legends in their own lifetimes!

In January 7, 1979, wannabe rock star Prince had just finished a performance in a small Minneapolis movie theater. The Warner Records representatives present were not impressed. It was obvious "their boy" was not ready for a tour. Prince couldn't believe it, if he was not ready for a tour how was he supposed to sell any records?

The label believed Prince was an excellent musician, but they knew he lacked charisma. He needed to develop the ability to get people excited about his music by getting excited about him. Instead of signing off on a concert schedule, they sent him back to the studio to record a second album. The first single of the new album, "I Wanna Be Your Lover," entered the Billboard charts. Finally, Warner saw enough momentum to risk sending the still-awkward performer on the road. A lucky break came when singer Rick James of "Super Freak" fame invited Prince to open for him on his 1980 Fire It Up Tour. "I felt sorry for him," James later recalled. At first, anyway.

By the end of that tour, Prince was commanding his audiences, leading call-and-response chants, wowing them with dance moves and flipping his guitars and microphone. Fans were so riled up by Prince's performances, James felt overshadowed. How did Prince get that good? By decoding-and mastering-the key strategies that constitute a charismatic rock performance.

Enhancing Your Charisma

Charisma is a complicated mix of many things, all of which can be managed and enhanced to bolster your image and draw people to your cause. The good news is that you already have many of the traits you need to build your charisma. You just need to uncover them and polish them up a bit. Here are ways to refine your image, build your charisma and create new and exciting opportunities for business, career and personal growth.

1. ENTHUSIASM

The first key to charisma is passion, enthusiasm, and excitement about your job, business, mission and life in general. People gravitate towards people with passion, people with energy, and people with drive. They seek to charge their own batteries from the electricity that flows from people of passion and enthusiasm. When asked to explain his remarkable success in life, author, Mark Twain summed it up in four words, "I was born excited!" The famous share their excitement with everyone they meet and begin to create an aura of positive expectancy in those around them. Positive vibes attract people like a magnet because everyone wants to feel excited. They want to be involved with winners. They want to feel confident in their future. Express your passion, express your enthusiasm. Express your joy for life and you will be a magnet for others.

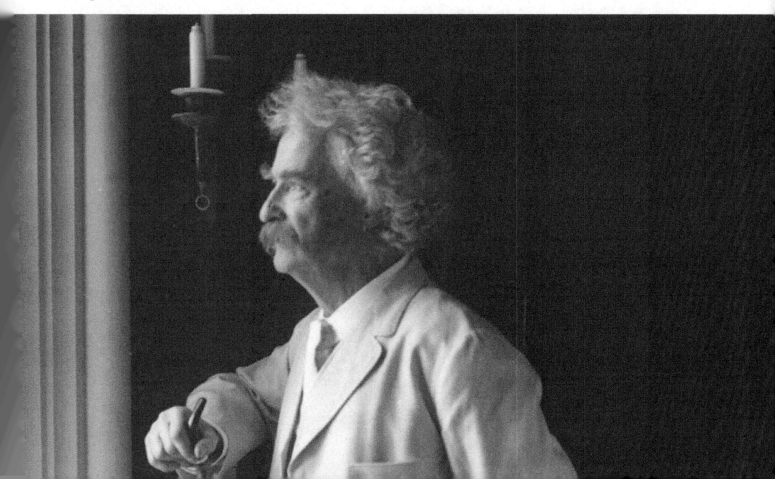

2. SELF-CONFIDENCE

The second key to charisma is self-confidence. People will only believe in you, follow you and buy from you if they think you have personal confidence in your own abilities and know where you are going or what you are doing. Go out of your way to develop a singular message defining your purpose. Use it in different ways, again and again, to create feelings of confidence and consistency in your performance. Confidence and commitment to purpose, more than anything, will draw people to your cause and enhance your charisma. You must act in control, but to enhance others who come with you, not to make them inferior.

No one had bigger dreams than a young Charlie Chaplin.

3. BIG DREAMS

The third key to charisma is to dream big dreams. Big dreams breed charisma. Why? Because so few people really dream big dreams. When they meet someone who does, they are instantly drawn to the concept. A wise man said, "Make no small plans, for only big dreams have the power to stir men's souls." Don't be afraid to share your big dreams with others. Oh, some may laugh. Some may scoff and shake their heads in disbelief, but underneath it all they will feel the power of the vision. People who do have big dreams like yours will always recognize and respect the trait in others.

Charlie Chaplin's childhood in Victorian London was fraught with poverty and hardship, making his eventual trajectory "the most dramatic of all the rags to riches stories ever told" according to his authorized biography. As his father was absent and his mother struggled financially, he was sent to a workhouse twice before the age of nine. When he was 14, his mother was committed to a mental asylum. Chaplin began performing at an early age, touring music halls and later working as a stage actor and comedian. At 19, he was signed to the prestigious Fred Karno Company, which took him to America. Chaplin was scouted for the film industry and began appearing in 1914 for Keystone Studios. He soon developed the tramp persona and formed a large fan base. Chaplin directed his own films from an early stage and continued to hone his craft. By 1918, he was the best-known figure in the world.

4. COMPETENCE

The fourth key to charisma is competence. Unlike some traits, competence cannot be faked. You simply must commit to being the best you can be in your field. You have to learn everything there is to know about your job or profession and never give up your quest for knowledge. Then practice, practice, practice.

As mentioned earlier, in his book, Outliers, Malcolm Gladwell suggested that it takes 10,000 hours to get really good at something. People feel comfortable following those people they know to be competent and yet always striving to do better. They may not always keep up, but they're glad you are out front.

5. LOOKING HEALTHY

The fifth key to charisma is looking healthy. People shy away from illness and pain. They avoid lethargic people who drain their energy. This is why famous people like Franklin Delano Roosevelt often hide their illnesses. By contrast, people gravitate toward healthy, energetic types. The healthier you look, the easier it will be to be seen as charismatic. It's little known that J.F. Kennedy suffered from birth with a terminal illness called Addison's Disease. If left untreated, this condition depletes the body's adrenaline, eventually causing death. By 1947 it was learned that the condition could be kept from deteriorating by using cortisone. In spite of this, Kennedy received last rites on five occasions before his death in Dallas.

Kennedy entered the Navy by using his family's influence to skip the physical, which he could never have passed. On top of this ailment, he also experienced chronic back pain due to a birth defect and not, as was variously reported at the time, as the result of an old football injury or the aftermath of his PT boat being sunk by a Japanese destroyer in World War II.

President Kennedy was in constant and agonizing pain, yet few would ever have guessed this from his public persona. Kennedy knew that the public wants as perfect a picture as you can possibly show them, so he never made his health problems or his pain public knowledge.

Rock star Mick Jagger goes to amazing lengths to stay in shape despite being in his 70s, as do Madonna, Cher and many others. Keith Richards not so much!

We have all experienced people who share their aches, pains, and illness with us in search of sympathy or empathy. If you must do this, don't give details of your ailments or indicate how bravely you are refusing to allow your problems to interfere with your performance. It's a well-known fact that people with charisma seldom get sick. Do your utmost to stay in shape. Shed a few extra pounds. Eat the right foods. Maintain an exercise program and, if you are having health problems, tell your doctor-not someone else.

Fitness doesn't have to be a chore. You can make it part of your everyday life. For example, when I play golf, I walk most of the time, rather than riding in a cart. When I change planes in Atlanta, I walk from terminal to terminal, rather than taking the tram. In Las Vegas, New York, and other cities where food and entertainment are close to the hotels, walk instead of taking a cab. Take the stairs rather than the elevator and you will quickly find that all these little actions add up to greater fitness. Having a fitness band that counts steps provides extra motivation for me to make sure 10,000 steps a day is my minimum. Remember, in the battle for fame everything counts, so make personal fitness a habit.

6. GIVING PEOPLE YOUR FULL ATTENTION AND PUTTING THEM AT EASE

The sixth key to building charisma is to build your people skills. While image can make a substantial difference, fancy clothes and catchy nicknames aren't worth a hill of beans unless you have the personality to back them up. Most famous people, in person, are people persons. They instinctively know there are no "little" people in life. They realize that in order to get anything done, they must depend on the help and goodwill of fans, soldiers, volunteers, teammates, and associates. With this in mind, they work hard at building good relationships with everyone they meet.

Make people feel comfortable with you. When meeting new people, always take the initiative. Very often, people hesitate to take the first step because they feel uncomfortable in unfamiliar surroundings or situations.

Give the person your full attention and focus. Look at him with a warm smile and grasp his hand palm to palm, firmly but not too hard. As you shake his hand, look directly into his eyes. For extra warmth, you might even put your left hand on his right shoulder. Studies show that points made while touching someone are far more likely to be remembered.

Introduce yourself, then ask the other person's name and start the conversation with pleasant and non-threatening questions. Take the initiative once again, by volunteering information about yourself and generally building good rapport. By being the leader in these situations you harness the power and assume control.

When you're with others, show that they have your full attention. I make a show of switching off my cell phone or closing my computer to show people in a meeting they're my only focus.

In Great Britain's 1868 elections, the race was down to two famous politicians, William Gladstone and Benjamin Disraeli. Both men projected power, intelligence, and knowledge. One woman who dined with each of them separately commented on how Gladstone had impressed her with his power but seemed to lack warmth. Disraeli, however, projected his presence and warmth as well as his power, making his dining companion feel fascinating and special. The woman commented, "After dining with Mr. Gladstone, I thought he was the cleverest person in England. But after dining with Mr. Disraeli, I thought I was the cleverest person in England." As you might expect, Disraeli won the election.

7. REMEMBER NAMES

The seventh key to charisma is the ability to remember people's names. This is a trait shared by many famous leaders. It was said of President Truman that he knew the first name of every single member of the very large White House staff. Julius Caesar was reputed to know the names of every solider in his legions. Taking the trouble to learn people's names can quickly add to your charisma. If nothing else, they'll be impressed by your excellent memory.

The importance of remembering a person's name was a central theme in Dale Carnegie's, classic book How to Win Friends and Influence People. He said, "A person's name is to him or herthe sweetest and most important sound in any language." When you first learn someone's name, repeat it back to them by saying "Hi, Sally" or "It's a pleasure to meet you, Sally." Also use their name when you end the conversation, it'll help immensely. Another trick is to try and connect their facial feature to someone else you know or a TV star of the same first name. If all else fails, make some note on your phone as soon as you part.

8. TELL GREAT STORIES AND SPEAK WITH CONVICTION

The eighth key to charisma is your ability to tell stories and the conviction with which you tell them. I was traveling with a good friend of mine who manages over a billion dollars when we met up for diner with a couple whose money he managed. I was shocked when he pulled a piece of paper from his pocket and proceeded to read off a few jokes to break the ice. That is not how you enhance your charisma.

Rock stars like Bruce Springsteen and Paul McCartney use anecdotes to add more meaning to their songs and connect with their audiences. I still vividly remember Bruce introducing his song "The River" at London's Wembley stadium in 1984. He talked about how he was fighting with his father and how his father kept saying, "Wait until the army gets you," then the subsequent relief his father showed after he was turned down for military service and so was not drafted to go to Vietnam.

There are five keys to speaking that will enhance your charisma.

1. GET YOUR POINTS ACROSS WITH STORIES.

Stories are less threatening, more emotional and entertaining, thus more powerful and remembered longer than basic points of argument.

2. NEVER SPEAK IN WISHY-WASHY TERMS.

Imagine Patrick Henry, saying, "Give me liberty or give me death, I think." or Churchill saying, "We will fight them on the beaches, as long as I can find the money to buy some tanks and can talk America into the war." Not quite as effective, are they? You must speak with total conviction about your plans. Use words like "I am sure" vs. tentative words like "I think," "I hope" and "I feel." You are an expert; you have talent; you are on your way up.

3. SELF-DEPRECATING HUMOR IS A GREAT WAY TO SEEM HUMBLE WHILE PROMOTING YOUR AGENDA.

My go- to start is, "All I ever wanted to be was a golf pro. Unfortunately, lack of talent held me back." I also have several anecdotal stories and some jokes that I have practiced and honed over many years that never fail to get a laugh. Anyone can find such anecdotes and get good at telling them with a little practice.

4. MODULATE YOUR TONES TO YOUR AUDIENCE AND SITUATION.

As a general rule you should speak quietly at first until you find some rapport and then gradually increase you volume and excitement.

5. BE RELEVANT.

Know what's happening in the world around you. People want to be with people who are in the know. Try to tie your stories into current events.

9. MAKE OTHER PEOPLE FEEL IMPORTANT AND INVOLVED

The cosmetics giant Mary Kay once said that the secret to her success was that whenever she met new people, she visualized them wearing a T-shirt with the words "make me feel important" boldly printed across the chest.

Napoleon knew well how to make his troops feel important, saying, "Give me enough colored ribbon and I can conquer the world." Notice, he said nothing about money, weapons or supplies-just pretty ribbons to decorate a worthy soldier's chest.

Compliment others wherever possible and follow up with a qualifier to prove your sincerity. For example, "That's a beautiful sweater" may or may not be taken at face value. However, if you add, "I gave one just like that to my wife last Christmas." it will make the compliment believable. After all, who would buy a sweater they didn't like? Followers will go a long way down the road for a leader with a powerful vision, but at some point they need more.

True Gentleman

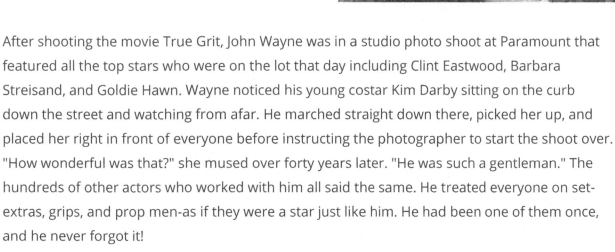

After shooting the movie True Grit, John Wayne was in a studio photo shoot at Paramount that featured all the top stars who were on the lot that day including Clint Eastwood, Barbara Streisand, and Goldie Hawn. Wayne noticed his young costar Kim Darby sitting on the curb down the street and watching from afar. He marched straight down there, picked her up, and placed her right in front of everyone before instructing the photographer to start the shoot over. "How wonderful was that?" she mused over forty years later. "He was such a gentleman." The hundreds of other actors who worked with him all said the same. He treated everyone on set-extras, grips, and prop men-as if they were a star just like him. He had been one of them once, and he never forgot it!

The common touch

Although she herself had enjoyed a life of privilege, it was Princes Diana's common touch that ultimately won the hearts of millions across the world. Her charisma was born not of her office but of her smile, her charm, and her constant work for numerous charities.

Another charismatic leader was Ronald Regan. Consider the story of Frances Green who was rebuffed at the White House guard station when she mistook an elaborate fundraising solicitation for a personal invitation to the White House. When word of this situation filtered back to the White House, a staff member arranged for a tour of the White House the following day.

During the tour, Ms. Green lingered near the Oval Office hoping for a glimpse of the president. As if he hadn't a care in the world with nothing of importance to occupy his time, Ronald Reagan waved her into the room. Frances, he said, "those darned computers, they fouled up again. If I'd known you were coming, I'd have come down to the gates and met you myself." Then he sat down and they talked for a while about things in California.

He made an old lady very, very happy. There are those who would see this as wasted time, but not Ronald Reagan. He understood the power of "little people."

Even the Famous Need Recognition

Even the famous can feel insecure. They need reinforcement that their vision is true. They need encouragement that the sacrifices are worthwhile. They need reassurance that their contribution, no matter how small, is important and has not gone unnoticed.

Often, in highly motivated or busy organizations, it's very easy to forget the simple little things that make a difference in everyone's performance. Fran Tarkenton, legendary quarterback of the Minnesota Vikings, recalled a close game in which time was running out and nothing was working. He decided that in order to create the break the team needed, they had to do something out of the ordinary. He chose a play that called for a quarterback block (not many of those in the playbook!) Sure enough, Tarkenton handed off the ball to the fullback, then, instead of dropping back, he ran forward and executed a perfect block on a stunned defensive player, allowing the Vikings to score a touchdown and win the game.

The next day, Minnesota coach Bud Grant reviewed film of the game and personally congratulated every player involved in the game winning play, except Fran. At the end of the meeting Tarkenton, who had sacrificed his body to make the play work, asked the coach whether he had seen the block and, if so, why hadn't he said anything? The coach responded, "Yeah, I saw the block. It was great, but you're always working hard out there, Fran, giving a hundred percent. I figured I didn't have to tell you."

"Well," said Tarkenton, "If you ever want me to block again, you do." No matter what our status and reputation, we all need to be told we've done a good job and, in my experience, the ones we think don't need it, often need it the most. (Maybe they even need their egos stroked!)

Everyone likes personal attention

Charismatic people are attentive to the small things, the human touches. They make their fans or customers feel good about buying from them. A birthday card, a handwritten note, a phone call, text or email just to say hi or thanks is often all it takes to develop a regular business relationship into a special relationship.

When all is said and done, it's the people, not the product, who make or break a company or career. The famous focus not only on the relationships they have with their fans and customers, but also on relationships with employees and suppliers. By making sure that everyone is treated with the respect and courtesy they deserve, you instill long-term trust and loyalty in all who come into contact with you while building your charisma.

10. CREATING A CHARISMATIC IMAGE

Creating a personal image that makes you stand out from the crowd will greatly enhance your charisma. I've devoted an entire chapter to this important topic, so I'll just give you one more, quick example.

Golfer Walter Hagen clearly understood the importance of image. He began his career as a professional golfer in the days when pros were not even allowed to set foot in the clubhouse. Unimpressed by the dismal accommodations made available to the pros, and tired of being treated like a second-class citizen, he decided to demonstrate his dissatisfaction publicly.

He started showing up for tournaments in a huge, chauffeur-driven limousine. He had his lunch served, complete with appropriate fine wines, in his car, which was conspicuously parked where everyone could see him. After lunch, he would change in his limo from his formal clothes into impeccable golfing attire and go to work. He waltzed around every course he played as if he owned the club, and the galleries loved him for it.

He threw lavish parties and often bought his losing opponents expensive gifts. His oversized actions made him the most famous professional of his era.

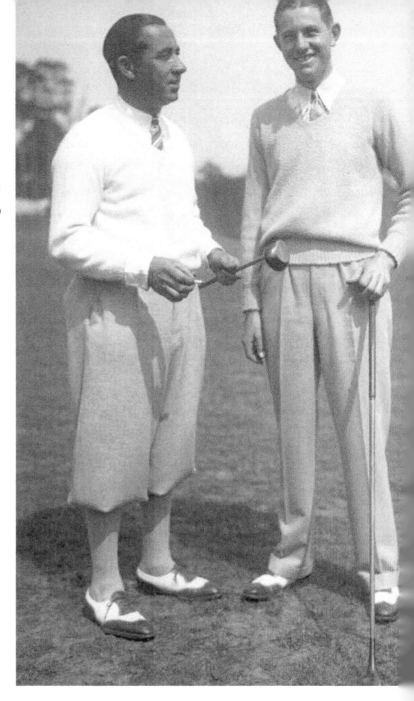

Many people credit Hagen with raising the golf pro from the rank of common laborer to that of the professional, recognized and admired by fans from every walk of life.

It was shortly after he achieved the status of a champion that country clubs gradually opened their doors to professional golfers, allowing them to use the locker facilities and other areas of the clubhouse previously reserved exclusively for members.

11. Fame Attracts Fame and Fame Builds Charisma

The eleventh key to charisma is the company you keep. Remember when you were a kid and your mother told you to keep away from Billy and Joey because they were a bad influence on you and always in trouble? Well the same holds true today, only the names have changed. People judge others by the company they keep, and you are no exception. Membership in golf, tennis, and yacht clubs can add to your charisma. While this is obviously not financially possible for everyone, there are many other opportunities to rub shoulders with the rich and famous and acquire a boost for your own image in the process.

The easiest way to do this is to become involved in your community, either in a business context with a Chamber of Commerce or development agency, or in a charitable way. The more visible you are in the community, the greater your chances of building your credibility, not only with associates, but also with others who see you in a leadership role.

Where charity is concerned, it stands to reason that people who selflessly donate their time and effort to worthy causes are people of means and respect in the community.

From a purely personal point of view, doing charitable work will almost always boost your own self-esteem and confidence. There is a true sense of

power and satisfaction in helping those less fortunate that yourself.

12. COMMITMENT BREEDS CHARISMA

The twelfth key to charisma is commitment. Just as few people dream big dreams, even fewer demonstrate true commitment. It is natural to be impressed by people who are committed. It doesn't matter whether you are committed to building a homeless shelter, raising money for a special school program, or taking your company to the next level. Commitment breeds respect. And respect helps build charisma.

What are you committed to? Hopefully, the answer is to your vision. So let it be known just how committed you are to seeing that vision through to its completion.

13. BODY LANGUAGE

The thirteenth key to charisma is body language. Charismatic people tend to stand and walk tall, with shoulders back and chest out. They tend to walk a little faster than most. They speak crisply and decisively. All of these traits create an air of importance in what they are doing and where they are going.

When all else fails, however, there is a simple, cost-effective and world-class way to help build or enhance your charisma: Smile! Sounds too easy, too trite? Well maybe it does, but I assure you the power of a smile is unsurpassed.

What do the following have in common: Julia Roberts, Rachel McAdams, Tom Cruise, Paul Newman, Arnold Palmer, and JFK? The list goes on. When you picture these charismatic people in your mind, don't they have a smile? Of course they do. It's part of the unique chemistry that makes each of them charismatic.

A smile defuses anger, removes doubt, encourages friendship, and builds camaraderie and trust. A smile inspires confidence in the person who is smiling and boosts the confidence of the person seeing it. A smile spreads a positive attitude, making people feel good about you and themselves. Smiling always reduces tension in others, and can make a bad situation appear less disturbing. Smiling will also build your reputation as a winner, especially if you smile when you lose. A smile acts as an instant energizer and makes you appear approachable and more attractive. A smile lets others know that you are good natured and that you have a sense of humor and enjoy life to the fullest.

In fact, a smile can and will make the best of just about any situation. An old saying goes, "Smile and the world smiles with you; cry and you cry alone." When you smile, and smile often, you build your charisma, even if it's only because people wonder why you are always so happy.

13. WINK, WINK. I KNOW WHAT YOU'RE THINKING!

In addition to a million-dollar smile, Ronald Reagan used simple physical gestures to generate charisma. At one White House meeting, a lowly staffer was startled to hear the president quoting directly from a memo he'd written the previous day. He was obviously surprised that the president read his memos. The president, noticing his surprise, winked at him. At another meeting, a female staffer sitting against the wall at the side of the room was shaking her head in obvious disbelief at the words of another staffer who was addressing the meeting. Wondering whether the president was believing any of the drivel they were hearing, she glanced over at him. She found Reagan looking directly at her, whereupon he threw another of his famous winks-just to let her know he was on the same wavelength.

14. QUICK THINKING

The fourteenth key to charisma is quick thinking. New research published in the journal Psychological Science says charisma may rely on quick thinking. In other words, people who can respond speedily to general knowledge questions or tasks tend to be seen as more charismatic.

"We had expected mental speed to predict charisma, as speed seemed like a critical underlying component to people's capacity to be interesting - and even a little unpredictable - in social interaction," Dr. Bill von Hippel, the lead researcher and a professor of psychology at the University of Queensland in Australia, told the Huffington Post. "But we were surprised to find that speed was more important than IQ in predicting charisma. Social intelligence is more than just knowing the right thing to say," Hippel said. "It's also the capacity to say it in a timely fashion."

15. MAKE A MEMORABLE FIRST IMPRESSION

The fifteenth key to charisma is to make a memorable first impression. First impressions are important because our brains naturally seek to reaffirm early assessments, not revise them. As such, once you've made your favorable first impression on someone, it will cast the rest of the relationship in a rosier hue. The opposite is also true, thus it's important you make the extra effort when meeting people for the first time.

16. SUCCESS BREEDS CHARISMA

The sixteenth key to charisma is success. I've saved this ingredient for last, since you obviously can't put the cart before the horse. But there is no doubt that success breeds success, and with success comes a measure of charisma.

Napoleon said, my power is dependent upon my glory, and my glory is dependent on my victories.

You can parlay small victories into bigger ones and build your charisma in the process.

Martin Luther King started on his way to becoming one of the most charismatic leaders of his time by organizing a local bus boycott in a small Alabama town. As a result of his success in this comparatively minor event, his reputation began to grow, allowing him to move on to bigger things like his original million-man march on Washington where he gave his famous "I have a dream..." speech.

Your victories will have the same effect for you. No matter how big or how small they are, share them with your friends and coworkers and you will sow the seeds of future greatness.

Make celebrating your little victories a habit. Use social media to thank fans, welcome new customers and highlight client successes. Remember, everyone loves a winner!

Charisma in Action

Even people who wanted to hate Bill Clinton found him so charismatic that after meeting him, they could not help but like him. Many people with polar opposite political views even became his friends. What was the key to Clinton's success? The use of many of the keys we have discussed are embodied in his approach. Clinton was known for having an excellent memory and could reportedly remember your full name, even if he met you years ago. Many people are quoted as saying "He looks at you like you are the most important person he's talked to that day. Even though you know you're not, you still feel like you are." He makes and holds eye contact better than almost anyone.

He is an active listener. He asks for opinions and does not dominate the conversation. He made physical contact. On many occasions he would place his hand on someone's shoulder, back, or forearm as he spoke, passing his energy on to them kinetically. He used his facial expressions and body language to convey his emotional state. Clinton would greet people with a smile in his eyes on a joyous occasion, and with sad eyes and an expression of empathy in moments of devastation. He always seemed to be successful in conveying the emotion he wanted the public to see.

He calibrated his vocal inflections and volume based on the amount of rapport he had established. If the rapport was strong, he would be more boisterous in his volume. If it was weak, he would have a more soft-spoken demeanor. Simple, but effective.

Clinton communicated in stories and always used a touch of self-effacing humor, like "I may not have been the greatest president, but I've had the most fun eight years." Can't argue with that. Self-effacing humor, when used effectively, is a hallmark sign of charisma.

He praised people publicly any chance he got, using the names of many people on his team. He had some unusual signature skills that made him stand out, like his saxophone talents. He was always seen hanging out with other successful people and he always seemed to be smiling.

He was a quick thinker and made a positive first impression on everyone he met, with an uncanny capacity to turn haters into friends. Clinton combined almost all of the keys we have discussed into his personality -- personality and charisma that allowed him to weather many personal and politically storms, much as his idol JFK had done three decades before.

A CHARISMA MAKE OVER - REMAKING THE GOLDEN BEAR

Let's take a look at how a young, talented professional went from being the butt of jokes to becoming the stuff of legends. Consider the case of two legendary golfers, each a legendary businessman and leader in his own right. Both built massive fortunes around their key asset, themselves. One was a natural who needed only to smile to unleash the power of his charisma. The other was not. In fact, he had to work very hard to acquire it. But both of them eventually prospered from their unique charismatic qualities.

In the early sixties, Jack Nicklaus wasted no time proving himself to be the world's best golfer, yet he was not immediately accepted by the golfing public. In spite of always being pleasant and polite with fans and fellow competitors, his image was hurting him badly.

The charisma was missing. When he joined the tour as a youngster, he was overweight, talked in a squeaky, high-pitched voice, and had a haircut like a Marine Corps recruit. The fans unkindly dubbed him Fat Jack. By contrast, the idol of the fans, Arnold Palmer, was articulate in a folksy way, handsome, well-dressed, and very charismatic.

Nicklaus was publicly gracious but privately distressed by the attitude of the fans. He did what any champion would do. Rather than crying about being misunderstood, he set out to change his image and build his own charisma. He became the consummate champion, both on and off the course. What effect did this image adjustment have on his career? It quickly won him favor with golf fans and, in the long term, helped him become one of the richest athletes in the world.

On the one hand we have the most naturally charismatic of players, with an image ten times larger than life. On the other is someone with the intelligence and determination to build and redefine his image. Both great champions demonstrate the importance of charisma, whether you start out with it, or develop it along the way.

You can improve your image by consciously adopting many of the traits that add up to charisma. For example, Nicklaus smoked in the early 1960s, but stopped after seeing himself on film, matched against Palmer in the playoff of the 1962 US Open. As he watched himself lining up a putt with a cigarette dangling from the corner of his mouth, he decided it was about the ugliest thing he had ever seen in his life and that it set a bad example to others, particularly youngsters. He never smoked on the course again.

Another change occurred towards the end of the 1960s when he decided to shed almost 50 pounds from his bulky 230-pound frame. Having made the decision, before the diet had even begun, he ordered new clothes to fit his target waistline. Sure enough, after a few months his new clothes were a perfect fit for a brand new, 180-pound Nicklaus. Even allowing his blonde hair to grow longer helped win the crowds over to him. To them he had been Fat Jack, a spoiled kid from Columbus with a squeaky soprano voice who was crashing King Arnie's party. Now he was trim and fit, his hair and clothes were in style, and he displayed a total respect for the game and all who played it. In this way he demonstrated not only his commitment to being a better role model, but also his excellent self-discipline. These adjustments to his image helped Jack become the undisputed king of the links, a position he would continue to occupy for two more decades.

Billy Casper, Unsung Hero

During this same era much was written that Billy Casper was the most underrated star in golf history, and the best modern golfer who never received the accolades he deserved. Casper developed his own self-contained style, relying on solid technique, determination, concentration, and perseverance. Never a flashy gallery favorite, and without any noticeable charisma, he earned a fraction of the off-course income enjoyed by Nicklaus and Palmer despite outplaying them both for many years. He was not considered one of the "Big Three" - Jack Nicklaus, Arnold Palmer and Gary Player. However, between 1964 and 1970, Casper won 27 tournaments on the PGA Tour, two more than Nicklaus and six more than Palmer and Player combined, during that time period. If Casper had developed his charisma it would have paid off...And it will for you too!

SUMMARY

Recognizing that we are a visual society, the famous go to great lengths with their demeanor. They always appear confident of future success, no matter what temporary troubles they may have to overcome. They are competent at what they do and strive endlessly to know more about their chosen field. They share their passion and excitement with the world. They look good, dress well, and stay in good physical condition. They work to develop a special trademark that sets them apart. Not just a logo or design, but an individual look, feel, or level of public acceptance that is not enjoyed by their competitors.

Once they have developed an image, they use every opportunity to emphasize and strengthen it. They work hard to build rapport and relationships with others they meet. They take care to be pictured and written about in a positive manner. They seek out other successful and respected individuals to be their friends and colleagues. They dream big dreams, and have an uncommonly high degree of commitment to see them through. Most important of all, they smile. Then, as time goes by, they build on small victories to raise themselves and others to even greater heights.

Define and cultivate your image and charisma carefully by taking all these aspects into account and, slowly but surely, you will find that others begin to gravitate towards you. They will seek you out for advice and counsel, going the extra mile to help you when they can. Once in a while they may wonder, perhaps a little enviously, what it is about you that sets you apart from the crowd. When building your charisma, it pays to be aware that it is the perception of reality that is important-not reality itself. People make decisions based on what they see and hear, not what is actually true.

What's more iconic than Jack Nicholson's toothy smile?

Action Plan

In this chapter, I've shown you how to make charisma tangible. Most people think that to possess charisma, you have to be born with it. But it is clearly a learned skill, even though many people develop a "presence" without realizing how they did it.

- How do you express your enthusiasm for life and your vision?
- How do you show others your self-confidence without being arrogant?
- Are others captivated by your big dreams?
- In what areas do you need to develop more competence to support your charisma?
- What regular exercise programs do you have to build your personal health?
- How do you put people at ease and demonstrate they have your full attention?
- What tricks can you employ to help you remember names?
- Work on a developing a few short anecdotes you can deliver with conviction that illustrate your talents.
- How can you make other people feel important and involved?
- What clothes, icons and symbols enhance your charisma?
- Do you socialize with people or in places that enhance your charisma?
- How do you demonstrate your commitment to your cause?
- How do you use your body language to make people comfortable with you and heighten your charisma?
- How do you adjust your responses to make them quicker?
- How do you go out of your way to make a memorable first impression?
- How do you ensure that you will have a series of small successes on which to build?

"A man with no enemies is a man with no character." - **Paul Newman**

9

THE YING AND THE YANG - FINDING THE PERFECT ENEMY!

People often disagree about politics, religion or social issues. Not only do they not agree, they often vilify the other side, and the debates can be heated -- one side is going to hell, the other is not. In every great story, movie or book, there has to be an enemy as a main character. You need to create your story that attracts others. You offer people benefits. You also have to have an enemy (an antagonist). It could be time, poverty or the dark forces of evil. If there was no antagonist, no struggle for the truth, no beating the odds, then it wouldn't be much of a story, would it? This is closely related to passion which attracts others to your cause and fame. You need to be a passionate protagonist.

Winston Churchill had the perfect cause and opponent when he rallied support for England to both survive and defeat the evil side in World War Two. He rose to the challenge, of course. But when the war was over he lost support and was basically kicked out as Prime Minister. Without the war cause, he had no yang to his yang and he was gone.

Many people find the concept of having an enemy hard to accept. When you take a strong stand for something – whether customer service or building a company – you will offend some people. They may be jealous or not want to look weak in comparison to you. Many people just want to blend in, be nice to people and get along with everyone. That simply does not what work in the quest for fame. Heck, it doesn't even work in everyday life. If you're going to stand for something, then you are against something else. A silly example is that if you like the Green Bay Packers, there is a pretty good chance that you hate the Chicago Bears. In soccer, the rivalry between football team fans like Manchester United and Man City, or Liverpool and Everton, Celtic and Rangers are the stuff of legends -- like English construction workers walking off the job for weeks because their hard hats were the color of the opposing city's team (true story).

You must have a reason for your dislike of the factors you're working to overcome or those who oppose your view. The clearer that reason is and the more often you repeat it, the more valuable it will be in helping you build your brand. Being a strong protagonist creates focus and provides contrast to your message, making it stronger. You need to be a clear protagonist to stir up passion, ignite your brand and accelerate it forward.

All famous brands have legendary stories that start with just one or two people as the protagonist(s) and an antagonist:

- Nike had Adidas, Phil Knight vs. Dessler
- Adidas had Puma before Nike, Dessler vs. Dessler
- Apple had Microsoft, Jobs vs. Gates
- Virgin Atlantic had British Airways, Branson vs. Big Faceless Corporation
- Southwest Airlines, the entire traditional domestic airline industry
- Ali had Frazer, Norton and Foreman
- The cool Swede Borg had the hot-headed New Yorker McEnroe, and the equally hot-headed Ilie Năstase, along with a loud Jimmy Connors
- Federer had Djokovick and Nadal
- Nicklaus had Palmer and Player
- The Beatles had the Rolling Stones
- The Sex Pistols had disco and the entire UK political structure as the enemy
- Rap bands wanted to destroy boy bands
- Christians don't like Muslims, who don't like Jews and so it goes...
- Trump and Hillary
- US and Russia
- Pro-Life and Pro-Choice

By taking a stand, by adopting a belief in yourself, your talent, your future, or your company you are automatically going to be taking an opposite position to many people. Few people who love Sinatra boast a collection of Eminem songs on their iPhone. That's okay. In fact, it's desirable to have an antagonist, an enemy against whom to rally troops to your cause. An enemy allows you to focus your energy, emotions and efforts AND it attracts fans to your cause while repelling non-believers. In other words, if you're not offending someone, you aren't offering an exciting alternative to others!

WHO DO YOU WANT TO BE?

There are many different protagonist positions you may choose to adopt.

THE SYSTEM IS THE ENEMY

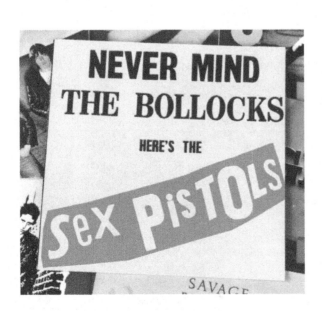

The Sex Pistols, a band with almost no musical talent, went down in history as one of the most influential bands ever with their firebrand rebellion against almost everything going on in the UK at the time. Their song "God Save the Queen," released in her silver jubilee year, was banned by the BBC, which of course sent it straight to number two (number one on independent charts). Drunk, and egged on by a reporter on live TV, they spewed a stream of profanity never before heard on British television. That got most of their live events cancelled, putting them in even more demand!

Crude, intensely emotional, and calculated to exhilarate and offend, the Sex Pistols' music and attitude were in direct opposition to the disco era music of Donna Summer; Earth Wind and Fire; and Trammps. The Pistols, along with the Ramones, the Clash and other New Wave acts of the time were the anti-disco antidote to the massive success of *Saturday Night Fever,* disco dancing and the Bee Gees!

Instead of dressing to kill in white suits and coiffed hair, they wore drainpipe jeans, leather jackets, T-shirts and hand-me-down sweaters. They sported spiked hair, mohawks often tinged with purple or green dye, or perhaps went skinhead. They wore Doc Martin boots, and for jewelry wore chains and safety pins everywhere, including in their ears and through their noses.

The government was the enemy; the queen was the enemy; the established class system was the enemy; disco was the enemy. They fought their battle on all fronts. Their message found a home with millions of disenfranchised teenagers short on job prospects, opportunities and money! Despite being together just two and a half years and making just one studio album, the band lived on in infamy.

You don't have to take on everyone, but being anti-establishment is often a successful way to get attention and attract followers.

FIGHTING YOUR LOCAL SYSTEM

The system that needs changing may not be the entire government, but just the one you have to operate in, like local zoning, visas, licensing, education or health care.

Being an advocate for "the people" against the system, which the majority of people may think is stacked against them in some way, is almost always a good approach. This can be seen on local TV in any ad for personal-injury lawyers springing to your aid against those "big bad insurance companies" for all your pain and suffering from last week's fender bender. Even better are the law/accounting firms that protect you from the IRS!

DAVID VS. GOLIATH – THE BIG CORPORATION IS THE ENEMY

The day Richard Branson launched Virgin Airways with just one plane in 1984, he declared war on British Airways. Dressed in a pirate costume, he climbed on top of a life-size model of arch rival British Airway's flagship Concorde parked outside Heathrow airport. He also changed the tail fin decals to read Virgin and put Virgin banners over the BA signs surrounding the plane. Of course all the British media had been alerted and were in attendance. His picture was splashed across the front pages of all Britain's daily papers, reaching millions of people in the process!

British Airways did everything in its power to crush Virgin Atlantic. The bad blood that existed from the beginning peaked almost a decade later in 1993 when BA had to pay damages of more than £600,000 ($1,000,000) to Branson and Virgin Atlantic. From the beginning, the entrepreneur positioned his airline as the challenger upstart to the might of BA. It was classic David vs. Goliath. Playing the "David" underdog against overwhelming odds appeals to lots of people. And the constant news of his fight took Branson's personal fame to new levels.

DAVE CARROLL VS. UNITED AIRLINES

Your fight can, of course, be much smaller. For instance, the small local car dealer or shop owner against the goliath dealership or Walmart. The local, family-owned, independent hotel or restaurant against the faceless franchises and the out-of-town suits who run them. The personal trainer against the two-story gym. The small church against the mega church. The independent lawyer or accountant fighting the big money downtown. Or even a little-known Canadian folk singer versus giant United Airlines.

In 2008, Canadian folk singer Dave Carroll and his band were on their way to the US to play a gig. During the trip his Taylor guitar was broken by United Airlines. When the air carrier wouldn't do anything about it after months of fruitless phone calls and letters, Carroll decided to take matters into his own hands with the only weapons he knew. Carroll, along with a few friends, wrote a song and recorded a video titled "United Breaks Guitars" that garnered tens of millions of views and led to appearances on all the major talk shows. Time magazine called Carroll's video one of the top 20 viral videos of all time. Today Carroll is a successful professional speaker who commands five-figure fees and specializes in customer service. He also wrote a book on his adventure, which is worth a read. I am sure his record sales went up as well. It's a classic example of the equalizing power of YouTube and social media in general.

THE OTHER COMPANY IS YOUR ENEMY
ENZO AND FERRUCCIO, THE PRANCING HORSE AND THE BULL

In the late 1950s Ferruccio Lamborghini had become very wealthy building tractors. Another local son, Enzo Ferrari had become famous building race cars. Some of these race cars were thinly disguised as road cars and sold to the public to finance his passion for racing, two of which Lamborghini duly bought. Lamborghini thoroughly enjoyed the performance of his Ferraris, but he did not like much else about them including their Spartan interiors. His main complaint though was that Ferrari's clutches were inferior and required constant trips to the factory in Maranello for replacement. As a builder of tractors, Lamborghini knew plenty about the mechanics of strong clutches, so he decided to approach Enzo about the problem and offer suggestions for improvement. Ferrari, never one to take complaints well and certainly not from a maker of tractors, rudely dismissed him. Thus a great rivalry was born and Ferruccio's hobby of driving fast cars turned into a passion for vindication.

Driven by Enzo's insult, Ferruccio got to work designing his car, and in just 4 months unveiled the Lamborghini 350 GTV at the Turin Motor Show in October 1963. By the end of 1964 Lamborghini sold his first 13 cars (renamed 350 GT). Although he sold them at a loss to keep prices competitive with Ferrari, the humble tractor manufacturer proved to be a formidable rival over the years.

In March of 1966, the Lamborghini Miura debuted at the Geneva Auto Show, and things have never been the same. The car was stunningly beautiful yet aggressive. But more importantly, the engine was transversely mounted, something that up until then had only been seen in Formula 1 racecars. Ferrari could not help but take notice.

Has someone rubbed you the wrong way? How can you use that slight to rally people to your cause. Success is always the best revenge!

WHEN FEAR OR IGNORANCE IS THE ENEMY

Watch any ad for colleges or online courses and the enemy will be fear and ignorance...

Without a degree, you will not be able to get a decent, high-paying job.

Without this course on digital marketing, your business may fail.

The reason you are fat is not because you eat too much and exercise too little; hell no, it's because no one ever showed you how to diet or exercise properly.

The reason you are broke is the nasty credit cards companies, not your inability to curb your spending.

If this model fits for what you do, you could be a champion of knowledge, enlightenment and personal improvement.

Growing up in the French Quarter of New Orleans, where lard was a food group and dessert mandatory, Richard Simmons weighed 268 pounds when he graduated high school. After trying every bizarre diet that came along with little success, Simmons finally took control of his weight by adopting a lifestyle of balance, moderate eating and exercise.

Shortly after Simmons prevailed in his own weight battle, he relocated to Los Angeles in 1973. Failing to find a health clubs that catered to anything but muscle builders, Simmons later opened his own exercise studio, originally called "The Anatomy Asylum." Having consulted with doctors and nutritionists to ensure the safety of the program, emphasis was placed on healthy eating in proper portions and enjoyable exercise in a supportive atmosphere.

Simmons' success as a fitness expert and advocate led to numerous local and national television and radio appearances including a four-year run on "General Hospital," followed by his own nationally syndicated series, "The Richard Simmons Show." The show ran for four years and received several Emmy awards.

Knowing that exercise and weight loss regimes must go hand in hand, Simmons created a series of products. He sold over 20 million copies of his 65 fitness videos, pairing lively music with rocking routines and humorous banter and encouragement.

Richard offers a routine for everyone, with titles that include:

"Sweatin' to the Oldies"

"Dance Your Pants Off"

"Party Off the Pounds"

"Disco Sweat"

"Blast Off the Pounds"

"Platinum Sweat"

"Sit Tight" (a workout designed for people who cannot stand up).

As the author of nine books, including the New York Times Best Seller, "Never Say Diet", Richard released his autobiography, "Still Hungry-After All These Years" in 1998. He is also the author of three best-selling cookbooks.

Alarmed by the growing epidemic of childhood obesity, Richard helped launch the "Fit Kids" bill in Congress. The effort is to ensure that physical education classes are reinstated or remain a part of the curriculum in public schools. Richard testified before a congressional committee and spoke of his own personal battle as an overweight child.

Simmons made weight the enemy!

SOCIAL CONDITIONS AS THE ENEMY

Frederick Douglass was the most famous African American of the Civil War era. He was a social reformer, abolitionist, orator, writer, and statesman. After escaping from slavery in Maryland, he became a national leader of the abolitionist movement in Massachusetts and New York, gaining note for his oratory and incisive anti-slavery writings. In his time, he was described by abolitionists as a living counter example to slaveholders' arguments that slaves lacked the intellectual capacity to function as independent American citizens. Northerners found it hard to believe that such a great orator had once been a slave.

Douglass wrote several autobiographies in which he described his experiences as a slave. His 1845 autobiography, *Narrative of the Life of Frederick Douglass, an American Slave*, became a bestseller, and was influential in promoting the cause of abolition, as was his second book, published in 1855, *My Bondage and My Freedom*. Douglass also actively supported women's suffrage, and held several public offices. Without his approval, Douglass became the first African American nominated for vice president of the United States as the running mate and vice presidential nominee of Victoria Woodhull, on the Equal Rights Party ticket.

Gandhi, Nelson Mandela and Martin Luther King all used the social conditions they were brought up in as the enemy, and while fame was not what they sought, their personal fame is what ultimately brought results.

Gandhi won freedom for India through peaceful demonstration. King and Mandela accomplished the same thing for equal rights. The social system -- the status quo -- was the enemy.

DON'T CRY FOR ME, ARGENTINA

Few people outside her native Argentina would know her today were it not for the hit Broadway musical (and Madonna movie) Evita. Maria Eva Duarte Perón, "Evita," was born in poverty in the rural village of Los Toldos as the youngest of five children. In 1934 at age 15 she moved to the nation's capital of Buenos Aires to pursue a career as a stage, radio, and film actress, which met with only modest success. There were few indications she would have major influence on the lives of millions of 20th-century Argentinians.

She met Colonel Juan Perón there on January 22, 1944 during a charity event at the Luna Park Stadium to benefit the victims of an earthquake in San Juan, Argentina. The two were married the following year. Juan Perón was elected president of Argentina in 1946. Eva was a skilled speaker, perhaps because of her training as an actress. She immediately decided to use her position as first lady to advance numerous causes such as women's suffrage. She founded and ran the nation's first large-scale female political party, the Female Peronist Party. She had a special connection with the poor, whom she called "mis descamisados" (my shirtless ones). She also started her own foundation to help them, often personally handing out cash. She became powerful within the pro-Peronist trade unions, primarily for speaking on behalf of labor rights. She also ran the ministries of Labor and health, and founded and ran the charitable Eva Peron Foundation.

Eva instantly became both loved and loathed by millions -- loved by those she wanted to help, and loathed by those who thought a woman shouldn't be an activist or who disapproved of her husband's autocratic rule. In 1951, Eva Perón announced her candidacy for the Peronist nomination for the office of vice president of Argentina, receiving great support from the Peronist political base, low-income and working-class Argentines. However, opposition from the nation's military and bourgeoisie, coupled with her declining health, ultimately forced her to withdraw her candidacy. . In 1952, shortly before her death from cancer at 33, Eva Perón was given the title of "Spiritual Leader of the Nation" by the Argentine Congress. She was given a state funeral upon her death, a prerogative generally reserved for heads of state. Even today, Evita has never left the collective consciousness of Argentinians. Cristina Fernández de Kirchner, the first elected female president of Argentina, and many other leaders, attest that women of her generation owe a debt to Eva for "her example of passion and combativeness."

THE OTHER STYLE IS THE ENEMY

Legendary horse trainer Pat Parelli promotes natural horsemanship. His enemy is people who train their horses with rough methods and devices that hurt horses. Since using a rough method is how the majority of trainers work, there are plenty of people who don't like Pat, or his equally talented wife Linda.

Former PGA-tour star and CBS announcer Bobby Clampett, now recognized as one of the top golf coaches in the world, thinks that all style-based golf instructors are leading their students down the wrong path. (As discussed elsewhere, style means how you swing the club.) Clampett says that the only thing all great players have in common is their position at impact. The style-based teachers naturally don't agree.

Famed British artist Sir Alfred Munnings, who painted the classic beauty of the English countryside, became wealthy and famous on both sides of the Atlantic. His paintings were owned by Rothschilds, Astors and members of the royal family. A friend of Churchill's, Munnings shared his passions for taking potshots at contemporaries, in his case Pablo Picasso and Henri Matisse. He hated modern art and felt that few modern artists had paid their dues or even learned to draw. In one letter trashing Picasso, he called him "a menace" and scrawled, "To hell with him. He never was a good artist. One of a group of the best leg-pullers this weary world…has ever seen."

Legendary martial artist and actor Bruce Lee created his own style of martial arts called Jeet Kune Do. His guiding principle was to absorb what is useful, blending the best techniques from many combat forms to make what he considered the most useful. Thus, he made instant enemies of all the traditional teachers, despite driving millions of people to their schools with his movies.

In my marketing business, I used proven direct sales techniques and longer-style copy. Many of my competitors, especially in the golf and hotel businesses, are more about design and style and use as few words as possible. Often their websites, emails and brochures are so *stylish*, with dark graphics and fancy scripted type, that they look good at a glance but no one can actually read them! They "claim" to be marketing companies but in reality, they are design companies who know little about generating sales.

If people can't read the words or there are too few words to make a real case for your product, you are unlikely to sell anything. (But everyone will "love" the way your brochure or website look.) My competitors choose style over function.

There will always be different styles of medical practice, lawyering, selling, marketing, coaching, painting, singing, farming and all other occupations.

Can you pit your unique style against a competitor's style to create an enemy?

CONTRARY BELIEF IS THE ENEMY

We all have firsthand knowledge of the divisions caused by religious belief. Various Christians, Muslims, Hindus and Jews have been at war for centuries. And it's not likely to change any century soon. Even within religious genres there are clear battle lines drawn between various sects – for example, Catholics, Baptists, Protestants, Methodists, Mormons, and so forth. There are many other beliefs that carry equally sectarian responses and therefore can intensify your message.

For instance:

- Political beliefs - Democrat vs. Republican, Conservative vs. Labour, Liberal vs. Monster Raving Loony Party (this is an actual political party in the UK).

- People for or against capitalism or climate change. One of the world's top climate change champions, along with former vice president Al Gore, is Oscar-award-winning actor Leonardo DiCaprio. His environmental activism dates back to the early 1990s where he began schooling himself on oceans and climate change, even taking private lessons in climate science. He has set up his own foundation to support biodiversity, ocean and wildlands conservation – as well as projects that focus on tackling climate change in general. Emma Watson, Bjork, Pharrell Williams and Arnold Schwarzenegger are other A-listers for the climate change cause. Donald Trump is not!

- The Atkins diet was all about meats and fats while Dr. John McDougal says vegan is the only way to live. Obviously, two very different camps.

- People who believe or do not believe in UFOs or life on other planets.

- Creationists and Darwinists.

- Those who champion Uber, AirBnB and Zipcar vs. those who want them regulated or shut down.

What key beliefs do you hold sacred that many of your peers or competition do not? How can you make this into a crusade or cause that will attract loyal followers?

LIVING CONDITIONS AS THE ENEMY

Motivational guru Anthony Robbins talks about being fat, broke and alone in his one-bedroom LA apartment. With no car, he took buses for two hours to work as a janitor in the middle of the night and was constantly hungry. Poverty and failure was the enemy and he vowed to slay it!

Rapper Eminem also used the poverty and dysfunctional nature of his upbringing as the enemy. He was living in a trailer park, his father left when he was a baby, and his mother was constantly spaced out on drugs.

Successful golfer Chi Chi Rodriguez was brought up in poverty in Puerto Rica. Calvin Pete went from migrant farm worker to the first black winner on the PGA, winning multiple times in the late '70s and '80s. Both made poverty the enemy in their quests for fame. So did South African superstar, Gary Player: "My mother died when I was eight, and my father worked 8,000 feet down in a mine. My brother went to war at 17 to fight with the British, while my sister went to boarding school. I'd come all the way home from school each night, by bus and tram, to a dark house, nobody there. I was eight. I had to cook my food, iron my clothes, and get up in the morning at five. I lay in bed every night wishing I was dead, crying. I became a champion because I knew what it was to suffer, To struggle. So I never gave up."

Think about your situation and past. Have you suffered abuse, beaten cancer, come back from injury? Are you a woman in a traditionally male business, a man in a traditionally women's business? How about very shy, short, a twin, and so on?

What conditions exist in your life or industry that can be challenged or changed? Make the commitment to go for a goal now despite what happened in the past.

THE OTHER GUY OR TEAM IS THE ENEMY

Many great sports rivalries help raise both the performance and the fame of their competitors.

For example:

- Borg, McEnroe and Connors
- Nicklaus, Palmer and Player
- Ali, Foreman and Frazier (The Big Three) and Norton
- James Hunt and Niki Lauder
- Michael Schumacher and Mika Hakkinen
- Lewis Hamilton and Sebastian Vettel
- Tom Brady, Aaron Rodgers and Ben Roethlisberger

It seems that when one player shines, two or three key contenders use that person's success as a target to motivate themselves to higher performance. In doing so the triumvirate, for it seems there are almost always three key players at any one time, creates a publicity machine far greater than anyone of them could do on their own. The public loves the drama of a good battle.

By picking someone more famous than yourself, you may be able to elevate your fame quickly. At the start it can be a variation of the David vs. Goliath story. But as your opponent gets involved with you, both of you will benefit. Some "feuds" can even be faked from the beginning to get attention. (Big time wrestling comes to mind.)

The Battle for Clients and Customers

The battle could just as easily be between Realtors, golf pros, attorneys, plastic surgeons, chefs, local bands or car dealers. In every town one person in any profession is more famous than the next. The quicker that person is you, the sooner the benefits of fame will flow to your door.

Having your sights on someone to beat makes it that much easier for you to focus.

FIGHTING MAD

After turning professional, Cassius Clay (who later changed his name to Muhammad Ali), won six fights in six months. Then in 1961, on a Las Vegas radio show to promote his seventh contest, he met the wrestler "Gorgeous" George Wagner whose pre-fight promotional skills got audiences very excited. As Ali later told his biographer Thomas Hauser, "George started shouting: 'If this bum beats me I'll crawl across the ring and cut off my hair, but it's not gonna happen because I'm the greatest fighter in the world.' All the time, he was yelling I was saying to myself, 'Man. I want to see this fight.' The whole place was sold out when Gorgeous George wrestled. I was there too and that's when I decided if I talked more, there was no telling how much people would pay to see me." Subsequently Ali, who was also quite handsome in his own right, talked often and talked loudly on his way to becoming "King of the World."

Unlike other boxers, Ali not only named all his fights but also gave all of his opponents nicknames to antagonize them and stir up hype in the media for the fight. The fight names included:

The Rumble in the Jungle
The Thrilla in Manila
The Fight of the Century

The nicknames included:

George Foreman, "The Mummy"
Joe Frazier, "The Gorilla"
Sonny Liston, "The Big Ugly Bear"
Oscar Bonavena, "The Beast"
Floyd Patterson, "The Rabbit"
Earnie Terrell, "The Octopus" (because of his ungainly boxing style)
Ernie Shavers, "The Acorn" (because of his shaved head)
Larry Holmes, "The Peanut" (because of the shape of his head)
Henry Cooper, "The Tramp"
Leon Spinks, "Dracula" (because of the gap in his teeth).

Ali also frequently called several boxers "bums" and "Uncle Toms" for not standing up to white domination.

THE GREATEST ENEMY OF ALL, DEATH

One sportsman, stuntman, daredevil -- whatever he actually was -- had the greatest opponent of all, death.

Said Evel Knievel, "They don't come to see me die, but they don't want to miss it if I do!"

Knievel missed no opportunity to play up his opponent in his press conferences and publicity tours:

"This is a very dangerous stunt."

"No one has ever done this before."

"This could be my last performance."
 (He always left you unsure about whether he meant retirement or death!)

"You can't ask a guy like me why I wanted to fly through the air. I was a daredevil, a performer. I loved the thrill, the money, the whole macho thing. All those things made me Evel Knievel. Sure, I was scared. You gotta be an ass not to be scared. But I beat the hell out of death."

Conquering death or injury goes back to at least the 1800s. It applies to professions from race car drivers to parachute jumpers to escape artists like Houdini. In the early days of motorcycles, riders would defy gravity in the "Wall of Death" using centrifugal force to ride inside a sphere.

In 2018 Tony Pender set a world record for chopping watermelons with a machete on his own stomach. It interested the Guinness Book of Records enough that they set up a new category for him to compete in.

You may not want to go over Niagara Falls on a tightrope or a barrel, but maybe you can come up with a daring stunt that fits your image.

… or maybe you can reverse it for a laugh by wrestling a dozen kittens instead of an alligator. Might work for a veterinarian!

HOLLYWOOD LOVES A GOOD FEUD.
IT KEEPS THEIR FAMOUS STARS IN THE NEWS AND PUBLICITY EQUALS FAME

- Tom Cruise vs. Brooke Shields; Tom called her out for taking anti-depression pills. (They have since made up.)

- Paris Hilton vs. Nicole Richie (This duo has not made up. Nicole, upset because she had not been invited to one of Paris's events, had a party of her own and played Paris's infamous sex tape on a big screen.)

- J-Lo's riff with Mariah Carey; the latter claiming in an interview she has never heard of her,

- Sylvester Stallone vs. Richard Gere; Gere spilled mustard on Sly's trousers.

- Letterman vs. Leno; the former thought he should have had Leno's job.

FINDING THE PERFECT ENEMY 343

- Martha Stewart vs. Gwyneth Paltrow; Martha thought Gwyneth's "lifestyle" advice was amateur and told her to stick to acting.

- Axl Rose and Slash's relationship was destroyed by the latter's collaboration with Michael Jackson whom Rose hated. Apparently, it was later revealed, because Rose had been a victim of child abuse.

- Hollywood's biggest feuder (and later Trump supporter, which caused even more feuding), Kanye West, has feuds with Taylor Swift, Jay Z, Justin Timberlake, and the list goes on for pages. Still, his best efforts will never match those of Hollywood's legendary feud between Bette Davis and Joan Crawford.

The decades-long catfight between Davis and Crawford is the quintessential feud of all time. It went on so long they actually made a miniseries out of it.

The feud reportedly started in 1935 when Davis fell in love with actor Franchot Tone, her co-star on the set of the movie Dangerous. Davis had a crush on Tone, but Crawford also fancied the actor and ultimately married him when the movie wrapped. From that moment on, the women were in an all-out war for roles and attention, making no secret of their hate for one another.

The feud escalated when the two worked together on the set of their 1962 movie, Whatever Happened to Baby Jane? Both gave virtuoso performances, although only Davis was nominated for an Oscar. Crawford allegedly campaigned against her. To put a cherry on top, Davis later accepted the award on behalf of the winning actress, Anne Bancroft, who could not make the event. Sadly, the feud played out the rest of their lives. Upon hearing of Crawford's death, according to the LA Times, Davis remarked "You should never say bad things about the dead, you should only say good. Joan Crawford is dead. Good!"

You may not be enough of a star now for people to care about your feuds. However, if you attack someone bigger than you, you might get extra attention and the attack may grow into a real feud. An attorney might attack unfair laws. Other good targets are politicians, bureaucracy, the IRS, and lawyers!

PUMA VS. ADIDAS SPLIT THE TOWN OF HERZOGENAURACH FOR 60 YEARS

Cain and Abel had nothing on this famous feud in Germany. The vicious feud between Puma and Adidas not only tore the Dressler family apart but divided the entire town for over sixty years!

In the 1920s, brothers Adolph and Rudolph were partners in the Dressler Brothers Sports Shoe Company, operating from a single room in the small German town of Herzogenaurach. Adolf (Adi) Dressler was the quiet, thoughtful craftsman who designed and made the shoes, complemented by the older Rudolph (Rudi) who was the extroverted salesman.

Despite both joining the Nazi party, their initial success came at the hands of black superstar Jesse Owens who wore their shoes on his way to winning four gold medals at the 1936 Berlin Olympics. (So much for Aryan superiority.)

The success brought by the huge spike in sales brought additional tensions to the brothers' relationship. It was already strained by the fact that their families lived in the same villa despite their wives not getting along.

Many incidents were said to have precipitated their conflict, but the most widely accepted one took place during World War II when the Allies were bombing Herzogenaurach. As Adi and his wife climbed into a bomb shelter already occupied by Rudi and his wife, he exclaimed, "The dirty bastards are back again," referring to the Allied forces. Rudi was convinced the remark was directed at him and his family. Thus, started a feud of Biblical proportions. There were many more incidents and bitter accusations of betrayal ending up in the 1948 split. Adi named his company "Adidas," a combination of his first and last names. Rudi attempted the same by first naming his company "Ruda" but eventually changed it to the more athletic sounding "Puma." The two built competing factories on opposite sides of the Aurach river. They quickly became responsible for much of Herzogenaurach's economy, with nearly everyone working for one or the other.

There were local businesses that served only Adidas or only Puma. Even people dating or marrying across company lines was forbidden. Puma was seen as Catholic and politically conservative, Adidas as Protestant and Social Democratic.

At the 1974 World Cup that was held in West Germany, Adidas was the official kit supplier to the Netherlands' football team, captained by superstar Johan Cruyff. All his teammates had the famous three stripes of Adidas on the sleeves of their orange shirt, but Cruyff had two. This was because Cruyff was sponsored by Puma who supplied him with their iconic Puma King boots, and he refused to wear the three trademarked Adidas stripes. The Dutch FA bowed to Cruyff's demand, and allowed him to play in a bespoke kit with only two stripes.

In business terms, it is Adi who has won. Adidas is by far the bigger company, employing 39,000 compared with Puma's 9,000. But it is the nature of the Adi- and Rudi-driven rivalry that has given both firms their fighting spirit, trying to outdo each other by securing endorsements with the world's top athletes. Herzogenaurach became known as "the town of bent necks" since people first looked at which company's shoes you were wearing before deciding about talking to you.

The rivalry split the town and meant that (officially at least) Adi and Rudi didn't speak to each other. The townspeople seem largely grateful for the rift. "Without the row we would not now be home to these two global players," says Klaus-Peter Gäbelein of the local Heritage Association.

Says local journalist Rolf-Herbert Peters, whereas the Berlin Wall fell 20 years ago, the antagonism between Adidas and Puma is still obvious to any outsider visiting the town.

It wasn't until 2009 that employees of both companies symbolized the end of six decades of feuding by playing a friendly soccer match. By then, the Dassler brothers had both died.

Even in death the animosity continued as the brothers were buried at opposite ends of the same cemetery, as far away from each other as possible

DEALING WITH THE ENEMY'S COUNTERATTACKS

Even if you don't want enemies, success and fame in any field will bring them into your life. The comments, reviews, posts and emails will be hurtful, insulting and often complete lies.

Just remember, even Mother Theresa had plenty of detractors, so what chance have you got of getting away unscathed by critics?

Do Not Back Down

It doesn't pay to waste too much time on petty rivals, but you shouldn't ignore their put-downs or comments on social media. While sometimes silence is the best policy, no response to repeated accusations can be damaging.

My preferred strategy is not to take a hater head on with an aggressive rebuttal but to be polite and goad them into saying something stupid, at which point others will leap to your defense.

Another strategy is to use humor to make light of the criticism.

"Don't try to explain it, just go sell it!" - **Colonel Tom Parker**

SUCCESS IS THE BEST REVENGE

By the late 1950s, Elvis Presley merchandise was selling like hotcakes, but not everyone was buying.

So, Presley's manager, Colonel Tom Parker, had an idea to get money from everyone by selling buttons with anti-Presley statements. These round badges looked similar to the "I Like Elvis" ones that were already being sold but instead read, "I Hate Elvis," "Elvis is a Jerk," and "Elvis the Joik*."

Parker signed a merchandising deal with Beverly Hills film merchandiser Hank Saperstein for nearly $40,000 to turn Presley into a brand name. With over 78 different items, from charm bracelets to record players, Presley merchandise had brought in $22,000,000 by the end of 1956. Parker, with his 25% share of profits, was finding many new ways to make money from his artist that managers before him could only have dreamed about.
Brian Bosworth, the famous and controversial American Seattle Seahawks football player, took a page from the colonels' playbook. Bosworth trash-talked Denver Broncos quarterback John Elway. When Denver played Seattle, 10,000 Seattle fans wore shirts that said "Ban the Boz." They didn't know it at the time, but the shirts were made by Bosworth's company.

Even in a gentlemen's game like golf, there are haters. Gary Player talks about going up against all-American hero Arnold Palmer. "When I went to America, I was this foreigner playing against Arnold Palmer; 20,000 people would shout: 'Tear him up, the little bastard! Go get him, Arnie!' I loved it! All the other players would say 'I can't play with Arnold Palmer, people shout at me and they scream at me!' But I loved it! I said 'Boy, you Americans, I'm gonna whack him right in front of your eyes, man!' Because I was prepared mentally (for the abuse). I taught myself as a young man. It was a divine intervention: I realized this was what it took to win tournaments."

When I first started out in the martial arts business I worked for two powerful and headstrong guys who ran a large chain of studios. When they fell out with each other, they both demanded my fidelity. I tried to stay out of it but by committing to neither of them I alienated both of them. This led to vandalism of my schools and threats of violence as they started a dojo war between the rival factions. This was right when I was about to publish my first manual, so instead of using my surname name, I used my middle names and used a model on the cover, not myself. I sold over $15,000 worth of manuals to their 200-plus schools without them knowing they were paying me!

WORKING BOTH SIDES

In Glasgow, the two big soccer teams are Celtic and Rangers who have a fierce and violent rivalry going back hundreds of years. A friend of mine goes abroad to Turkey to get some winter sun, and there is a famous Celtic-themed bar that plays anti-Rangers songs which get everyone all riled up and, of course, drinking more. All the fans love the Turkish guy who owns the bar, thinking he is a hardcore Celtic fan -- little do they know he also owns the Rangers bar 10 minutes away that does the exact same thing in reverse.

FINDING YOUR ANGLE OF ATTACK

In my martial arts business, I made the enemy martial arts billing companies. At the time they took 10% of a school's tuition revenues in return for some self-serving advice. I advocated independence from their clutches and to instead take my independent advice!

In the golf business, the big management companies and the third-party tee-time companies hated me as I exposed their shady business practices and poor marketing efforts weekly on my social media networks. This created a large audience who agrees with and follows me, and a small audience who side with the big bad guys.

- Could your enemy be greedy commission takers while you charge a flat fee? Or perhaps the reverse, you charge commission, but your flat-fee competition has multiple add-on charges that end up costing the client more?
- Do you offer a large number of choices vs. competitors' limited options?
- Superior business methods and innovation vs. competitors' old techniques that don't work anymore?

- Some future sound, vibe, feel, looks, taste vs. the ways of the past?
- More certifications, awards and qualifications vs. your competitor lacking in credibility?
- Speedy response vs. the sloth of your competitors.
- You have fewer listings or clients because you are more particular vs. those big outfits are the enemy?
- You have more listings or clients because you are better vs. those smaller companies don't have your resources?
- Only old people…listen to that, dance that way, use Facebook, drive that brand etc., vs. the young do this….
- That style of teaching, art, fashion used to be popular vs. now this is trending…

It's your story, you can position the enemy however you choose. And don't be afraid to have opponents. Having an "enemy" makes your position clearer and more attractive to your audience.

SUMMARY

Every great movie has an enemy and every great band is the same. You need an antagonist to position yourself against and make your message clear. You are the hero against the government, the crazy rules, ignorance, high commission rates, unfair business practices or inferior competition. Perhaps the other style or belief system is the enemy maybe even death itself. Having a ying and a yang always creates more interest in your struggle and more media attention.

Whatever position you adopt others will disagree and in this world of instant feedback take to social media to voice their opposition. Have a plan for dealing with the "haters". Try humor and have some stock graphics and responses ready so you waste little time on them. Always remember success is the best revenge!

One man can change an evil empire .... ?

ACTION PLAN

- Who is your enemy?
- Why are you going up against them/it?
- Why should people rally to your cause?
- Do you have a style of teaching, painting, singing, acting, creating, selling, working that is clearly different from your major competition?
- Why is your method better, more relevant, progressive, trendy?
- Are you passionate enough about your method or style to call out non-believers?
- What specifically will you solve or create?
- How will you use your enemy to motive yourself and your team?
- Write your story of good versus evil.
- How will you respond to the negative response of others?
- Do not blind yourself to unseen threats from other possible usurpers.
- Have some creative stock responses to the haters so you don't let them get away with much, but don't waste too much time either!

"Words are, of course, the most powerful drug used by mankind." – **Rudyard Kipling**

10

THE FAMOUS DON'T LEAVE THEIR PUBLICITY OR LEGACY TO CHANCE

After leaving office, Winston Churchill was asked by a young reporter how he expected history to view him in light of his many political and military failures, especially the WWI Dardanelles campaign. Churchill cheerfully replied that he expected history to view him very favorably. The reporter asked, "Why?"

Churchill, already several volumes into writing a definitive history of World War II, cheerfully replied, "Because that's the way I intend to write it." Few people know that Churchill actually made his living by writing and in addition to mountains of newspaper articles and speeches, published 93 books in his lifetime.

Churchill was by no means the first famous person to shape how his legacy was seen. In fact as a keen student of British history, he would no doubt have known that Alfred the Great, king of Wessex, employed two monks to write his biography, so as to preserve his legacy as long ago as 880.

You don't become Alfred "The Great" by relying solely on the goodwill of medieval reporters.

Alfred the Great

Indeed, there are constant opportunities for people at all levels to influence the way people think about you. I became the world's leading expert on the martial arts business simply by claiming the title. I am now also the world's leading expert on golf-related marketing. When I claimed the titles I may have been a trifle premature, but over time I have backed up this personal positioning with real substance. You can do the same.

New businesses and small businesses in general will only survive and grow if they attract attention. Unless your product or service is in such great demand that people work to find you, it up to you to use creative marketing to publicize yourself. When you are new, people expect some creativity or brashness, so don't be afraid to use "guerrilla marketing" techniques that are aggressive, novel, or funny. For example, Pets.com was able to turn a silly sock puppet into a nationally recognized spokesperson.

It's easiest to get publicity if you have something truly unique.

For instance, if people buy clothing online they're going to worry about fit. Zappos.com, an internet shoe store, was one of the first to deal with this fear by offering free, easy returns. This reassured customers who worried about buying shoes they could not try on. It dealt with a real issue and got Zappos lots of publicity. Their easy-return policy became a standard for the online shopping.

A very old concept in marketing is called **preempting the truth** in which you make a claim that applies to everyone in your category, but nobody else uses it.

An example would be the tax lawyers on the radio who tell you they'll handle everything (you don't have to see the IRS yourself) and that, unlike accountants, the IRS can't make them testify against you because of lawyer-client privilege. This has the added advantage of making them look better than their accountant competitors.

Anita Roddick was the founder of The Body Shop, which has made billions of dollars since the 1970s. She was an early celebrity in the business-environmental area. The company was one of the first to prohibit the use of ingredients tested on animals and one of the first to promote fair trade with developing countries. These policies continue to be used by more and more businesses today.

Surprisingly, public relations as we know it today grew up in the American Wild West.

Buffalo Bill Cody had his own press agent, considered by many as the first P.R. man, Major John M. "Arizona John" Burke who was an early pioneer of many modern marketing techniques.

Although he was never in the military and didn't come from Arizona, the Stetson-clad "spinmeister" was a master of the media.

Burke's remarkable innovations included celebrity endorsements, press junkets, press kits, publicity stunts, op-ed pieces, mobile billboards, custom publishing, and product licensing deals, most of which had never been seen before.

They helped attract 50 million people to Buffalo Bill's Wild West Show, making it the first great entertainment property in the world. In the process, Burke methodically built up the almost mythic western hero image of Buffalo Bill that survives to this day.

According to the *Detroit Free Press,* "With his broad-brimmed black Stetson, his long, curly white hair, his cigar stuck jauntily between his lips, and his enormous diamond horseshoe pin crowning his cravat, he was known in virtually every newspaper office in the country,"

Jesse James, the most celebrated bandit in Western history, loved his notoriety. One time he even wrote his own press release about a robbery, which he handed to the engineer of the train before riding away with his men. (He wanted the newspaper to get the story right!)

General George Custer was a "media celebrity" in his lifetime. He valued good public relations and used the print media of his era effectively. He frequently invited journalists to accompany his campaigns.

One Associated Press reporter, Mark Kellogg, died at the battle of the Little Bighorn. Journalists' favorable reporting contributed greatly to his positive reputation, which lasted well into the latter part of the 20th century. Custer himself enjoyed writing, often writing all night long. According to friends he was seriously considering it as a career once he retired. He wrote a series of magazine articles of his experiences on the frontier which were syndicated in newspapers across the country, and eventually were published book form in 1874 as *My Life on the Plains*.

Meanwhile, back on the East Coast, P. T. Barnum became the most famed promoter of his era, perhaps ever. Barnum wrote in his book, *Humbugs of the World*, that the term humbug "consists in putting on glittering appearances—outside show—novel expedients, by which to suddenly arrest public attention, and attract the public eye and ear." And Barnum wanted to make it clear such a practice was justified. "There are various trades and occupations which need only notoriety to insure success," he claimed, concluding no harm, no foul, so long as at the end of the day customers felt like they got their money's worth.

Ever the perfectionist, P.T. Barnum requested that the New York *Evening Sun* newspaper print his obituary a couple of weeks before his death so that he would have a chance to read it before he actually died. Barnum approved of the write-up.

Ivy Lee opened a "counseling office" in 1904. He was the first famous PR (publicity) man. One of his first clients was the Pennsylvania Railroad. In 1906, he used the "press release" to distribute the company's "news" about an accident before reporters received other versions of the story. It worked like magic and he went on to work for all the major railroads and Mr. Rockefeller himself.

Fidel Castro had already suffered one failed revolution and spent two years in jail when, several years later, he returned from self-imposed exile in Mexico with a band of 80 troops. The new revolution was a disaster from the start with only a couple of real sailors to operate the ship in poor weather. The boat eventually ran aground on a sand bank a mile off the East Cuban shore and arrived three days late of their intended rendezvous with other guerrillas on land. That group had already been defeated, and government soldiers were waiting for Castro's men as they waded ashore. Only 22 of the 80-plus in Castro's band survived, and they fled to the hills.

While Castro was an amateur general, he did know the value of good PR. While hiding in the hills, he got word to a New York Times writer that he was open for an interview. Weeks later, a writer from the New York Times was led to their mountain camp. Castro talked for hours about his revolution. Carefully planned interruptions made it sound like he was running battle: "The commander from Unit Two has just arrived to see you, Comondante" said an aide.

"YES, later," replied an irritated Castro waving him away. Castro went on to say that while Batista's units had 200 men, his band of just 30-40 were more mobile and beating them badly. He claimed had many units hiding in the hills. The writer took it all in and fell for the charade. The fact was, all 22 of Castro's men in the revolutionary army were in the camp! The story of Cuban rebel leaders and the struggle for independence ran on the front page of the New York Times and made Castro an instant worldwide celebrity. He milked this fame to drum up a wildfire of local support, taking command of the country a short while later.

Now that's the power of good PR even for a bad guy!

NOW SOME AMAZING NEWS: YOU OWN YOUR OWN MEDIA COMPANY!

In the past, getting coverage from newspapers, magazines and TV stations was a pretty hit - and-miss and expensive affair, even with a good PR company. You had no control over when or if they ran your story, not to mention how the edited version might appear. Today you have no such problem because you own your own TV, radio, newspaper and magazine. Yes, you are a media mogul although you may not have thought of it that way.

- Your Facebook, Instagram and Twitter accounts are your newspapers with daily stories
- Your blog and LinkedIn are your magazines, with posts weekly if not daily
- YouTube is your TV station, with satellite stations on Twitter, Facebook and LinkedIn
- And your podcast is your radio station
- You have even more reach through other synergistic alliances you have with people who can distribute your content
- All your content can also be found on your website, which generates additional traffic to your media accounts
- Most important of all are the people on your email list who receive your newsletters

If you add up all your fans, followers, emails, website traffic, blog traffic and the groups you belong to, your media reach is most likely larger than your local papers or TV stations. This is real star-making power at your fingertips. These online media resources are too valuable to ignore. You must make a constant effort, daily in my case, to increase your reach in every way possible.

While all the social avenues offer potential, your most important asset will always be your email list that you own. The rest you just rent and must accept the whims of Facebook, LinkedIn or Google. Therefore, no matter which of the following ways you use to increase your fame, make every effort to end up with email addresses. And don't ignore snail mail -- that may come in handy too.

All things being equal in the "Fame Game," he with the biggest database, and therefore the biggest audience, wins.

TOP 20 PRACTICAL WAYS TO ENHANCE YOUR PERSONAL BRAND AND BUILD FAME IN YOUR MARKET!

This is a bulletproof blueprint for getting your brand to the top of your profession, organized by the amount of time, money, and effort it takes to accomplish each task.

1. ALWAYS BE GROWING YOUR EMAIL DATABASE

Nothing is more important than this. All things being equal, he with the biggest database wins. Professional A has 10,000 emails, professional B has 1,000 emails. This means professional A has a ten-to-one advantage that's almost impossible to beat by any other means. Try to incorporate email growth into everything you do. Email your list high quality content regularly, preferably weekly.

2. BLOGGING

A quick, easy, cheap, effective way to get your knowledge, views, causes, sounds, movies and expertise out to clients, fans and prospects.

Many people have become famous by blogging alone and it was certainly a big key to my success in the golf industry.

The *Huffington Post* started out as Adriana Huffington's blog. A blog also made the *Drudge Report* big for Matt Drudge. Celebrity gossip site *TMZ* also started out as a blog for American lawyer, Harvey Levin. You can frequently see Harvey hosting his own TV show or appearing as a guest on celebrity-related matters on CNN, FOX, and other networks. All three managed to leverage the popularity of their blog to build a personal brand and fortune for themselves.

Tim Sykes started blogging to document how he turned $12,000 of his Bar-Mitzvah money into over $1 million dollars. He has gained Internet fame for being an authority on penny stock trading.

Tucker Max was blogging about his drunken, womanizing exploits before the phrase "blogging" even existed. Tucker's blog attracts hundreds of thousands of visitors weekly who like to read about his "interesting" exploits. Because of Tucker's blog, he was able to get a book published which The *New York Times* called "...highly entertaining and thoroughly reprehensible..." No wonder it was on The *New York Times* best sellers list for 100 weeks.

Brian Clark is the founder of *Copyblogger*. He started the blog back in 2006 as a resource for entrepreneurs to learn to be better copywriters, content marketers, and all around "kings of content." The blog has since grown to become an authoritative source on creating killer content for the web. With 100K+ subscribers, Brian leveraged his readership to launch several spinoff companies.

There are hundreds of other examples in every profession where a blog proved to be the catalyst to produce fame in a specific industry.

Blog Tips

- Be personal; let your personality come through. Do not write politically correct corporate speak, be real, be you! If that turns some people off, that's OK, it will attract others
- Tell stories, people love stories
- Be topical. Tie your blog posts into what's going or in the world or in your industry
- Be punchy, to the point

- Choose great headlines that either provide clear benefits or shock the reader; for instance, people like lists such as "Ten Ways To…"
- Choose great graphics that demand attention!
- Add a call to action at the end of every post. What should the reader do next: watch your YouTube video, listen to your music, download your special report, connect with you on social media, donate to your cause or buy your book?
- Blog as often as possible
- Blog with a strategic purpose in mind
- Email blog updates to your lists and share on all your social media

I have several blogs, fan pages and groups for different niche markets that I serve, These include: authors/experts/speakers, golf, martial arts, horse owners and entrepreneurs. You may want to consider segmenting your blogs based on the groups of people you serve.

Now for the best part: if you blog even 3-5 days a week, you are going to have enough info for a nice booklet or a chapter of a book at the end of the month. Do that every month and you are going to have a bunch of micro books or enough info for a single full book.

3. FACEBOOK

The most important use of Facebook is to use their powerful data and Facebook ads to build your email lists. Target the people and geography you want to reach through Facebook ads and drive them to your opt-in landing page. There give them some information or reward for opting in. This is one of the simplest, cheapest and most powerful ways to grow your audience.

Next use Facebook to distribute your blog, YouTube, LinkedIn and other content.

Then develop a strategic approach to other information you post. Make sure everything you post on your fan page supports your position. The key to Facebook content can be defined in three words engage, educate and entertain. If you post content that meets these criteria, people will be happy to read your sales message.

Here are a couple of examples of post from my Golf Industry Facebook page that does all three key things and sells my book at the end. Humor is an effective weapon on all social media!

4. START YOUR OWN FACEBOOK GROUP

There are certain advantages to starting your own Facebook group, not least of which is the ability to invite people via entering their email address, along with more control over content in the group and the audience itself.

5. START YOUR OWN SOCIAL MEDIA

While it's harder to get people to show up on a regular basis, you can bypass Facebook entirely and create your own similar social network with all the same features except you control everything! My friend Pat Parelli has Parelli Connect with many thousands of users, while his wife Linda has a couple of thousand fans on her Pegasus Personal Growth social engine.

6. LINKEDIN

LinkedIn is like Facebook for business people and will put you in touch with a professional crowd. LinkedIn has three ways to build your audience: posts, articles and groups.

Posts are limited to 1300 characters or you can post a video. I post daily and use all 1300 most days. Choose graphics carefully to attract more readers and followers. You can make quick custom graphics for free using services like canva.com or get interesting stock images cheap from places like dreamstime.com.

Articles are LinkedIn's version of a blog. Repost your blog articles on their platform. Articles can be as long as you like but should contain lots of pictures to break them up. Once again, great headlines and the photo you choose make a huge difference to how big your audience becomes.

Groups. The real power of LinkedIn kicks in when you share your articles and posts with the members of the various groups you are involved in. My dozen golf industry groups alone give me a combined potential audience of over 150,000 people. My marketing groups are over 500,000, while my leadership groups are over 100,000.

Be active in commenting and supporting other people on the platform and don't forget to start your own LinkedIn group. The very act of starting a niche group attracts like-minded people to your cause and builds your fan base.

One other benefit of LinkedIn, not available on Facebook, is that you can download the emails of all your connections, thus making it a great way to grow your email lists.

7. SLIDESHARE

LinkedIn also owns SlideShare, a platform that allows you to reach audiences most interested in digesting your various materials via PowerPoint shows.

Below is an example of a slide deck I created to build my brand and promote my book *Cowboy Wisdom* in an entertaining way. PowerPoint has plenty of nice designs to choose from, or for an extra ten to twenty bucks you can buy a custom template that suits your needs, as I did here.

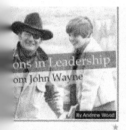    

8. E-NEWSLETTER

It takes time but you can quickly build a small loyal following and grow it. I have built my golf industry list to 79,000, my horse lover list to 28,000, my martial arts list to 18,000 and my golf traveler list to over a million. My hotel industry list is 150,000, plus various other smaller niches lists giving me a total email audience of almost two million people. A high-quality e-newsletter helps build your database fast!

9. SPEAKING OR PLAYING TO A LIVE AUDIENCE

Not everyone can do it well, but performing live is a very powerful tool to build your fame. If you can't speak well, take lessons or courses. Speak, preach, and perform wherever you can; every audience grows your fan base. Every appearance before an audience adds to your fame. Every audience can be primed to buy or at the very least be added to your email list. Video every presentation so you can use clips on your social media pages or create residual income from them via courses and webinars. Running your own events can also be very lucrative.

10. GUEST ARTICLES ON OTHER BLOGS OR MAGAZINES

The more articles you get out in your industry, the more quickly your reputation will grow. Make sure all your articles have a resource box with a headshot, short bio and a link back to your website! Let people know they can repost your stuff as long as they publish the resource box.

11. SPECIAL REPORTS, BOOKLETS OR MICRO BOOKS

Easy, effective, and you can get someone else to write it using your ideas if you have trouble getting them down on paper. There are few things as strong for personal branding as writing a book! But let's face it, not everyone has the time, ability, or inclination to write one. If you just don't have a book in you, you can still benefit from a much simpler form of publishing. Write a short 10-20 page booklet on your specific field of expertise. Have a graphics person design a nice layout, print it up, and give it away to anyone who will take one.

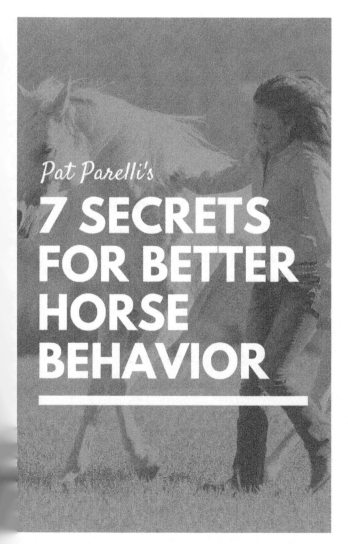

My first attempt at this was a simple five-page effort, photocopied, folded in half, and stapled in the middle. It made a nice little 20-page booklet and was titled *How to Design an Ad that Works.* After sending it to The *LA Times* every year for four years in a row, they published a nice little story on how small business owners could get the booklet for free to help them with their ads. That story brought in over $25,000 in business and made a nice addition to my press kit.

I have used this tactic many times in many different fields. Sometimes I write them for my clients, other times I have people write them for me. Booklets always make a big impression on people and help build your reputation.

If you are a golf pro, write a booklet on 10 ways to stop a slice. If you are a chiropractor, write a booklet on the 12 ways to avoid back trouble. It you are an attorney, write a booklet on what to do if you are involved in an accident. If you are a big corporation, as many of my clients are, you can use this tactic to show your clients you care about them. One of the major insurance companies I worked with published a whole series of booklets to help their clients improve their businesses. Not one had anything to do with insurance, but all had something to do with building the company's reputation as an insurance carrier that cared about the success of their clients.

Getting Your Booklet Out

Once your booklet is published, the next trick is to get it out so it attracts the attention you desire. Start by giving booklets out to all your existing customers and asking them to pass the information along to a friend. Next, look for others who are strategically aligned to your business. In the martial arts business we got hospitals and doctors' offices to give away our booklets on building self-esteem in children. I got speakers bureaus to give out my booklet A Meeting Planner's Guide to Successful Events, and even customized the booklets with the individual bureaus' phone numbers on them. We had banks, toy stores, and hairdressers give away our booklets on building confidence in kids. The possibilities for distribution are as endless as your imagination. Also, don't forget the press when it comes to your booklet. Let them know it's available to help their readers with their choices, problems, and businesses by sending them a copy along with a professional press release.

Then of course if you don't want to go to all the trouble of printing you can just make it a downloadable pdf from your website and use it as an opt-in device to build your database. Better still you can make it a micro book on Kindle.

Micro Books

The beauty of Kindle is that the publishing process is really easy. What Kindle is good for is building your brand and allowing you to test concepts, titles and covers in the real world. It also puts you into a market of people who have simply never read printed books, sad, but true. There are lots of low-priced services that will turn your manuscript into a Kindle - format book, and while the upload process to self-publish is easy it can also be outsourced. You can also choose to sell your info.

Make sure you have a page in your book that encourages people to visit your website and subscribe to get some kind of value-added extra so you can collect the emails of people who bought your book. Otherwise you will never know who they are!

12. WRITE A BOOK

This the most prestigious and longest-lasting tool to build your personal reputation in any field. As mentioned earlier, if you blog strategically two to three times a week you can painlessly write a book a year, or you can always hire a ghostwriter.

Nothing builds your stature and credibility in any industry like a book. How many people have you met who were "going" to write a book? The time and effort deters many as did the cost of self-publishing in the past. Now with print-on-demand publishing anyone can create a book for a very small investment.

Being published in book form puts you head and shoulders above most in your industry and it even makes you some money. All of my books have made me money, but not all made a lot of money. The upside is that a book is the best sales tool you will ever have for selling consulting or additional professional services. I love to write. If you don't, you can still have your thoughts and ideas turned into a book with the help of a college student or professional ghost-writer.

I use Amazon KDP (formerly CreateSpace) for my print-on-demand books. The final product looks great and you can use them to ship your books for you. The cost per book is very low, and flat-rate shipping is cheap, except overseas. A downside is the delivery time overseas. You can charge a different shipping price for international customers to offset having to use more expensive shipping. Being able to have a physical book in your hands without having to shell out tens of thousands of dollars is nice!

In the days and weeks that followed the death of Billy the Kid, there were several articles, written mostly in New Mexican newspapers and dime novels that depicted the Kid's death in ways that put lawman Pat Garrett in a bad light. Garrett took control and coauthored a biography of Billy the Kid. As he wrote in the introduction to *The Authentic Life of Billy the Kid*, "I am incited to this labor, in a measure, by an impulse to correct the thousand false statements which have appeared in the public newspapers and in yellow-covered, cheap novels."

First, Garrett wanted to publicly respond to the speculative accusations against him about Billy the Kid's death that were being printed. Many people had begun to gossip about the unfairness of Garrett's final encounter with the Kid.

Second, he wanted to set the record straight regarding the more notable incidents that had involved the notorious outlaw, beginning with his early life and leading up to his untimely death. Garrett, who did not consider himself a writer, called upon his friend, Marshall Ashmun "Ash" Upson, to ghostwrite this book with him and shared equally in the royalties.

This is exactly how you make sure your story is told the right way!

P.T Barnum owed much of his fame to the runaway success of his autobiography *The Life of P.T. Barnum, Written by Himself* was first released in 1854 and was then continuously re-edited and re-issued over the following decades. New editions and appendices appeared on a near-annual basis, and Barnum helped increase sales by putting the book in the public domain and allowing anyone to publish it. He even instructed his widow to write a new chapter that chronicled the events of his 1891 death. All told, the book sold more than 1 million copies during Barnum's lifetime.

13. AUDIO DOWNLOAD OR PODCAST

The beauty of audio programs is that you don't have to spell check or typeset them, and most need little editing. Audio programs are also portable and so can be utilized on the road or on a plane. I remember with great fondness all the programs I bought and listened to on audio-cassette in the early Nineties by Earl Nightingale, Brian Tracy, Jay Abraham, Dan Kennedy, Nido Qubein, Harvey Mackay, Mark McCormack, Michael Gerber and just about every business program Nightingale Conant offered at the time. Many of them I wore out and bought again and again. If you have never listed to the vintage classic *Lead the Field*, you should!

Without a doubt, every one of them played a part in my future success and, ultimately, that's the best thing about the info business, using your knowledge to help people. These days it's quite possible to do a high-quality recording and edit it right on your laptop!

The interview format is one I used early on in the martial arts business that was very popular. I simply interviewed successful school owners about how they grew their businesses.

How they started?
Did they ever struggle?
What was their breakthrough moment?
What was their most successful method of attracting students?
What books, audios and people influenced them?
What advice they would give to someone starting out?

I'd interview a different person each month, asking pretty much the same ten or twenty questions, but the answers and stories were always different. This is an easy way to quickly come up with a quality product. People in every industry or life situation want to hear from others who have succeeded in their business or have dealt with the same challenges they face in their personal life. And you don't have to write anything!

Once you have such audios, you can then send them out to be transcribed and instantly create special reports or a chapter for your next book!

The other format I have frequently used is the basic "How to" or "Ten Ways" format, both of which work very well on audio if you tell them in an entertaining way. My friend Pat Parelli does monthly "Pat Talks" in the horse world where he combines information on how to train your horse with lots of great stories.

You can reverse this idea and answer your own questions or give your own reasons:

- The ten questions most home owners ask when they want to sell a home
- Ten things you must do to protect yourself from lawsuits
- Seven secrets to writing a best-seller

You can use your audios to promote your brand, generate leads or, in many cases, to generate income as well. Sell your audios as MP3 files, stream them from within a membership portal or put them on iTunes.

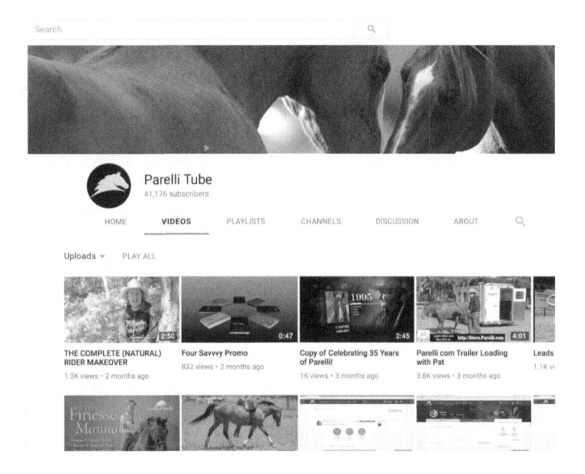

14. YOUTUBE

Don't leave getting on TV to chance. Once you are on YouTube you are on TV. It doesn't matter what it cost you to film it, you are up there just like Tom Cruise! Being on that screen is an incredibly powerful tool in self-branding. Simple self-videos have launched many famous careers from all walks of life.

Justin Bieber skyrocketed from obscurity to fame thanks to YouTube videos of him performing as a preteen. The Biebs was posting his homemade music when he was 12 years old and those videos convinced execs at Island Def Jam Recordings to sign Bieber to a huge deal before he was even able to drive. Interestingly enough, Bieber is largely responsible for the rise to fame of another young recording artist. Carly Rae Jepsen was already popular in her native Canada but didn't hit the road to U.S. fame until the Biebs tweeted that "Call Me Maybe" was "possibly the catchiest song I've ever heard."

Michelle Phan's success as a makeup guru on YouTube led to the launch of her own line of cosmetics.

Comedian Bo Burnham first started making people laugh back in 2007 with the original comic songs he uploaded to YouTube. These included "Bo Fo' Sho" and "My Whole Family Thinks I'm Gay" - and rode the remarkable response to a deal with Comedy Central Records before his 18th birthday and then on to his own show.

Soulja Boy, the Chicago-born hip hop artist, relied on fans of his MySpace and YouTube channels. His best known hit, "Crank That," was originally self-published online. He was eventually discovered there by hip hop producer Mr. Collipark and eventually signed a record deal. (The song would go on to hit #1 on the Billboard Hot 100.) Soulja Boy has since earned well over $10 million!

Logan Paul's YouTube features slapstick adolescent pranks in short films and comedy sketches. Paul also posts a daily vlog. His vlog channel has a following of over 17 million people and that made him a tidy $12.5 million last year!

Kate Upton, the supermodel who's been featured on the cover of *Sports Illustrated* multiple times owes part of her success to a couple of YouTube videos. Upton was struggling to find work when she posted a video of herself "doing the Dougie" at an L.A. Clippers game; the video was quickly viewed millions of times and gained her 170,000 Twitter followers. Upton doesn't have any trouble finding work now; she's earned millions from modeling and advertising jobs over the past few years.

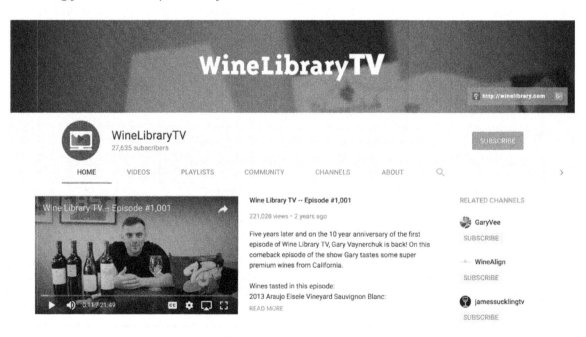

YouTube is not just for entertainers and models, it's also for serious business people and professionals. Gary Vaynerchuk hosted a video blog on YouTube called *Wine Library TV*

from 2006 to 2011. It featured wine reviews, tastings, and wine advice. The show was produced daily at the Wine Library store in Springfield, New Jersey. It grew his father's wine store business from $4 million to $60 million a year. He went on to fame and fortune with a multimillion dollar digital marketing agency and is the author of several best-selling books.

Havard Rugland, a Norwegian soccer player, became a YouTube hit after uploading his "Kickalicious" video featuring impressive trick shots. That video eventually found its way into NFL circles and Rugland signed with the Detroit Lions as a free agent. Nice – well, nice if it wasn't the Lions!

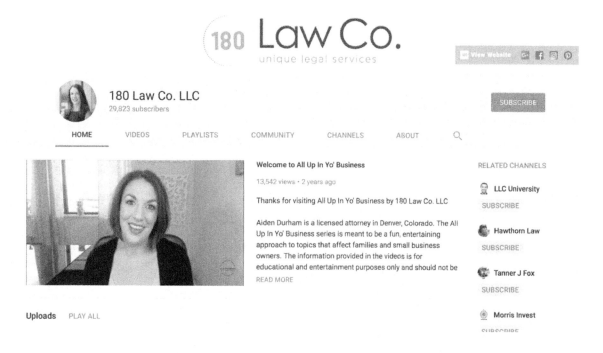

Adien Kramer has 30,000 subscribes for her YouTube channel on small business law and I'm betting she gets all the business she can handle from this one media alone.

Many YouTube celebrities succeed with just the built-in camera on their laptop, but you can take it to the next level and produce your own show. I was able to produce a nice 30-minute show called *Martial Arts Business Magazine* for just $1,500 a month. The show was quick paced and patterned after *PM Magazine*. I also regularly do 30-minute shows on various topics in the golf business. Here is an easy way for you to get started:

- Film your sales demo, seminars, or insights.
- Get someone to interview you with a series of questions that positions you well in your industry. Then edit it all into your own show!

15. CREATE COURSES, WEBINARS OR ONLINE EVENTS

Webinars give you a chance to run an online event using your videos or slide shows and give you the ability to answer questions in real time when you do them live. This helps you connect with your audience. Then you can make additional money replaying the webinar at other times in the future. You can also package your live events after the fact as webinars. The online course market has exploded over the last few years but so too has the competition. There are thousands of out-of-the-box tools to help you create online programs quickly, and monetize them with almost no technical skill -- which is a huge plus for me given my lack of technical know-how!

As always, specialization is the key. You can take your special reports, manuals and books and easily chop them up into an online slide show format that's ideal for online courses. You can add videos or audios to spice things up. In short, all of your available content can be used to create great online courses to expand your brand and position you as the authority.

One thing to remember with all of your information is that people have their favorite way of learning. Some people (like me) love to read, others would rather watch a video, and still others would rather listen. . Some people like the idea of self-paced learning while others just want to head right for the info they most need as fast as possible. You too may have you own preferences, but the savvy marketer will include as many ways as possible to build their brand!

16. INSTAGRAM, TWITTER, PINTEREST AND OTHERS

Depending on your market, your main social media may not be Facebook, LinkedIn or YouTube. Both Obama and Trump made great use of Twitter to expand their brands. So do Lady Gaga and many other entertainers, but for most I feel Twitter is of limited use as the primary way to get famous. Instagram is another matter, and many are using that media as their push off point.

Tana Ashlee is an MMA model who got most of her exposure on Instagram. The beautiful and very fit Tana took to Instagram to share photos and workouts with her followers. Today she is a personal trainer with her own business in Las Vegas, Nevada.

Amra Olevic was a girl from Brooklyn with a beauty blog who worked for MAC and loved make up. Rezy, as her fans call her, would post selfies on Instagram every day and explain the make-up she had used. Girls started going crazy over her stunning beauty and her make up techniques. Amra then moved to LA where her fame sky rocketed and she became the famous make-up guru she is today. These days Ms. Olevic has her own eyeshadow palette through makeup giant Anastasia, as well as her own line of lipsticks through Lipland.

17. EXPAND YOUR NETWORK AT EVERY OPPORTUNITY

The more people you know, the bigger your audience. Always be expanding your social networks-- the *real* ones where you actually meet people and shake their hands. Join clubs, go to parties, support charity events; see and be seen at every opportunity.

18. EXPAND YOUR REACH

Enlist your current clients, customers, friends, family and fans to help. Make it easy for current contacts to give referrals and to share your image-building content. Always suggest they share your content with a friend.

Partner with other people to expand your reach. When I started consulting in the martial arts business, Panther Productions, supplier of over 80% of the world's martial arts videos, partnered with me to produce a business series. I got the standard 10% royalty, but I also got a full page in their catalog mailed to thousands of people. Later I partnered with Macho Products, a supply company who promoted my books and videos to their massive list. Next, I partnered with a billing company who also promoted me to their clients. Then an insurance company with a martial arts school product. In a matter of 12 months I was hitting my entire market from multiple angles.

Look for synergistic ways to get your content in front of other people's audiences. A lawyer might run an article in an accountant's e-newsletter and vice versa. One band could promote another band to their fans. I frequently get Northern golf clubs to promote Florida resorts to their e-lists in the winter in return for a couple of free vacations, a true win-win situation. The more places you and your content are seen, the quicker your fame grows.

19. ASK FOR REVIEWS, RECOMMENDATIONS, FEEDBACK AND TESTIMONIALS

This not only reinforces your position of preeminence among your existing fans but also provides great ammunition *to* get more. Anytime someone asks for a small favor, I ask that in return that they review one of my books or provide a testimonial to help build my brand. At the end of every live seminar I hand out review sheets that ask open-ended questions like, "What did you like best?" I often offer a free gift for filling in the review sheets, which they only get if they hand in the review. 95% of people do so, providing me with a wealth of new testimonials at every event. I keep all in a folder, post them on social media and add them to my Amazon author page as they happen.

20. CAREFULLY DESIGN YOUR OWN PRESS KIT

Write your own bio, maintain an up-to-date portfolio of flattering photographs of yourself, and have a couple of magazine-length articles written about you, your work, or your mission in life. Whether you are running a nonprofit organization, a small department, a major company, or the local blood drive, there are always opportunities for PR. Local papers, regional magazines, newsletters, web sites, and local cable stations all offer opportunities for enhancing your status in the community. The better prepared you are to provide detailed information about yourself or your organization, the more publicity you will receive.

Often, overworked and underpaid reporters will run your pieces verbatim, and when they do, as Churchill pointed out, the results are usually favorable. You can also put a press kit on your website so that journalists can use it 24/7.

Your Bio in Multiple Forms.

You will use your bio in multiple ways, on your website, blog, LinkedIn, guest articles, and as an introduction for speeches or from radio and TV hosts. One bio does not fit all purposes and if you left it to others to edit as they see fit they will no doubt leave out the most important part for that particular situation. Therefore, you must compile a biography in multiple forms from the long form to the 15-second intro exactly as you want them delivered, thus leaving nothing to chance.

Your Media Kit Should Include:

- Portfolio of pictures
- Long bio, short bio, book bio, video bio, LinkedIn bio and tiny bio
- Resource box for guest post
- Pre-written profile articles about you, your company, products, books, songs, shows, etc.
- 20 questions and answers about you
- Copies of published articles from magazines, newspapers and blogs
- Some short two-minute video clips
- Testimonials, endorsements and awards from others

All these items should be made available from the media section of your website or blog

21. A WEBSITE INCORPORATING ALL OF THE ABOVE

This takes time, money, and effort, but you can incorporate almost all of the above elements into one website, so people can watch you, listen to you, read your articles, and interact with you. You should also include marketing automation, so your website follows up for you automatically based on your visitors surfing habits. This is like having a full-time salesperson on your team and will significantly increase your reach and conversion rates.

If you will work through the above list from start to finish, you will have legendary status in your industry.

The best part of all these branding activities is they can all be converted into residual income in one form or another. A book becomes a course, a seminar becomes a video which is then transcribed and becomes the outline for a book.

SUMMARY

You cannot leave your fame to the whims of the media or mere chance. You must have a carefully crafted plan to expand your brand. The truth is you already own your own media company, now let's put it to use. Your most powerful weapon will be your email list. Do everything in your power to grow it. Blog often and use the reach of Facebook, LinkedIn and other social media daily to get your content in front of as many people as possible. Start your own groups for added power and control. Depending on your audience, use SlideShare, Twitter, Instagram and Pinterest. However, make sure you focus first on the big three: Facebook, LinkedIn and YouTube.

Publish your own booklets and graduate to your own book; nothing says professional credibility like a book. Put your book on audio or cut it up into podcasts and YouTube segments to expand your audience. Create webinars and other online events or courses. Expand your personal network of real contacts (the type you shake hands with) at every opportunity. Ask for reviews and get people to share your content. Design you own press kit so it's easy for others to promote you when opportunity calls. Last be not least, incorporate as many of these ideas as possible into your website.

SUMMARY

You cannot leave your fame to the whims of the media or mere chance. You must have a carefully crafted plan to expand your brand. The truth is you already own your own media company, now let's put it to use. Your most powerful weapon will be your email list. Do everything in your power to grow it. Blog often and use the reach of Facebook, LinkedIn and other social media daily to get your content in front of as many people as possible. Start your own groups for added power and control. Depending on your audience, use SlideShare, Twitter, Instagram and Pinterest. However, make sure you focus first on the big three: Facebook, LinkedIn and YouTube.

Publish your own booklets and graduate to your own book; nothing says professional credibility like a book. Put your book on audio or cut it up into podcasts and YouTube segments to expand your audience. Create webinars and other online events or courses. Expand your personal network of real contacts (the type you shake hands with) at every opportunity. Ask for reviews and get people to share your content. Design you own press kit so it's easy for others to promote you when opportunity calls. Last be not least, incorporate as many of these ideas as possible into your website.

Ted Turner did not leave his media to chance. He started his own network, CNN.

ACTION PLAN

- In your quest for fame you cannot afford to leave your press to the whims of others. You must take decisive action to use your media empire to its full advantage. The total sum of your reach when you add all of your media together is very large!
- Whatever marketing you do, try and get your audience members to give you their email addresses.
- Blog at least weekly. Many people have become famous by blogging alone.
- Use your email, Facebook page, LinkedIn and groups for article and video distribution. Cross post everything in the appropriate part of your website for easy access.
- Join targeted LinkedIn and Facebook groups to rapidly expand your audience,
- Create your own group of like-minded people or fans.
- Create some slide shows on SlideShare.
- Post on YouTube often; consider creating your own show with you as the star!
- Create a special report, white paper or booklet to show your expertise on a topic and grow your mailing list.
- Write a book -- nothing says credibility like a book!
- Create some online courses.
- Speak to live groups.
- Have a presence on other social sites that make sense for your market, including Twitter, Instagram, Pinterest and others.
- Increase your personal contact network at every opportunity.
- Coordinate with others to increase your distribution.
- Ask for reviews and testimonials.
- Create your own press kit and add it to your website providing easy access to others who may wish to write about you in their blogs and magazines. The more complete with pictures, videos, interviews and prewritten articles, the more likely you are to score free PR.
- Just remember not to believe your own press clippings.

"I won't be a rock star. I will be a legend." - **Freddy Mercury**

11

SHOWTIME - DELIVERING A LEGENDARY PERFORMANCE!

Whether you are a rock star or a Realtor, whether your performance is on stage, or behind a desk, the success of your efforts comes down to communication. This includes the words, sounds, body language and actions that create an emotional response in your audience, whether that audience is 20,000 fans in a stadium or one person to whom you are trying to sell a house. Without the ability to communicate and connect with your audience, fame and the wealth and opportunities that surround it simply cannot become yours.

It's a fact that your success in business life will be based largely on your ability to communicate with others—those above you and those below you, those on your team and those you wish to attract, those you serve and those who serve you. When you master performance skills the doors of opportunity will be flung open to you.

Famous people are by in large great performers and great performers are great communicators, although not all start out that way.

As mentioned earlier, Churchill, perhaps the greatest orator of the 20th century, stuttered badly as a child and took speech therapy even as an adult.

Yet, history has witnessed the power of Churchill's unique ability to use the English language to marshal people into action and save a bruised and battered Britain from the Nazis.

Lincoln was by no means a natural speaker, yet his eloquence grew with practice. The Gettysburg Address lasted just over two minutes and contained fewer than 300 words, yet what power those words held. They moved an entire nation with their power and eloquence.

FAME AND DESTINY OFTEN HANG ON A FEW WELL CHOSEN WORDS

These two legendary orators illustrate beautifully the point that the entire fate of a nation, company, sports team or career can hinge on a single speech, song or sales pitch. One that evokes passion, that rallies pride and stirs uncommon motivation to act, perhaps even instills an undying commitment to see that action through to its successful conclusion. Make no mistake about the power of the spoken word to change the fortune of anyone. Nations have been brought back from the depths of despair.

Companies have been saved from the brink of disaster by the power of a few well-chosen words spoken with feeling and eloquence.

I have witnessed the fortunes of an entire company, filled with mistrust and bursting with rumor and discontent, change in less than an hour after a sterling speech by the CEO. The world of sports is full of powerful stories like, "Win one for the Gipper!" about turning around the fortunes of a downtrodden team, brought back from the dead by a legendary coach to clinch victory in the Super Bowl, the World Series or the World Cup. The famous know the power they wield with every word they speak, therefore they take great care in planning all of their communications.

STEPS TO A POWERFUL PRESENTATION AND PERFORMANCE

Let's look at the steps to building a POWERFUL performance no matter the size of your audience or purpose of your mission. These techniques work whether you are selling your songs, products, or cause. They make a great roadmap for a speech, sales presentation, concert, marketing material -- or even TV script!

1. ALL COMMUNICATION IS PERSONAL

All communication is *personal* communication whether speaking to a convention of 5,000 people or five sales prospects in front of you. It pays to remember that people listen and respond as individuals, not as groups. Each person in your audience, no matter how big or small it is, relates to your words in a personal way. Even if 5,000 individuals get up and applaud you, they still have to do it one by one. It's the ability to touch the individual that motivates the group to act.

2. CREATE A LEGENDARY PERFORMANCE!

The famous don't merely sell, sing, preach or present -- instead they perform.
Your every interaction should be a performance not a meeting, sales pitch, lesson or speech. You need to develop a carefully orchestrated, scripted and rehearsed performance, so that it becomes a part of your being that is totally natural.

Although I quit high school at 15, I did pass a GED test to take advantage of a golf scholarship at Palm Beach Junior College. Of all the teachers I had in college, I can only remember the name of one. Although I love reading now, at the age of twenty-one the idea of studying the works of Shakespeare, Milton, Coleridge, and others long since dead held little interest for me.

In my English Literature class, the story was completely different. I can still picture Professor Watson B. Duncan dancing over the stage with surprising grace despite his advancing years. I can hear him as if it were yesterday yell lines from Milton's *Paradise Lost*, "Threw him headlong flaming from the ethereal sky," he would roar with the passion of an accomplished actor as he threw his arms around wildly. He referred to William Shakespeare simply as The Big S. Though he stated boldly that had Milton not died so young we might well be talking more about the Big M instead. His classes were so popular they were held in the auditorium. One day as I entered, I found the place almost pitch black, yet with everyone already in their seats. Suddenly a spotlight shone on the stage, Professor Duncan appeared, and he asked if we knew what day it was. After all the obvious answers were exhausted, he pulled back the curtains to reveal a giant cake complete with several hundred candles. Today is The Big S's birthday. Come up and get some cake in celebration.

Watson B. Duncan was in his late sixties, of average height, and a little overweight. He wore square glasses and had a shock of bright white hair a little like Einstein's. He was not the type of man you would expect to relate to a bunch of kids a quarter of his age. He was a scholarly man and knew his subject intricately, but this was true of a lot of other people on campus whose names have long since been forgotten, alas along with much of their teaching. People did not forget Watson B. Duncan though. They did not cut his classes, and they didn't fall asleep in the back row. In fact, people used to sneak into class just to hear him.

Watson B. Duncan did not teach class, he *performed*. Duncan was well known as a gifted actor; he performed frequently in the Shakespeare Festivals. His teaching style reflected that avocation. He was flamboyant, dramatic, and rendered his material quite unforgettable. He had unshakable enthusiasm for his subject and it oozed from him in his mannerisms, in his tone, and in his words. Although many of us in college were working two jobs and out late the night before, when we left his class, we felt recharged and revitalized. Watson B. Duncan had more enthusiasm than any teacher I have ever met, and we were all helpless under his spell. Generations of students remember his shout of "ME MISERABLE!," a trademark of his *Paradise Lost* lectures, and recall his classes as some of the most memorable experiences of their college years.

3. THE POWER OF A PASSIONATE PERFORMANCE

The key to Watson's remarkable talent? Passion, a passion and energy that created a magnetic force around him drawing people under his spell in much the same way you see others such as motivational speaker Tony Robbins ignite crowds, horsewoman Linda Parelli enthrall equestrians or Lady Gaga create a room of screaming "monsters." Steve Jobs was passionate about design, he loved his new products, and wore that parental pride and enthusiasm on his sleeve with every Apple launch "It looks pretty doggone gorgeous," he said with a big smile after showing the iPhone for the first time. Jobs often used words such as "cool," "amazing," or "gorgeous" because he believed in them.

Your audience wants to feed off your passion. Let it shine through in your conversations, put movement into your body language and let excitement ring in your voice! After all, if you're not excited about your music, cause, lesson, product or service that you are, pitching why should anybody else be?

4. SET YOUR OWN STAGE

Rock bands these days go to enormous expense to set the right stage. A stage that gives the right sound, the right feel and the right lights makes the band's performance even more memorable. You too have a stage, whether it's your office, your car, or you own personal corner of a hotel lobby. When in your control the stage should be set with the upmost care and attention. Remove any type of clutter that is likely to distract a prospect's attention and not aid directly in building your image.

I'll tell you a funny story about furniture (although not so funny at the time) from my days in the karate business. It's one that helped me understand at an early age the importance everything plays in both sales and the experience you provide to your customers. It's amazing how unconnected you think it would be, but it's not.

Furniture, like everything else I am talking about, is all part of the very complicated experience that goes into the decision-making process of the human mind.

When I first opened my small karate school I went big with a $900 Chinese desk with carvings, two *carved* dragon chairs at $450 each (a lot back then) and a large Chinese painting. After a really great first year, my studio was broken into and both the chairs were stolen. I replaced them with normal cheap office chairs and thought little about it except for wanting to catch the thieves who stole my fancy chairs.

Surprisingly a lot of the parents and students noticed and asked, *"What happened to the dragon chairs?"*

I told them they had been stolen.

"Will you be getting some new ones?" They questioned.

I had really not thought about it as I didn't realize that they mattered to my business, and they would be expensive to replace. But sure enough over the next few days it was confirmed they really did matter. One student told me he had signed up because of the furniture. We looked like a cut above the other schools with their cheap desks and metal chairs and because of that they were willing to pay more and sign up with me. It was a very interesting lesson in human psychology. Do whatever you can to enhance the feeling people get from your office, store or teaching space.

In some cases, like selling a country club membership, the last place I want sales staff to take a prospect is their dingy windowless office. Instead I encourage membership salespeople to find a corner of the clubhouse to ply their craft. At golf schools, I suggest putting the students name behind a triangle stack of balls, just like they do on the PGA Tour. A simple little stage trick like this can greatly enhance the experience of your brand.

Where you are not in control of your own "stage," say in a hotel lobby or Starbucks, always get there first and sit in a corner with your back to a wall so the person you are meeting is not looking out the window or across the entire store. You want to try and minimize the distractions in his view, so they focus all their attention on you.

If selling or meeting on the road, investing in a conversion van with four nice captain's chairs and table might make more sense than the typical high-end SUV. Now you really have a mobile office. Even on the phone I try to set the stage. Whenever I get a phone call I immediately stand up, run a voice check, and answer on the third ring (ideal according to AT &T). Then I start pacing; movement makes anyone sound more excited on the call. There is more energy and enthusiasm in your voice than slouched in a chair or sitting at a desk. When the phone rings stand up and be up!

Where you meet and how it feels matters to your audience and to your own performance. Chose and set your stage with care.

5. ENGAGE YOUR AUDIENCE QUICKLY

"Hello, Miami, how ya doing tonight?" are the first words of just about any rock band to connect with the local audience.

"It was just another boring Monday, but it was about to get a lot more exciting. Of course I didn't know at the time, but in 45 minutes I'd be dead." Great start to a novel or mystery movie to hook the audience.

"What's the best score you ever shot?" Question to a golf audience, immediately putting them in a pleasant state of mind.

"What's your favorite color or what was you very first car?" Salesman on a car lot disarming typical customer resistance.

You should start your presentation by encouraging your audience to participate.

Ask them a question.
Tell them a quick personal story.
Grab their attention.

People are alarmingly quick to form opinions. If you don't make a connection fast, you will spend the rest of your time trying to regain your credibility and the audience's attention.

There are numerous techniques you can use to build rapport with your audience.

Here are just a few.

Dates

Do you remember where you where the day President Kennedy was shot?

The day man landed on the moon?

Where were you the day the Berlin Wall came down? How about on 9/11?

Each of these events has very special meaning, depending on your age. Few people old enough to remember forget where they were, when they heard about each of these events.

It "zones" people into a specific time, a feeling that can be shared by an entire audience no matter how large or small.

There may be special dates or events involving you and your audience that can be recalled to create the same results. If so, use them to your advantage.

CREATING FEELINGS IN YOUR AUDIENCE

Think for a moment of the song *My Way*. Whom do you see in your mind?

Elvis? No, Elvis sang the song, as did Sid Vicious and a hundred others, but that song, written by Paul Anka, is forever burned in the minds of millions as Frank Sinatra's theme song. I bet you can see Ol' Blue Eyes right now, alone in the spotlight, impeccably dressed in a black tux and bow tie, giving it his all.

When you think of that image and that song, doesn't it make you smile just a little? Doesn't it make you feel just a little happier? No matter what position in life a person holds, that song hits home and brings with it a certain glow, a certain feeling that can't be taken away. Playing the song can put your audience in a receptive mood. The same with playing the theme tune from certain movies Like Rocky or Star Wars.

Motivational speaker Tony Robbins opened his seminars for many years with Tina Turner's "Simply the Best" to get his audience in the mood to being the best they could be! Many sports stars like Rory McIlroy and Cam Newton fire up their personal performances by listening to rock or rap music before they play. Inspirational music is played throughout every NFL game and most other pro sports in the USA to inspire the crowd.

Anecdotes everyone can relate to.

In 1985 I saw Bruce Springsteen at Wembley Stadium in London on his "Born in the USA" tour that was the singer's reflection on the plight of American veterans returning home from Vietnam. It was a very hot day and he played for over four hours. What I remember most was the story he told about constantly fighting with his father for having his hair too long. His father kept telling him "wait till the army gets you! They'll cut that hair and make a man out of you."

Finally, his number came up and he had to go the draft board which would most likely mean he'd end up serving in Vietnam (which also gave him an alarming chance of never coming home). Fortunately for him, he failed his Army physical and was given a status of 4-F (unfit for duty) owing to a concussion from a motorcycle accident. It was a powerful story, made even more powerful by his angry father's heart-felt relief at him failing, despite their troubles.

Images

The same is true of putting your audience in the mood with strong visual images. Think for a moment of the Statue of Liberty, the Eiffel Tower, the pyramids, or Big Ben. In the briefest of moments, we have all visited New York, Paris, Egypt and London. This is a powerful force in building rapport and gaining the attention of your audience. Employ mental images the audience can relate to and they will quickly tune in to what you are saying.

Whatever method you employ to get the audience on your side, do it quickly. Make sure that it relates to your main topic, then smoothly transition to the next step.

6. EXPLAIN WHY THEY SHOULD LISTEN TO YOU—WHAT'S IN IT FOR THEM?

"Tonight, we have a great show for you. We are going to play some of your old favorites and a few of our new tunes that you might be hearing for the first time!" - **Any given rock band!**

"In the next fifteen minutes I am going to tell you how to double or triple your teaching income." - **Sales pitch**

"Guys, one team today will be watching next week's game at home. Here's what we need to do to make sure it's not us." - **Any Coach**

You have people in front of you—at a convention, your office or theirs, in a locker room or classroom. You have their attention with your opening statements but in many of the audience members the unasked question remains: Why should they "really" listen to you?

Your early communication should always provide a clear benefit for the audience. Why should they give you their undivided attention for 5 minutes or 55 minutes? What problems are they going to solve by listening? What rewards are they going to receive? How will they be better, happier, more fulfilled people after listening to you? Will you give them the inspiration they seek? The meaning they want? The path they should take to increase their productivity, income or meaning?

Conversely, you could also tell them what will happen if they don't heed your words. If they don't get on this new trend, they will be left in the dust. If they don't plan for retirement, they will be forced to live in poverty. If they don't help this cause it will mean untold calamity for millions. If they don't "dig" this sound or technology, they will quickly be irrelevant. Whatever direction you take, make the reasons for listening to your words overwhelmingly compelling.

This is also a good time to tack on a few of your credentials to show why you are qualified to speak on these issues. Keep it short and to the point. People are not interested in your entire life story -- yet. They only want to know that you are credible in your positioning and that you can help them improve their lives in some small way or provide at least few moments of happiness just for listening.

7. FRAME YOUR PRESENTATION AGAINST AN OPPONENT

Steve Jobs was a master of explaining the problem with current technologies before having his product arrive like the cavalry to save the day. For example, when launching the I-phone, Jobs said the problem with current smartphones was that "they're not so smart and they're not so easy to use." Jobs showed several smartphones from competitors and highlighted their weaknesses. In launching the iPad, Jobs argued that it fit in between a smartphone and a laptop and would have to be better than both those products at certain key tasks such as: browsing the web, enjoying and sharing photographs, watching games or reading e-books

Your way, cause, sound, system, product or service must be compared against the inferior options.

8. MAKE YOUR KEY MESSAGE CRYSTAL CLEAR

Just like an email subject line or billboard, your key message should be very clear and succinct. Jobs was also a master of this. When unveiling the I-phone, Jobs proudly proclaimed, "The i-Phone is going to reinvent the phone." The headline, "Apple reinvents the phone," was the only sentence on the slide. He repeated the headline several times during the presentation. A search for the phrase on Google turns over 150,000 links, most of which are directly from articles and blog posts covering the launch presentation.

Other memorable themes from Jobs' presentations include:

"Music, calls and internet." – introducing **iPhone.**
"1000 songs in your pocket." – introducing **iPod.**
"Touch your music." – introducing **iPod touch.**
"The world's thinnest notebook." – introducing **MacBook Air.**

Don't save your best points for a climax. Hit them with both barrels right away. If you don't capture their attention and interest with your first few points, it's almost certain they will be mentally adrift by the time you arrive at the last few.

9. SEND IN THE TROOPS

Once you've made your key points, back up your position with logic, proof, and more anecdotes. Quote well-known people who share or endorse your point of view. Give real-life examples of people proving your theory or world view. Use history, biographies, statistics and any tool you can find to add believability to your point of view.

For example, let's say you were discussing the importance of setting a goal to success: In his biography, *My Story*, Jack Nicklaus, the greatest golfer in history, recounts that at an early age he set a goal of winning more major championships than anyone had ever won. He decided to plan his schedule and his life around these key events. It was this ability to plan, set goals, and focus on them that allowed him to become such a great champion.

Abraham Lincoln also valued the importance of goals and good planning. He said, "I shall prepare and one day my time shall come." Planning worked for me, too. The turning point in my own life came when I sat down one day with a yellow pad and actually asked myself what I wanted to do with my life.

In the previous two paragraphs, in a few short sentences, I shared my own personal story and used golfing legend Jack Nicklaus plus a quotation from Abraham Lincoln to back up my point. That puts me in pretty powerful company, don't you think?

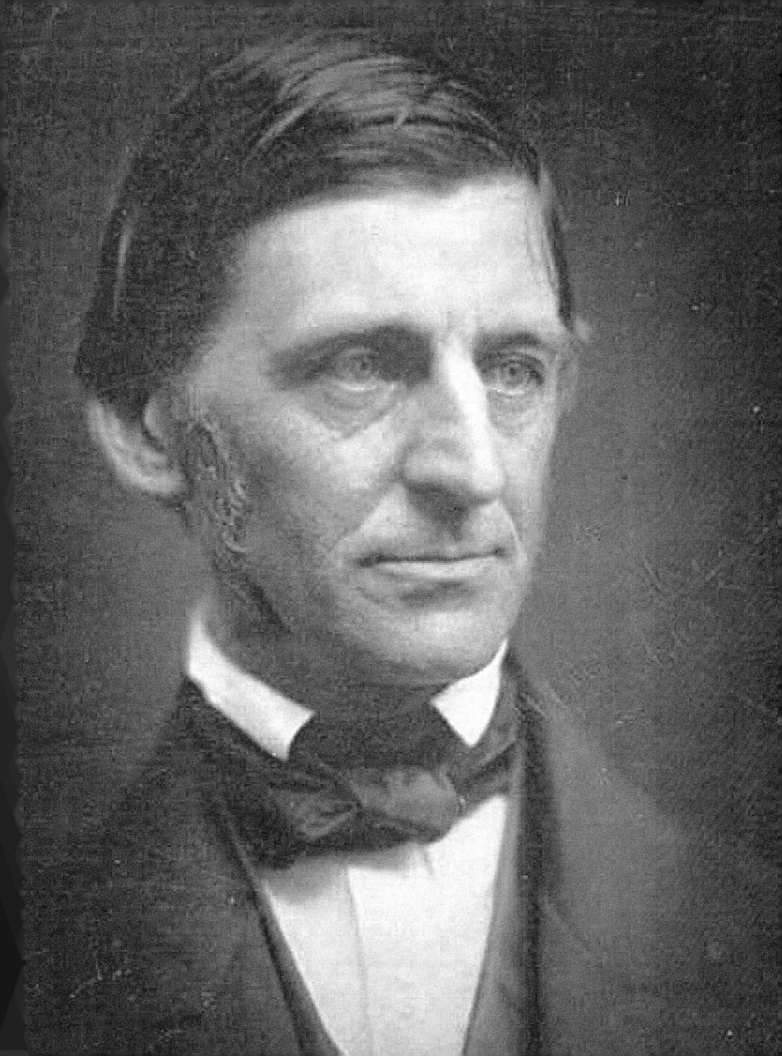

It doesn't matter how good your message is if you don't hold an audience's interest. The more different ways you can back up your point of view with the most interesting range of dynamic people, personal anecdotes, and quotes, the greater your chances of successfully delivering your message.

10. MAKING THE EMOTIONAL CONNECTION

Ralph Waldo Emerson once said that it is a luxury to be understood. To be famous, it's a luxury you cannot afford to be without. You must make sure that you are connecting with the audience emotionally. After all, most great salesmen know that sales is simply emotion backed up with logic and—make no mistake— communicating is selling your ideas. Sure, they are listening to you, but are they *hearing* you?

Connecting on all three levels

Most people process information in one of three ways.

- Visually
- Kinesthetically
- Aurally

Visual people want you to paint them a picture with your words. Kinesthetic people want to feel your words, while aural people want to hear your sounds. If you talk to aurally-centered people in strictly visual terms, you might as well be talking in a foreign language. They simply will not connect with your message. Intertwine all three learning styles into your presentation so that no one is left out in the cold. For example, in the following paragraph I will use words that will appeal to all three groups, rather than talking strictly in visual terms (which is how I happen to connect to things).

Setting goals is like climbing a giant ladder. With each step upwards, you begin to feel the charge of energy running through your veins as you breathe in the sweet-smelling scent of success and hear your name being called by those who finally recognize your accomplishments.

"San Antonio, I can't hear you." *Aural* typical shout out from the band at any rock concert to stir the emotions of the crowd. "Put your hands in the air." *Kinesthetic*, the audiences sways to and fro with their hands clapping above their heads. "Let's light it up." *Visual*, the audience lights up the arena with their cell phones.

In addition to using the three key learning traits, bring as many senses into play as you can. Ask your audience to picture things, listen to things, hear things, taste things, and experience things. The more senses you activate in support of your key points, the greater connection your audience will have with your messages. Make them laugh, make them cry, fire up their pride, and get them emotionally charged to do something with your message.

11. USE POWER WORDS AND PHRASES

When speaking, it's important that you don't use wishy-washy terms. You must be precise in your message and your choice of words. Imagine Patrick Henry saying, "Give me liberty or give me death, I think." It kind of changes the whole power of the thing, doesn't it?

Or how about Winston Churchill saying, "I have nothing to offer you except blood, sweat, tears etc., etc., etc." Would that kind of wishy-washy talk have motivated a nation into action?

I think not. "Take no prisoners!" is a much more powerful image than, "Take as many prisoners as you can and let me know how you did." Make confident, bold statements; use clear precise wording to remove all ambiguity. As legendary painter Pablo Picasso said, "In painting as in life, one should act with bold strokes."

Painting with words

Top performers paint pictures with their words. If you study any of the world's great speeches, you will find them alive with imagery – images that people can relate to, picture in their minds and see with a clarity that makes them real.

Churchill did not merely say, "We will fight in Europe." He said, "We will fight them on the beaches, we will fight them in the hills, on the landing grounds and in the air." He painted a very clear picture of all the places we would fight in order to gain victory.

Martin Luther King, in his "I Have a Dream" speech, did exactly the same thing to bring people together by touching on different parts of the country in his address. Instead of saying, "We have to pull the country together," he described landmarks in several different states, a strategy that involved people on a much more individual basis.

Today rap stars frequently use references to specific desirable luxury bands like Gucci, Prada , Bentley, Rolex, and Cristal. They also use the names of other celebrities.

12. THE POWERFUL PAUSE

Perhaps the most underused tool of powerful speaking is, strangely enough, not speaking at all but the sound of silence. In our efforts to get a message across, we often put forth an endless barrage of words without giving the listener time to think or let the words soak in. John Wayne had his unusual gait, his gravelly voice and the tendency to pause mid-sentence for extra effect.

The deliberate pause gives greater weight to the statement you have just made and allows the audience to actually think about what you just said, rather than letting it pass in one ear and out the other.

Repetition

Another common characteristic of most great performances is repetition. The key theme is repeated over and over, almost like a chorus in a song (often in groups of three). The "I Have a Dream" speech is a perfect example, as are many of Churchill's speeches. Reagan, Obama and Trump all repeated their key message again and again. "The best days of America are yet to come," "Change" and "Make America great again," respectively.

13. USE HUMOR

Humor is another way to reach out and touch the audience, and keep them interested. But it shouldn't be used just to get a laugh. It must connect to the story or point you are about to make. It also helps if you aim the humor at yourself. Self-deprecating humor makes you more human, more real, and avoids the possibility of insulting anyone.

Many years ago, I saw Don McLean perform at the Coach House in San Juan Capistrano. It's a small, intimate venue and our group was close to the stage. He started to strum the opening bars to "American Pie," stopping every now and then to talk.

A lot of people ask me what this song means. *strum, strum*

Some people think it's about the '60s. *strum, strum*

Some people think it's about Buddy Holly. *strum, strum*

Some people think it's about Elvis. *strum, strum*

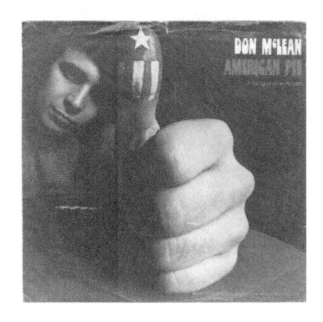

They've studied this song at Harvard. *strum, strum*

They've studied this song at Yale. *strum, strum*

Tonight, for the first time ever, since you are such a great audience, I'm going to share with you what American Pie really means to me. *strum, strum.*

We were all on the edge of our seats as he had always been very elusive about the true meaning of the song.

What American pie means to me is... *strum, strum*

I don't have to work another day in my life because, unlike the Beatles, I own all my songs!

A, long, long time ago...

His moment of humor made the entire show.

When Steve Jobs first told his audience that Apple was going to introduce a mobile phone, he said, "Here it is." Instead of showing the iPhone, the slide displayed was a photo of an iPod with an old-fashioned rotary dial on it. The audience got a kick out of it, laughing and clapping. They had been played and Jobs was enjoying their reaction. There were many funny moments, including a prank call. Jobs was demonstrating the maps feature to show how easy it was to find a location and call the number. He found a Starbucks nearby and called it. A woman picked up the phone and said, "Good morning, Starbucks. How can I help you?" Jobs said, "I'd like to order 4,000 lattes to go, please. No, just kidding. Wrong number. Bye bye." The audience cracked up.

Having two or three short, humorous stories is a must, as is having a handful of jokes you can tell well in mixed company along with a few one-liners, all of which should enhance your key points in some way. Remember, the world's best comedians are funny only because someone wrote funny material. They tested it on small audiences, kept the stuff that worked and practiced their delivery. You can do the same. Humor is memorable, and memorability is important to fame!

14. PROVIDING THE PATH

By now you have the audience captivated with your stories. You've established your position with proof and maintained their interest with humor and anecdotes. You've used powerful language and they are in the palm of your hand. Now what do you want them to do? The greatest percentage of sales are lost simply because people are never actually asked to buy. Similarly, when addressing a group, the power of the moment is often lost because the speaker fails to demand action from his listeners.

Lay out a plan of action. The steps you want them to take. Make them simple. Present them in an easily understood format. You know, 1, 2, 3…the type of specific information people need in order to enact change. Many people are inherently lazy. Showing them a path is not enough. You must help them take the first few steps of the journey.

Country legend Emmylou Harris knows exactly what she wants her audience to do at the end of a show and it's not buy her records!

Emmylou is an avid dog lover who takes her dogs on tour with her. She parades them across the stage at the end of her concerts, sharing the message that adopting a pet from a neighborhood shelter is an honorable and rewarding thing to do. Those who contribute to the cause are often given special perks at her shows, including the ability to meet her backstage, take a photo with her and get an autograph. She founded Bonaparte's Retreat, a Nashville-based dog rescue organization, and Crossroads Campus where both people in need and animals in need can help each other prepare for the future. Her own fundraising event is aptly dubbed Woofstock!

15. EXPLAIN THE BENEFITS OF TAKING ACTION

As we all know, people do things for their reasons, not yours. Help them by explaining in simple yet vivid detail exactly why they should listen to you and why they should follow the course of action you have prescribed. What's in it for them? Will they make more money? Feel better about themselves? Increase their status? Contribute to a better world? Win a war?

Ask for some kind of commitment. Challenge them to act in their own best interests. Challenge them to act in the interests of others. Invite them to buy into the dream, for without action there can be no change in the status quo, and without that there is no leadership.

16. NONVERBAL COMMUNICATION

Ralph Waldo Emerson once said, "What you do speaks so loud, I can't hear what you are saying." I devoted a good deal of space in other chapters to body language and creating an iconic look for yourself , so I'll note here only that your costume is a big part of the show and that eye contact, facial expressions and body language count big in the performance department.

Voice quality

There are great voices, deep and rich, and there are whiny voices. Speech coaches can help you speak better, breathe better, and sound better but, in the grand scheme of things, you need to be yourself, but your best self. Barbara Streisand and Rod Stewart both make millions with their voices and couldn't be much further apart in sound quality. Although there have been many famous people like Arnold Schwarzenegger who spoke with strong accents, Stallone who has a slight slur or others who spoke too fast or too slow, you should attempt to minimize such problems. But when all is said and done you have to be you. You must speak from the heart to be believable. Don't try to become some kind of TV news-anchor clone.

Having said that, nothing kills a speech faster than talking in a monotone. Vary the pitch of your voice with higher and lower tones. Speak loudly or speak softly to emphasize points. Tempo, too, plays an important part in breaking up the way you sound and increasing your audience's attention span. The real key is to speak with as much energy, conviction, volume, and speed control as you can muster. Listening to yourself on audio will help a great deal.

17. CHOOSING THE RIGHT AUDIENCE

It's very important that you pick the right audience for your message.

Late in his career Elvis was the biggest act Las Vegas ever had, but early in his career Colonel Tom Parker, his manager, made a big strategic mistake with Presley's career. He booked him into a four-week Las Vegas engagement, misjudging the reaction of the older, more reserved audiences that Las Vegas attracted. While Presley was a hit among the youth of America, the middle-aged audiences found him to be something of an oddity. Some viewed him as a clown-like figure, wiggling his hips for screams like a monkey for peanuts. Others found his manner of performance vulgar and more suitable for late-night gentlemen's clubs. After a very cool reception during his first few shows, Parker cut Presley's appearance to two weeks. Presley would later remember the event as one of the worst moments of his career. Even Elvis needed to preach to the choir, not try to convert the heathen. A message you should heed!

Sinatra 1947 - The Real Reason Some Fans Screamed Louder Than Others

In the 1940s, Frank Sinatra—or Frankie, as he was known at that time—became America's first national teen idol.

Sinatra later recalled a series of shows he performed in 1942 at a New York City Theater. "The sound that greeted me was absolutely deafening. I was scared stiff. I couldn't move a muscle." Not to take anything away from his legendary voice or his ability to excite the throngs of females that swarmed to every show, but the "bobbysoxer craze" Sinatra incited had a little help. George Evans, Sinatra's publicist, auditioned girls for how loud they could scream, then paid them five bucks and placed them strategically in the audience to help whip up the excitement.

18. PREPARATION AND PRACTICE

Very few people are gifted salesmen or presenters by accident. All great performances are a result of careful planning, tireless practice and constant tweaking of all the elements: the setting, stage, lighting, costume, music and scripts. Brent Schlender, co-author of *Becoming Steve Jobs*, told *Fast Company Magazine* that Jobs would spend months preparing and rehearsing "exhaustively" for public appearances. "I once spent an entire day watching him run through multiple rehearsals of a single presentation, tweaking everything from the color and angle of certain spotlights, to editing and rearranging the order of the keynote presentation slides to improve his pacing," Schlender said.

Churchill often spent days writing, rewriting, and practicing a one-hour radio speech. Lincoln spent over a week working on the two-minute Gettysburg address. Mark Twain once wrote a long letter to a friend and apologized for its length, but noted that he simply hadn't the time to write a shorter one! It takes enormous skill and effort to get a message across with brevity and clarity but, oh, how much more powerful the message becomes.

Mick Jagger doesn't wing it, spending 2+ months preparing for tours.

The Rolling Stones talked about getting ready for an upcoming tour. "Personally, I start preparing about two months before the tour starts," said the 70-something Jagger. "So, I have to up my fitness level and I have to start singing every day, doing practices and a bit of dancing." To maintain his iconic moves, Jagger spends time in front of a mirror in a dance studio. Charlie Watts also noted how the band has to prepare double the material for these special shows, and has to also double their fitness for extra-long sets. All great performances are a result of scripting, choreography, practice and tweaking. You should do likewise with yours. Remove words that hang you up and replace them with others. Change out the one liners or jokes that fall flat. Embellish the ones that work.

Where possible, tape record or videotape your performance so you can go back later and critique it. Using the steps outlined here, a few small changes in style and presentation can turn an ordinary speech into a real experience that motivates people into action.

Communication is not, of course, a one-way street. You must elicit feedback and encourage dialog at all levels with the people you lead. Invite feedback via letters. Invite feedback via e-mail. Invite feedback via phone. Most importantly, invite feedback in person. Like great coaches, all great leaders look back on any speech, meeting, or sales presentation and analyze performance. From this feedback, and from honest personal appraisal, the legendary leader reassesses what worked and what didn't. Which jokes got a laugh and which ones got blank stares. What was made clear, as noted by approving nods, and what must not have been so clear, as demonstrated by the number of questions or puzzled looks you got on a specific point.

SUMMARY

To get famous, you must give a legendary performance in your art. Whether that art is singing, selling or teaching, your communication must be memorable and all communication regardless of the crowd size must be personal. Start by setting your own stage. Add to that a large dose of passion for your subject. Connect with your audience quickly using dates, images, song and anecdotes to get them in the mood. Tell them why they should listen to you and explain your credentials. Hit them with your biggest message first then frame it against an enemy to give you message extra punch.

SUMMARY

To get famous, you must give a legendary performance in your art. Whether that art is singing, selling or teaching, your communication must be memorable and all communication regardless of the crowd size must be personal. Start by setting your own stage. Add to that a large dose of passion for your subject. Connect with your audience quickly using dates, images, song and anecdotes to get them in the mood. Tell them why they should listen to you and explain your credentials. Hit them with your biggest message first then frame it against an enemy to give you message extra punch.

Back up all your key points with proof and make an emotional connection by using all three modalities of learning. Use powerful words, humor, and don't forget to pause or repeat your key message. Provide the path for what should happen next and explain the benefits of taking action. Never forget that non-verbal communication is important and picking the right audience is critical. Above all practice; repetition and tweaking is what makes good people great and great people famous!

One performance at woodstoick made jimmy hendrficx a legend!

ACTION PLAN

1. All communication is personal; no matter how big or small your audience is you must touch the individual.

2. Famous people don't communicate, sing, teach, coach, lead or sell, they perform!

3. Set your stage up for success.

4. Passion is the fuel of a great performance.

5. Engage your audience quickly with: A bold statement, dates, images, a dramatic picture, music, a personal anecdote

6. Explain why they should listen to you.

What will the biggest benefit be to your audience from what you say? (If you can't define a benefit for them, why should they listen!)

What problem will they have if they don't listen and understand your message?

What is you most important credential that shows why they should listen to you? (For instance, you've dealt successfully with the problem they face. Or you've profited from the action you recommend.)

- Case studies or examples
- Testimonials
- Examples of famous people
- Logic

7. Make your key message crystal clear.

8. Frame your presentation against the "enemy."

9. Send in the troops.

10. Make emotional connections.

Include visually oriented words in your presentation. Paint a visual picture with words. Use words like "see" and "picture this."

Include kinesthetic words in your presentation. Use words like "feel," "smell," and "touch."

Include aurally oriented words in your talk. You'll be able to "hear" the birds. Their sweet "sounds" permeate the forest.

Bring their senses into play as much as possible with other words like "taste" and "touch."

Win over your audience's emotions by appealing to their pride, their goals, and their fears. People generally make decisions emotionally and then rationalize them.

11. Use powerful words and phrases

Use strong, declarative sentences. Don't imply a question at the end of your sentences.

Use pauses for emphasis. Eliminate weak space filers like "um" from your sentences. All you have to do is tell yourself to stop saying "um" and you will.

Repeating key phrases three times is a power rhetorical tool. List your key phrase.

12. The powerful pause.

13. Use humor.

14. Provide a path of action. What do you want to tell people to do?

15. Explain the benefits of taking action.

16. Non-verbal communication.

Create a "presentation" outfit with the right clothes and shoes. Do you need to buy anything new?

Other nonverbal cues like tone of voice, posture, eye contact, and facial expressions simply take practice.

17. Choosing the right audience for your performance. Don't waste your time trying to influence the wrong audience. Who are your key constituencies?

18. Preparation and practice create great performances.

12

PERSISTENCE, THE TURNING POINT TO FAME

"Now remember, things look bad, and it looks like you're not gonna make it, then you gotta get mean. I mean plumb, mad-dog mean. 'Cause if you lose your head and you give up, then you neither live nor win. That's just the way it is." - **Clint Eastwood as The Outlaw Josey Wales**

Almost all famous people have the character trait of persistence since almost no one gets famous overnight. They have the determination needed to see a project through to the end, no matter what. They know Murphy's Law will rear its ugly head when least expected or invited. They know that there will be setbacks, curve balls, and sometimes total failure along the road to fame. Because they understand and accept these facts, they are better equipped mentally and physically to handle adversity. They recover quicker from setbacks. They acknowledge lost battles when they occur and get back on track with the task at hand —winning the war.

According to President Calvin Coolidge, "Nothing takes the place of persistence," and if history is any judge, he was certainly right. Almost all of the world's success stories are about rising from the ashes of failure or despair. They are about people who are fired from one company, only to persist and rise rapidly to the top in another. People like Lee Iacocca, fired by Henry Ford, only to be appointed president of Chrysler and save it from total financial ruin in a matter of months after taking over. He became a national business hero and the ultimate proof that success is the best revenge. Walt Disney was fired as a young newspaper reporter by an editor who told him that he lacked good ideas and was void of creativity. Baron Hilton, founder of Hilton Hotels was so desperate for cash to meet payroll in his struggling San Antonio Hotel that he kept his hotel chain going with a loan from a bellboy of just $300. Ray Kroc's McDonald's was once on the verge of bankruptcy, even with 200 stores in operation. Phil Knight almost went bankrupt twice, even when Nike was a $20 million a year business. Many generals, such as George Washington, have been humiliated in one battle but have later returned to win the war's decisive victory.

Persistence is the ingredient that truly separates those stars at the top from the also-rans and wannabes. Like all the other ingredients, it can be easily learned, and putting it into action is as easy as deciding to just do it. Persistence has been quoted and demonstrated by those at the top as the reason for success more than any other factor. From Washington to Reagan and from Edison to Eminem, this one lesson can be learned in the biographies of every famous person in the world.

"I had never really known who John Dunbar was. Perhaps because the name itself had no meaning. But as I heard my Sioux name being called over and over (Dances with Wolves), I knew for the first time who I really was." — **John Dunbar, in the film *Dances with Wolves***

COSTNER'S LAST STAND

By the early 1990s, the Western genre was all but dead in Hollywood. Actor Kevin Costner had met a man in acting class named Michael Blake who had pitched him an idea for a

Costner told him he'd have more chance pitching a book. Broke and couch surfing from friend to friend, Blake wrote the book about the Plains Indians and a cavalry lieutenant. The book was rejected by over thirty publishers before it was published. Blake, who at various times stayed with Costner, tried to get him to read the book, but he wouldn't. After overstaying his welcome, he eventually left and ended up washing dishes at a Chinese restaurant in Phoenix for minimum wage. Blake continued to pester Costner for financial help and to read his book. When Costner finally relented, he was stunned. "It was the clearest idea for a movie that I'd ever read," Costner recounted.

Costner wanted to make the movie, but no studio would finance a $15-million, three-hour western epic, where half the dialogue was not even in English. Eventually he secured overseas funding and later Orion came in for over half. The film went way over budget and Costner funded the shortfall from his own pocket.

The book no one wanted to publish became a film no one wanted to fund and eventually one no one wanted to direct. After being turned down by three of the biggest names in Hollywood, who wanted wholesale changes Costner would not approve, Costner decided to direct the movie himself.

Once shooting on location began, with weather ranging from twenty to one hundred degrees on a set that included thirty-five hundred buffalo, three dozen teepees, three hundred horses, two wolves, and an army of Native American extras, things were challenging at best.

Hearing about the film's production difficulties, budget problems, and countless delays, many in Hollywood started to call the risky project "Costner's Last Stand," while others dubbed it "Kevin's Gate," in reference to the wildly over-budget Western flop Heaven's Gate.

In the end Costner was vindicated. Dances with Wolves won seven Academy Awards, including Best Picture, and grossed more than $425 million, the highest-grossing western ever! Costner made over $40 million for his trouble, and the Sioux made him an honorary member of their tribe. Surely one of the few white men to enjoy that honor.

John Wayne had similar struggles to get his movie, The Alamo, made and was all but broke when it finished, having financed much of the filming himself. And Sylvester Stallone's Rocky is the stuff of legends.

A MAGICAL RAGS TO RICHES STORY

J.K. Rowling first came up with the idea of a boy whose parents had died discovering he was a wizard on a delayed train to Manchester. But it would be seven years before that idea would become a book. Rowling's teenage years weren't particularly happy. She says she came from a difficult family situation, including her mother's 10-year battle with multiple sclerosis that took a toll on her and the family. After her mother's death, which traumatized her, Rowling left for Portugal for a fresh start where she became a teacher and married a Portuguese TV journalist. She gave birth to her daughter, Jessica, in July 1993 but the marriage didn't last the year. To make matters worse, Rowling was fired from her teaching job for daydreaming. She was now an unemployed single parent. Rowling and Jessica returned to the UK to live in Edinburgh, Scotland, where she lived in a mice-infested flat, struggling to raise her daughter on a welfare check of £70 a week. She had suicidal thoughts and a battle with deep depression, but her young daughter kept her going. Unable to spend money on heating, she regularly warmed up in cafés, where she revisited the idea of *Harry Potter*.

Rowling said, in a 2008 Harvard University commencement speech, "An exceptionally short-lived marriage had imploded, and I was jobless, a lone parent, and as poor as it is possible to be in modern Britain, without being homeless... By every usual standard, I was the biggest failure I knew." But she managed to write the first book.

After sending her manuscript to 12 different publishers and getting rejected by every single one, Rowling began losing confidence in her book. Finally, the editor at Bloomsbury Publishing company sat down to read the manuscript. And so did the editor's 8-year-old daughter. The little girl loved the opening chapters, and begged him to read the whole thing. This made the publisher agree to publish Rowling's novel. But Rowling was left with a warning: that she should get a day job because she wouldn't make any money writing children's books. Once *Harry Potter and the Sorcerer's Stone* was published though she proved everyone dead wrong.

Today Rowling is the author of the best-selling book series in history. The books have been translated into 73 languages, sold 450 million copies and accrued over $20 billion through movie adaptations and sponsorships. She is also one of the richest women in the world. The very best thing her fame has given her, she wrote on her website, is the absence of worry. "I have not forgotten what it feels like to worry whether you'll have enough money to pay the bills. Not to have to think about that anymore is the biggest luxury in the world."

10 STEPS TO INCREASING YOUR LEVELS OF PERSISTENCE

There are 10 steps that you can take to maximize your persistence.

1. BE OVER-PREPARED

Start each quest with a deck stacked in your favor. Know your goals, vision and strategic plan. Know your talents, weaknesses, product, staff, resources, customers, fans and competition.

Have backup plans.

Anticipate objections.

Eliminate roadblocks.

Be over-armed with solutions.

The clearer you are about your goals and objectives, the harder it will be to sidetrack you and slow your progress. The clearer you are about your vision, the easier it will be to attract support and action, especially in times of trouble. The better you know your support organization, managers, and employees, the better you can gauge their unique strengths and weaknesses in helping you with the task at hand, thus avoiding a host of problems associated with hiring or asking the wrong person to do the job.

The better you know your competition, the more likely you are to anticipate their next moves and plan your strategy accordingly. You are therefore less likely to be blindsided by a pricing, marketing, or technological breakthrough. The better you know your customers, donors, partners or fans, the better you can anticipate their wants and needs.

Finally, the more you practice and learn about your art and field, the more competent and confident you will become. As Abraham Lincoln said, "I shall prepare and one day my time will come." This statement is never truer than in the face of adversity. The importance of good preparation cannot be overstressed.

2. EXPECT IN ADVANCE THAT THINGS WILL GO WRONG

Despite being over-prepared you must anticipate some setbacks or failures along the way. Not everything will go according to plan. Things can and do go wrong. Don't let any lost sale, missed opportunity, financial setback, mechanical problem or poor performance become an emotional downer. Don't allow any situation to adversely affect your attitude for more than the briefest of moments. Self-pity is not part of the makeup of the famous. Use setbacks as motivation to try harder; remember no one made it to the top without them.

In the words of William Blake, "Mistakes are easy, mistakes are inevitable, but there is no mistake so great as the mistake of not going on."

3. REFRAME YOUR SITUATION TO THE POSITIVE

Many of the most famous people in history have experienced the ignominy of failure many times over. The difference is in how these great people viewed their failures. Many refused to look upon them as failures at all. Rather, they considered them, as did Edison his thousands of unsuccessful attempts to design a light bulb, as successfully demonstrating how not to accomplish a particular task. By eliminating another idea that didn't work, the path to success became clearer. This is a classic example of reframing.

Almost all discovery involves a painful process of eliminating things that don't work in the hope of eventually finding something that does. Learn to treat each setback you encounter as another way not to reach you goals. You'll never have to waste time doing things this particular way again. Instead, you will regroup and try a different approach, knowing you are now closer to your goal. By genuinely learning from your experiences, you can view your own setbacks as steps to success. As my good friend Linda Parelli, world famous horse trainer, says, "That was interesting, now let's try something else!"

4. ANALYZE WHAT WENT WRONG AND TAKE CORRECTIVE ACTION

After each incomplete sale, failed campaign, poor performance or personal setback, take the time to step back and analyze what went wrong. Top performers play it back in their minds and try to find the words or solutions that might have made the difference. Hindsight is always 20/20. Use hindsight to future advantage by not making the same mistake, or a similar one, again –which brings me to one of my all- time favorite quotes. Einstein defined insanity as "doing the same thing over and over and expecting different results."

After each setback, pause for a moment to redefine your approach. First, when analyzing why things went wrong use only facts—not fiction. Many times, we jump to wrong conclusions to rationalize our failure. One way to avoid this is to ask yourself, "How do I know this conclusion is true?" Often, you'll find it is not true and you must look elsewhere for the real reason for the setback. Look at your timing. Was it good? Look at your marketing and your sales approach. Look at all aspects of your project and clearly define why your plans did not work out the way you wanted.

If you can't understand why you were rejected, solicit the help of those who rejected you, your fans, co-workers, shareholders, competitors, or customers. Ask them why they turned you down. Then ask them how you could change your approach to be more successful. This will actually build rapport for you with the people who rejected you. They'll respect you for asking, and may even reconsider you. You can do this later or immediately. In fact, this is a famous sales close for immediately after you've been rejected called variously the "foot in the door close" or the "Columbo close" (after the TV detective's habit of asking one more question on his way out the door).

Ronald Reagan, The Great Communicator

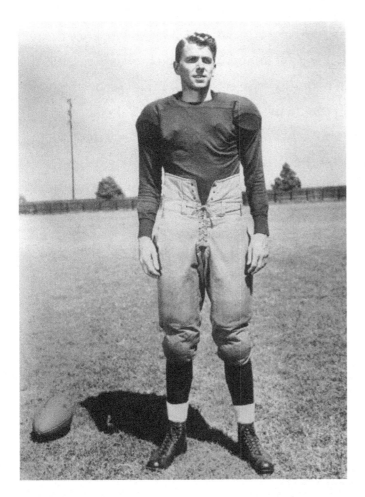

In his biography, President Ronald Reagan talks of the small things that happened in his life that proved to be turning points. A pivotal moment in his life was when he applied for a job as head of the sports department at a new Montgomery Ward's store. They were looking for a local high school sports star, and, because Reagan had been a football player, he was convinced he would get the job. Fortunately for him, he lost out to another local sports star. This was a bitter disappointment to the young Reagan, yet, had he gotten the job, he might well have stayed in that small town for the rest of his life.

His failure to win that job persuaded him he should travel to Chicago and try getting into radio. He dreamed of being a sports announcer but was turned down by every single station where he applied. He did, however, leave with some good advice. He was told to start out by trying a smaller station in a rural area.

Discouraged but determined, Reagan set off again in search of a job in broadcasting, this time at smaller stations. Within a few weeks, he struck pay dirt, and all because he took action and continued to take action until he reached his goal. In the face of rejection after rejection, Reagan persisted and finally landed the position he wanted. He was ecstatic with his new job and the excellent salary it offered. From the start, however, things did not go at all well, and he was soon told he would be replaced. This, of course, came as another bitter disappointment. Fortunately, the radio station asked him to stay on for a few days to assist his replacement. Instead of indignantly refusing, as many others might have done, Reagan agreed. Before the end of the week, the person hired to replace him had decided not to accept the job, and Reagan was asked to stay on until another replacement could be found. This he again agreed to do, but only if the station's most experienced announcer would spend time with him each day. He wanted to understand what he had done wrong and how he could do better in the future, so he could find work with another station.

His employer agreed to this condition and, as often happens when people seek out and accept good advice, Reagan improved his performance so rapidly the station stopped looking for a replacement.

THE GREATEST MISTAKE IN ROCK HISTORY

It was New Year's Eve 1961. A quartet of very young and very hopeful rock musicians stuffed themselves into an old van and headed for London, Their audition at Decca Records was strangely set for New Year's Day, 1962. The journey to London would have normally taken five hours but, with snowy condition and their driver getting lost, the freezing trip took ten.

They finally arrived in London around 10 PM, but instead of wisely resting up for the biggest audition of their lives, they indulged themselves liberally in some New Year's Eve drinking. The recording session started at 11 AM the next day and lasted about one hour. The boys' nervousness was evident, although they became more confident as the set progressed.

It wasn't a "great" audition, but after the 13-song set ended, everyone seemed happy enough. Mike Smith the DECCA Records man informed the young hopefuls that he "saw no problems." He'd let them know his decision "in a few weeks" after his boss reviewed the tapes. All left the audition believing the contract was as good as signed and went back to their normal routine of playing clubs while waiting for their big break!

After nervously waiting for a happy verdict for several weeks, their manager, Brian Epstein, finally got through on the phone to Decca Records A&R man Dick Rowe. Rowe was not impressed, "Groups with guitars are on the way out," Rowe informed him bluntly. Rowe continued by saying that "the Beatles have no future in show business" and condescendingly advised Epstein that, "You have a good record shop down there, Mr. Epstein, why don't you go back to that?" Epstein, aghast, told Rowe, "You must be out of your mind!" and told him his boys were someday "going to be bigger than Elvis Presley." Rowe, no doubt, suppressed his laughter and rolled his eyes. After the initial shock and bitter disappointment wore off, the Beatles regrouped and signed with rival EMI a few weeks later which at the time was no sure thing!

Although he later went on to sign The Rolling Stones and many other top acts, Dick Rowe went down in music history as "the man who turned down the Beatles."

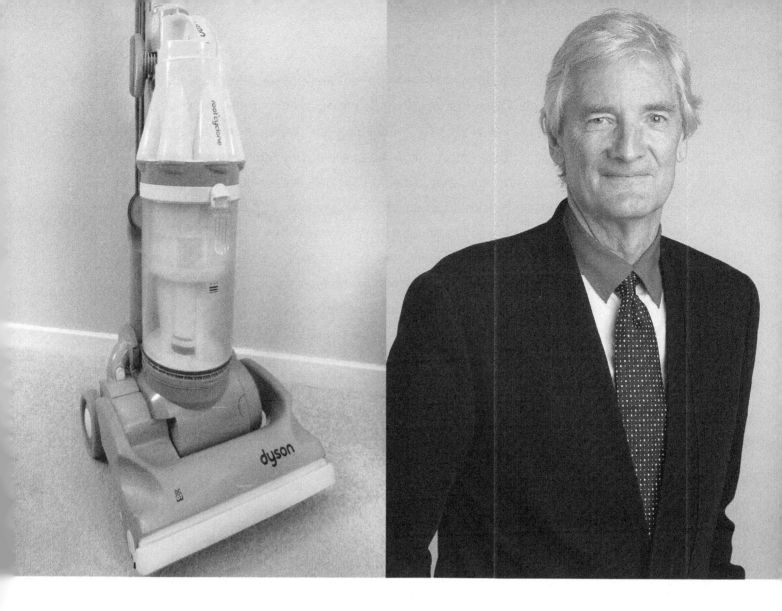

5. DEVELOP A "PLAN B"

Sir James Dyson, an engineer by trade, had the idea to create the world's first bagless vacuum cleaner when he became frustrated with his Hoover vacuum and its loss of suction. His revolutionary idea was to use the concept of cyclonic separation.

Partly supported by his wife's salary as an art teacher, after five years and 5,126 failures Dyson finally got it right. When he finally did, after six years of struggles, he was astonished to discover that no distributor in the UK would take on the revolutionary product as it would have disturbed the valuable £100 million market for replacement dust bags.

Switching tactics, Dyson launched a hot pink version of his vacuum in the Japanese market. It won an industrial award in Japan and in 1986, three years after its first introduction, he was awarded his first US Patent for it. However, manufacturers still didn't want to take it on so Dyson formed his own company, in 1993 at the age of 46, to market the product.

Dyson's breakthrough in the UK market came more than ten years after the initial idea, when he starred a TV advertising campaign that emphasized that, unlike most of its rivals, the Dyson vacuum did not require the continuing purchase of replacement bags. The slogan "say goodbye to the bag" proved more attractive to the buying public than a previous emphasis on the suction efficiency that its technology delivers. Ironically, the previous big change in domestic vacuum cleaner design had been the introduction of the disposable bag – users being prepared to pay extra for the convenience. The Dyson Dual Cyclone became the fastest-selling vacuum cleaner ever made in the UK. It outsold some of the companies that rejected his idea, becoming one of the most popular brands in the UK. In early 2005, it was reported that Dyson vacuums had become the market leaders in the United States by value. Today, Dyson is worth more than £3 billion, all because of his refusal to give up. He struggled through times of failure, sorrow, and regret, but he persevered.

Jay-Z has sold more than 36 million records, but his early days of trying to break out from the streets of Brooklyn to king of the rappers were fraught with disappointment. Jay-Z told MTV of his troubles. "I went to every single record label, and they were like, 'This guy is terrible. He's nothing.'" So he took matters into his own hands and started his own record label Roc-a-Fella Records and releasing his debut Reasonable Doubt on his own. "I could have easily been like 'Maybe what I'm talking about ain't right! Nobody wants to sign me!' That would have stopped the suffering," he said. "But I didn't."

Based on what you discover when you analyze your setbacks, be your own coach. Develop alternate plans, assuming, of course, that you didn't have a plan B, C and D already in place.

6. STAY FOCUSED ON YOUR VISION

In times of trouble, change, or crisis, it pays to keep your vision in mind and to summon up renewed energy and enthusiasm to share that vision with those who support your cause. A vision should be like a guiding star, keeping you focused on the end result and not allowing you to be drawn into skirmishes along the way that are unrelated to your goal. Keeping your eye constantly on the prize will allow you to dispense with failure quickly and readjust your course decisively.

Take every opportunity you can to surround yourself with images of what success means to you: Get brochures on new cars, boats or bikes, find images of beautiful homes, clothes, a retirement villa on the beach or other things that you could obtain as a result of achieving success. Each time you see or visualize those images, you trigger the thoughts, feelings, and actions that make them more likely to materialize in your life. Visualize the success you will achieve despite any temporary setbacks.

Jim Carrey who's brought us some of the highest-grossing comedies of all time such as *The Mask*, *Dumb and Dumber*, and *Ace Ventura*, had a long and arduous path to fame. He grew up in a lower-income family with a father who struggled to keep jobs. At 15 he had to drop out of high school to earn money as a janitor just to help feed the family. He was booed off stage on his first comic stand-up at a club called Yuk Yuk's in Toronto. When he finally got an audition for the famed show *Saturday Night Live*, he failed to land the part.

Carrey was undeterred and stayed focused on his vision of himself as a top comedian. After he achieved box office stardom, i n an interview with Oprah Winfrey, he talked about how he used the Law of Attraction by writing himself a check for $10,000,000 million dollars for "Acting Services Rendered." He kept the check in his wallet for seven years until he received a $10,000,000 million dollar payment for his work in Dumb and Dumber.

No One in Hollywood History Held Out for Fame More Profitably Than Stallone

Sylvester Stallone challenges started early in life. Complications his mother suffered during labor forced doctors to use forceps during his birth which accidentally severed a nerve in his face. As a result, the lower left side of his face was and is paralyzed, including parts of his lip, tongue, and chin, an accident which gave Stallone his snarling look and slightly slurred speech. In middle school, his speech and facial paralysis became a thing for others to make fun of so he joined a gym and started body-building to frighten those who bullied him.

After high school, Stallone dreamed of being an actor. What he found instead was a big dose of rejection, failure and a string of agents telling him he talked funny, walked funny and couldn't act. Short in stature and short on options, Stallone first starring role was in the soft core pornography feature film *The Party at Kitty and Stud's*. He was paid US $200 for two days' work. Stallone later explained that he had done the film out of desperation after being evicted from his apartment and finding himself homeless for several days. He has also said that he slept three weeks in the Port Authority Bus Terminal in New York City prior to seeing a casting notice for the film. In the actor's words, "it was either do that movie or rob someone, because I was at the end – the very end – of my rope. I was so broke I sold my dog for $25." (The film was released several years later as Italian Stallion, in order to cash in on Stallone's newfound fame.)

1975, Stallone saw the Muhammad Ali – Chuck Wepner fight also known as the "Bayonne Bleeder." That match was like a flash of divine inspiration when for a brief moment Wepner knocked Ali to the canvas. That night Stallone went home, and after three days he had written the rough script of for *Rocky*. Now he had to sell the idea to a producer which lead to nearly 1500 rejections. Says Stallone in a video he did for the film school archive "I was on casting call and I was not right for the part but on the way out I told them I do some writing and I have story about boxing. They said let's take a look at it, but if I hadn't turned around at that door my whole life would have changed. That's why I always tell actor and writers keep talking and maybe you'll hit a nerve. I have to give them credit for their insight and willingness to take a chance. They were really enthusiastic about the script but they here not enthusiastic about me playing the part. I can't say I blame them there were a lot of stars at the top of their game Robert Redford, Ryan O'Neil, Burt Reynolds but I thought this opportunity is not coming round again. If I give up now and this is a hit I think I'd throw myself off a building."

Producers Irwin Winkler and Robert Chartoff offered Stallone, whose net worth hovered around $100, $25,000 for his script. He said not unless he stared in the movie. They kept upping it $100,000, $150,000, $200,000. Said Stallone, "My $40 car had just blown up an I had to take the bus everywhere, but I couldn't sell out on my dream." When they offered him $360,000, Stallone still refused. Eventually, he accepted just $35,000 and a percentage of the film's sales but he got to star in the movie. Six months before Stallone had sold his dog to help make ends meet. Stallone eventually talked the family into giving Butkus back so that the dog could star in the movie, the actor explains:

"The other family had owned him for six months," Stallone says. *"They weren't exactly thrilled, but I said, 'Please.' I said, 'This dog belongs in the movie.' He had suffered along with me for two years. I said, 'Please let him have a shot in the movie.'"*

Mercifully, the family relented and Stallone's dog starred in two *Rocky* films. He even appears in the credits as Butkus Stallone.

Rocky was made on a budget of under a million dollars, shot in 28 days, and almost always in one take. It earned $225 million in global box office receipts becoming the highest grossing film of 1976. It was nominated for ten Academy Awards, including Best Actor and Best Original Screenplay nominations for Stallone. The film went on to win the Academy Awards for Best Picture, Best Directing and Best Film Editing.

7. KEEP YOUR SENSE OF HUMOR

On March 30, 1981, President Reagan, aged 70, was shot, along with James Brady and a bodyguard during an assassination attempt. Arriving at a Washington, DC, hospital, Reagan refused a wheelchair and walked to his room where he promptly collapsed. In his book *Rawhide Down*, Del Quentin Wilber says, "Reagan was far closer to death than was previously thought. One paramedic, on seeing the president enter the hospital, thought, 'My God, he's Code City,' meaning he was about to die. The doctors at first could not stop the internal bleeding, and Reagan ended up losing more than half his blood. Surgeons made repeated attempts to find the bullet. They had almost given up when it was discovered, only an inch from his heart. The slug was a devastator round, designed to explode on impact. Fortunately, the shot that hit Reagan had first deflected off the armored door of the presidential limo. Had the bullet exploded in his body, Reagan would almost certainly have been killed."

Moving in and out of consciousness and with death potentially staring him in the face, Reagan never lost his sense of humor or stage presence. He demonstrated his remarkable courage and persistence by joking about his situation with a series of memorable one-liners.

As the nurse took his hand to check his pulse, he quipped, "Does Nancy know about us?" When he wife showed up at his bedside, he borrowed from famous heavyweight boxer Jack Dempsey, saying, "Honey, I forgot to duck!" As a doctor prepared to operate, Reagan cracked, "I hope you are a Republican!" The following day, with a tube stuck in his throat, making speech very difficult, he sent a series of handwritten notes to concerned aides, including one that read, "I'd like to do this scene over again, starting back at the hotel."

Those who maintain a sense of humor in times of trouble always gain our respect and admiration. Reagan, charismatic to begin with, rose to astonishing levels of popularity in the aftermath of the attack. *Washington Post* journalist David Broder noted, Reagan "was politically untouchable from that point on. He became a mythic figure."

Humor, of course, does more than merely comfort those around us. When we laugh we release endorphins in the brain that make us feel better. It gives us more energy to tackle the problems we face and our positive frame of mind attracts others to our aid. Keep whatever makes you laugh close at hand for a good dose when needed.

8. DO NOT TAKE REJECTION PERSONALLY

One reason so many people never learn to become persistent is because they take every rejection, setback, or failure personally. They somehow equate their idea, product, service or song with their personal self-esteem. The famous can never afford this self-indulgence for there will be plenty of rejection before fame.

Everyone gets rejected on the way up, authors, singers and salesmen more than most. But whatever your profession you must not take rejection personally.

Just look at this collection of "losers:"

Herman Melville's masterpiece, *Moby-Dick*, was turned down by multiple publishers, some of whom had creative suggestions for the author. One publishing house wrote: "First, we must ask, does it have to be a whale?" When he finally did get published, Melville still ended up paying for the typesetting and plating himself.

"You'd have a decent book if you'd get rid of that Gatsby character." This rather drastic revision was suggested to F. Scott Fitzgerald about his masterpiece *The Great Gatsby*.

Animal Farm by George Orwell was rejected because "there is no market for animal stories in the USA."

Harry Potter and the Sorcerer's Stone was rejected 12 times and J. K. Rowling was told "not to quit her day job."

Lord of the Flies by William Golding was rejected 20 times before it was published.

"I haven't the foggiest idea about what the man is trying to say. Apparently the author intends it to be funny." Joseph Heller decided to name his satirical book about World War II after the 22 rejections he received: *Catch-22*.

Dune by Frank Herbert was rejected 23 times before it was published and Herbert was already an established author.

The Wizard of Oz was rejected by every publisher, even though Baum had published several similar books. He had to pay for the first publication himself.

Carrie by Stephen King was rejected 30 times before it was published. King was so discouraged he tossed the book into the trash. Fortunately his wife then went through the trash to rescue it and convinced him to re-submit it. Today, King has over 50 novels and has sold over 350 million copies of his work.

Can you imagine what King's life would be like had he given up? It's difficult to imagine that such a successful author was once rejected so many times.

Gone with the Wind by Margaret Mitchell was rejected 38 times before it was published.

Zen and the Art of Motorcycle Maintenance by Robert M. Pirsig was rejected 121 times before it was published.

He was fired as his role as contributor to the *San Francisco Examiner* in 1889 because he was told by an editor, "I'm sorry Mr. Kipling, but you just don't know how to use the English language."

During his screen test for MGM, the studio's talent scout wrote on his report to describe the man auditioning: "Can't act. Can't sing. Slightly bald. Can dance a little."

Who was the man who, according to the talent scout, could only "dance a little?" The man was Fred Astaire!

THE MUSEUM OF MODERN ART

NEW YORK 19

11 WEST 53rd STREET
TELEPHONE: CIRCLE 5-8900
CABLES: MODERNART, NEW-YORK

THE MUSEUM COLLECTIONS

October 18, 1956

Dear Mr. Warhol:

Last week our Committee on the Museum Collections held its first meeting of the fall season and had a chance to study your drawing entitled Shoe which you so generously offered as a gift to the Museum.

I regret that I must report to you that the Committee decided, after careful consideration, that they ought not to accept it for our Collection.

Let me explain that because of our severely limited gallery and storage space we must turn down many gifts offered, since we feel it is not fair to accept as a gift a work which may be shown only infrequently.

Nevertheless, the Committee has asked me to pass on to you their thanks for your generous expression of interest in our Collection.

Sincerely,

Alfred H. Barr, Jr.
Director of the Museum Collections

Mr. Andy Warhol
242 Lexington Avenue
New York, New York

AHB:bj

P.S. The drawing may be picked up from the Museum at your convenience.

Today, the MOMA owns more than 100 of Warhol's pieces, including Gold Marilyn and Campbell's Soup Cans, both created in 1962!

Ironically, Steven Spielberg was rejected from the University of Southern California School of Theater, Film and Television three times. He was eventually accepted by another school, a school that he dropped out of to pursue directing. While the lack of a diploma did not hold him back, Spielberg finally completed his BA in 2002.

When she was trying to start her career, modeling agencies told Norma Jean (Marilyn Monroe) she should consider becoming a secretary.

After just one performance, at the Grand Ol' Opry, manager Jimmy Denny fired Elvis Presley. He reportedly told him, "You ain't going nowhere, son. You ought to go back to driving a truck."

Yes, people much more famous than you have suffered ridicule and rejection. Get out of the habit of beating yourself up mentally when things go wrong. There are plenty of other people out there who are only too willing to do it for you, and they won't charge you a dime! By blaming yourself, you are breaking down your level of persistence and resolve.

By all means, analyze what went wrong, but don't take the rap personally. Simply focus on a new angle of attack and use your mental energy to come up with a new solution. Realize that past failures mean nothing. They are gone and can't be replayed. You are concerned only with the future. You start each new day with a clean slate. It's up to you what you do with that day. The past does not reflect what will happen in the future.

And by the way, not all failures are really failures. Many times when people who have rejected you see or hear from you several more times they become impressed by your persistence and respond positively in the end.

9. THE EXPERIENCE FACTOR

"Experience is what you get when you are looking for something else." I read that interesting quote by Mark Twain on the back of a matchbox when I was a teenager. Gaining "experience" often means disappointment.

Professional sports offer a very good look at the experience factor. Each year in the Super

Bowl or FA cup final, the two best teams in the country come together for one afternoon. One of them is going to lose and will then be faced with two options—they can quit and admit they just aren't good enough to achieve the pinnacle of success, or they can chalk it up to experience and try again next year. Naturally, they opt for experience and try again.

Michael Jordon who scored 32,292 points, earned six NBA championships and five NBA MVP titles was cut from his high school basketball team. He once said:

"I have missed over 9,000 shots in my career. I have lost almost 300 games. On 26 occasions I have been entrusted to take the game winning shot and I have missed. I have failed over and over and over again in my life. And that is why I succeed."

Despite Steve Jobs incredible fame as an innovator, he suffered many failures: the Apple Lisa. Macintosh TV, the Apple III, and the PowerMac G4 cube. Most devastating of all was being fired from Apple. Jobs saw this move as an incredible personal failure that he had been pushed out of the company he had worked so hard to grow.

He later shared in an interview, *"What had been the focus of my entire adult life, was gone. It was devastating."*

Not devastating enough to stop him. He would later go on to found NeXT (which was a failure) and spin Pixar off into its own entity after purchasing the animated division of Lucas Films (which became a hugely profitable deal). When he returned to Apple, the additional experience he had gained while away helped him find immortality with the iPod, iPad and the iPhone.

People will forget that you were wrong on a lot of smaller efforts as long as you kill it on the big ones. Imperfection is a part of any creative process and of life.

We must risk failure to succeed in bigger ways!

10. ADAPT IF NECESSARY BUT DON'T STOP REACHING FOR THE STARS

Her childhood dream was to be a figure-skater but she failed to make the US Olympic team. Eventually she became a fashion editor at Vogue. She worked there for 17 years but left when she was turned down for the editor-in-chief position. It was while she was looking ahead to her own wedding, at the age of 40, that she became frustrated with the lack of stylish wedding dresses available and decided to design her own. Today Vera Wang is a fashion designer to the stars and worth an estimated $400 million.

Having emerged as Formula One's star driver amid a 1975 world title win Niki Lauda was leading the 1976 formula one, championship battle again. Then with just six races to go Lauda was seriously injured in a horrific crash at the 1976 German Grand Prix at the Nürburgring On the second lap, Lauda lost control of his Ferrari at high speed due to a suspected rear suspension failure and crashed into the barriers before bouncing back on to the track, and the car caught fire. The vehicle was then hit by two other vehicles whose drivers immediately stopped got out, along with a third who stopped to help. The three pulled Lauda out of the burning car, and the race was stopped. Lauda was sent to the hospital with severe burns and was fighting for his life after inhaling hot toxic fumes and suffering severe burns in which he lost an ear.

Miraculously, he survived, and incredibly Lauda missed only two races, before appearing at the Monza press conference six weeks after the accident with his fresh burns still bandaged. He finished fourth in the Italian GP, despite being, by his own admission, absolutely petrified. F1 journalist Nigel Roebuck recalls seeing Lauda in the pits, peeling the blood-soaked bandages off his scarred scalp. Although he narrowly lost the title to James Hunt that year, he won his second world championship the following year and his third in 1984. He went on to start an airline and run the Mercedes Formula, One team. Nothing could stop the champion nicknamed "Super Rat."

SUMMARY - SHOULD YOU TRY AGAIN?

It is truly amazing how many turning points in the lives of famous people come down to the same decision. Should we try again, or should we throw in the towel and settle down to a life of mediocrity.

There is absolutely no better long-term solution to success than single-minded, bulldog determination. Of course you must have a capacity for making changes to deal with fluctuations in market conditions, which in today's world happen at a fever pitch. Entire industries are disrupted and vanish overnight. Jobs come and go, forcing career changes when people least expect them. Unforeseen events can bring emotional and financial calamity to someone who is unprepared. Counter this danger by being constantly aware that things can sometimes go badly wrong. Prepare contingency plans to deal with the worst-case scenario and always be on the lookout for new horizons that offer expanded opportunities. The famous waste no time in self-pity or recrimination but instead concentrate on setting new goals and moving forward. They treat each new set of problems as opportunities to improve and to profit from their own experience. Your desire and determination to succeed must never waver. All it takes is a positive attitude, a new plan, and unrelenting persistence.

As famed radio commentator Paul Harvey so aptly put it, "In times like these, it pays to remember there have always been times like these."

Like most famous people, Walt Disney endured many failures and humiliations before his ultimate triumph.

ACTION PLAN

- Are you mentally prepared to deal with multiple setbacks and rejection?
- Have you anticipated what could go wrong?
- How will you reframe temporary disappointments?
- Are you willing to honestly analyze what went wrong?
- What is your Plan B?
- Can you stay focused on your vision?
- What can you do to heighten the feeling of success you will feel when you reach your goal?
- How will you maintain a sense of humor and stay upbeat?
- Can you separate personal rejection from professional rejection?
- How will experience help you reach your goals?
- Are you willing to adapt to new conditions or opportunities?

Howard Schultz may not be a famous as some but his coffee sure is...

FINAL THOUGHTS

Now you have a formula for fame, a blue print to becoming the most noted person in your profession whatever that profession is and in whatever geographical area makes sense to you. Work carefully through these twelve key factors and build or enhance each one for they are the DNA of fame. With fame comes a new world of opportunity, business, connections and money so you can live life on your terms.

1. Create your back story fill it with authentic details and emotions about how you came to be the person you are.

2. State your claim as an expert, a performer or the leader of a cause.

3. Build your confidence in yourself and in others by constantly building your competence. Commit to being, a life-long learner of your craft.

4. Find a signature sound, the name, catch phrases and tunes that work for you.

5. Develop a signature look that is uniquely yours and sets you apart from the crowd.

6. Use carefully crafted photographs and videos to build you image.

7. Create a legendary performance.

8. Build your charisma with the right smile, body language and personal traits.

9. Create your own rituals ones that resonate with your audience and turn them into raving fans.

10. Don't leave your press to chance write your own story and exploit then that story on your own media channels.

11. Find a protagonist a person, company or viewpoint that's the antithesis of yours for both contrast and to rally your troops behind you against the enemy!

12. And above all persist in the pursuit of your dreams.

I wish you luck, but with the talents you have, I don't think you'll need it!

Andrew Wood
Marketing Legend
Andrew@LegendaryMarketing.com

ABOUT THE AUTHOR
ANDREW WOOD

Born in Oxford, England and growing up in the midland county of Shropshire, Andrew Wood immigrated to America in 1980 to pursue a career as a professional golfer. Unfortunately, lack of talent held him back and he accidentally found himself running a small karate school in Southern California. After struggling to survive for 18 months as a small business owner he decided to focus all his attention on marketing. This focus soon paid off and he increased his income to six figures while still in his twenties.

His initial interest in marketing turned into a passion and he quickly turned the single school into a national franchise of over 400 units.

After selling out of the karate business in the late 90's he moved to Florida where he founded Legendary Marketing, a business designed to combine his passion for golf and travel with his marketing expertise.

Legendary quickly built a name for itself in the golf industry with innovative websites, social media, and online campaigns. Over the last decade, Wood has worked with over 1500 golf clubs, resorts and developments, in over twenty countries. His clients include properties in the USA, Canada, England, Scotland, Ireland, France, Spain, Russia, the Caribbean, and Morocco to name just a few.

Author of over 40 books including; Million Dollar Laptop, Cowboy Wisdom, Cunningly Clever

Marketing, Cunningly Clever Selling, Cunningly Clever Entrepreneur, The Golf Marketing Bible, The Hotel Marketing Bible, Confessions of a Golf Pro and many more. He is considered the world's leading expert in golf, resort and real estate marketing and spoken to thousands of audiences worldwide on this and other topics from his books. A pioneer in internet marketing his creative talent, out of the box ideas and copywriting skills are at the core of his expertise. Regarded as one of the top marketing minds in the world his ability to generate leads and increase income!

In his spare time he travels the world, plays golf & tennis, writes books and occasionally races cars!

FOLLOW ANDREW

Web: www.marketinglegend.com
LinkedIn: cunninglyclever
Facebook: andrewwood1836
Instagram: marketinglegend
Twitter: @cunninglyclever

OTHER BOOKS BY ANDREW WOOD

Legendary Advice—101 Proven Strategies to Increase Your Income, Wealth & Lifestyle

Legendary Achievement—How to Maximize Your True Potential & Live the Life of Your Dreams

Million Dollar Laptop

Cunningly Clever Marketing

Cunningly Clever Entrepreneur

Legendary Selling

Legendary Leadership

Making Your Business the One They Choose

The Traits of Champions (with Brian Tracy)

The Joy of Golf

The Golf Marketing Bible

The Golf Marketing Bible Vol. 2

The Hotel & Resort Marketing Bible

The Golf Sales Bible

Golf Marketing Strategy

How to Make $150,000 a Year Teaching Golf

Desperately Seeking Members (as Harvey S. McKlintock)

Confessions of a Golf Pro

Cowboy Wisdom (with Pat Parelli)

No One Gets Out Alive - How to Create a Life Well Lived!

CREDITS

Jean-Claude Van Damme, page 6
© Featureflash | Dreamstime.com
File ID: 30289187
License: Editorial

Chuck Norris, page 7
© Carrienelson1 | Dreamstime.com
File ID: 26911253
License: Editorial

Bruce Lee, page 7
National General Pictures
(https://commons.wikimedia.org/wiki/File:Bruce_Lee_1973.jpg), „Bruce Lee 1973", marked as public domain, more details on Wikimedia Commons:
https://commons.wikimedia.org/wiki/Template:PD-US

Paris Hilton, page 8
Toglenn at English Wikipedia
(https://commons.wikimedia.org/wiki/File:Paris_Hilton_3.jpg), „Paris Hilton 3",
https://creativecommons.org/licenses/by-sa/3.0/legalcode

Yoko Ono, page 8
Marcela Cataldi Cipolla
(https://commons.wikimedia.org/wiki/File:Yokoono2.jpg), „Yokoono2",
https://creativecommons.org/licenses/by/3.0/legalcode

Jackie Kennedy Onassis, page 8
None
(https://commons.wikimedia.org/wiki/File:Jackie_Kennedy_on_her_wedding_day,Rhode_Island,September_12,_1953.jpg), „Jackie Kennedy on her wedding day,Rhode Island,September 12, 1953", marked as public domain, more details on Wikimedia Commons:
https://commons.wikimedia.org/wiki/Template:PD-author

Kim Kardashian, page 8
Toglenn at English Wikipedia
(https://commons.wikimedia.org/wiki/File:Kim_Kardashian_2009.jpg), „Kim Kardashian 2009",
https://creativecommons.org/licenses/by-sa/3.0/deed.en

Buddy Holly, page 9
Coral Records
(https://commons.wikimedia.org/wiki/File:Buddy_Holly_&_The_Crickets_publicity_portrait_-_cropped.jpg), „Buddy Holly & The Crickets publicity portrait - cropped", marked as public domain, more details on Wikimedia Commons:
https://commons.wikimedia.org/wiki/Template:PD-US

Aryton Senna, page 9
StuSeeger
(https://commons.wikimedia.org/wiki/File:Ayrton_Senna_1991_United_States_GP.jpg), „Ayrton Senna 1991 United States GP",
https://creativecommons.org/licenses/by/2.0/legalcode

Elvis Presley, page 9
Lindsey Turner
(https://commons.wikimedia.org/wiki/File:Elvis_Presley's_Grave.jpg), „Elvis Presley's Grave", Cropped by Andrew Wood,
https://creativecommons.org/licenses/by/2.0/legalcode

Dale Earnhardt, page 10
Darryl Moran
(https://commons.wikimedia.org/wiki/File:Dale_Earnhardt_-_NASCAR_Photography_By_Darryl_Moran.jpg), „Dale Earnhardt - NASCAR Photography By Darryl Moran", https://creativecommons.org/licenses/by-sa/2.0/legalcode

Pamela Anderson, page 12
Darren Stone
(https://commons.wikimedia.org/wiki/File:Pamela_Anderson.jpg), „Pamela Anderson",
https://creativecommons.org/licenses/by-sa/2.0/legalcode

Steve Jobs, page 12
Matthew Yohe
(https://commons.wikimedia.org/wiki/File:SteveJobsMacbookAir.JPG), „SteveJobsMacbookAir", Cropped by Andrew Wood,
https://creativecommons.org/licenses/by/3.0/legalcode

Justin Bieber, page 13
Daniel Ogren
(https://commons.wikimedia.org/wiki/File:Justin_Bieber_at_Easter_Egg_roll.jpg), „Justin Bieber at Easter Egg roll",
https://creativecommons.org/licenses/by/2.0/legalcode

Ray Kroc, page 14
Unknown
(https://commons.wikimedia.org/wiki/File:Ray_kroc_1976.jpg), „Ray kroc 1976", marked as public domain, more details on Wikimedia Commons:
https://commons.wikimedia.org/wiki/Template:PD-US

McDonald's, page 14
Bruce Marlin
(https://commons.wikimedia.org/wiki/File:McDonalds_Museum.jpg), „McDonalds Museum",
https://creativecommons.org/licenses/by-sa/2.5/legalcode

Richard Branson, page 15
NASA
(https://commons.wikimedia.org/wiki/File:Richard_Branson.jpg), „Richard Branson", marked as public domain, more details on Wikimedia Commons:
https://commons.wikimedia.org/wiki/Template:PD-US

Colonel Sanders, page 15
Edgy01 at English Wikipedia
(https://commons.wikimedia.org/wiki/File:Colonel_Harland_Sanders_in_character_(cropped).jpg), „Colonel Harland Sanders in character (cropped)",
https://creativecommons.org/licenses/by-sa/3.0/legalcode

Bruce Jenner, page 16
Duncan Rawlinson/ @thelastminute/ Duncan.co
(https://commons.wikimedia.org/wiki/File:Bruce_Jenner_2012.jpg), „Bruce Jenner 2012",
https://creativecommons.org/licenses/by-sa/2.0/legalcode

Caitlyn Jenner, page 16
Web Summit
(https://commons.wikimedia.org/wiki/File:Caitlyn_Jenner_2017.jpg), „Caitlyn Jenner 2017",
https://creativecommons.org/licenses/by/2.0/legalcode

Eminem, page 18
DoD News Features
(https://commons.wikimedia.org/wiki/File:Eminem_-_Concert_for_Valor_in_Washington,_D.C._Nov._11,_2014_(2).jpg), „Eminem - Concert for Valor in Washington, D.C. Nov. 11, 2014 (2)", Cropped by Andrew Wood,
https://creativecommons.org/licenses/by/2.0/legalcode

Phil Knight, page 19
Neon Tommy
(https://commons.wikimedia.org/wiki/File:Philknightfootball.jpg), „Philknightfootball",
https://creativecommons.org/licenses/by-sa/2.0/legalcode

Ted Bundy, page 21
Unknown
(https://commons.wikimedia.org/wiki/File:FBI-360-Ted_Bundy_FBI_10_most_wanted_photo.jpg), „FBI-360-Ted Bundy FBI 10 most wanted photo", marked as public domain, more details on Wikimedia Commons:
https://commons.wikimedia.org/wiki/Template:PD-US

Jim Furyk, page 23
PGA golfer Jim Furyk
© Droopydogajna | Dreamstime.com
File ID: 50490279
License: Editorial

Elon Musk, page 31
Steve Jurvetson
(https://commons.wikimedia.org/wiki/File:Elon_Musk_2015.jpg), „Elon Musk 2015",
https://creativecommons.org/licenses/by/2.0/legalcode

Harrison Ford, page 34
Harrison Ford
© Starstock | Dreamstime.com
File ID: 58056735
License: Editorial

Joel Osteen, page 36
Justin Brackett
(https://commons.wikimedia.org/wiki/File:Joel_Osteen_Preaching_At_Lakewood_Church.jpg), Cropped by Andrew Wood,
https://creativecommons.org/licenses/by-sa/4.0/legalcode

Charlize Theron, page 40
Gage Skidmore from Peoria, AZ, United States of America (https://commons.wikimedia.org/wiki/File:Charlize_Theron_(36042687682).jpg), „Charlize Theron (36042687682)", https://creativecommons.org/licenses/by-sa/2.0/legalcode

Oprah Winfrey, page 41
© Laurence Agron | Dreamstime.com
File ID: 90841854
License: Editorial

Bruce Lee, page 42
A statue of Bruce Lee in a 'ready to strike' pose. The statue wa
© Atosan | Dreamstime.com
File ID: 57529724
License: Editorial

Bruce Lee's headstone, page 42
FLJuJitsu (https://commons.wikimedia.org/wiki/File:Bruce_Lee_1.JPG), „Bruce Lee 1", marked as public domain, more details on Wikimedia Commons: https://commons.wikimedia.org/wiki/Template:PD-self

Gary Player, page 43
Unknown (https://commons.wikimedia.org/wiki/File:Gary_Player_with_wife_and_her_mother_1961.jpg), „Gary Player with wife and her mother 1961", marked as public domain, more details on Wikimedia Commons: https://commons.wikimedia.org/wiki/Template:PD-US

Prince Harry, page 47
Prince Harry will attend the annual ICAP Charity Day
© | Dreamstime.com
File ID: 47607860
License: Editorial

Muhammad Ali, page 50
PA (https://commons.wikimedia.org/wiki/File:Muhammad_Ali_fights_Brian_London_on_August_6,_1966.jpg), „Muhammad Ali fights Brian London on August 6, 1966", Cropped by Andrew Wood, https://creativecommons.org/publicdomain/zero/1.0/legalcode

Ted Williams, page 51
Apex Photo Company (https://commons.wikimedia.org/wiki/File:1939_Ted_Williams.png), „1939 Ted Williams", marked as public domain, more details on Wikimedia Commons: https://commons.wikimedia.org/wiki/Template:PD-US

Steven Spielberg, page 64
Gage Skidmore (https://commons.wikimedia.org/wiki/File:Steven_Spielberg_by_Gage_Skidmore.jpg), „Steven Spielberg by Gage Skidmore", Flipped by Andrew Wood, https://creativecommons.org/licenses/by-sa/3.0/legalcode

Tom Brady, page 66
© Jerry Coli | Dreamstime.com
File ID: 73710053
License: Editorial

Beyonce, page 67
Beyonce Performs in Concert
© Michael Bush | Dreamstime.com
File ID: 128889119
License: Editorial

Cristiano Ronaldo, page 68
Анна Нэсси (https://commons.wikimedia.org/wiki/File:Cristiano_Ronaldo_2018.jpg), „Cristiano Ronaldo 2018", https://creativecommons.org/licenses/by-sa/3.0/legalcode

Winston Churchill, page 69
PA-Press Association (https://commons.wikimedia.org/wiki/File:Winston_Churchill_1949.jpg), https://creativecommons.org/licenses/by-sa/4.0/legalcode

John Wayne, page 70
Unknown photographer (https://commons.wikimedia.org/wiki/File:John_Wayne_-_still_portrait.jpg), „John Wayne - still portrait", marked as public domain, more details on Wikimedia Commons: https://commons.wikimedia.org/wiki/Template:PD-US

Elvis Presley, page 71
Metro-Goldwyn-Mayer, Inc. Reproduction Number: LC-USZ6-2067 Location: NYWTS -- BIOG (https://commons.wikimedia.org/wiki/File:YoungElvisPresley.jpg), „YoungElvisPresley", marked as public domain, more details on Wikimedia Commons: https://commons.wikimedia.org/wiki/Template:PD-US

Winston Churchill, page 71
British Government (https://commons.wikimedia.org/wiki/File:Churchill_1881_ZZZ_7555D.jpg), „Churchill 1881 ZZZ 7555D", marked as public domain, more details on Wikimedia Commons: https://commons.wikimedia.org/wiki/Template:PD-UKGov

Eminem, page 72
DOD News Features (https://commons.wikimedia.org/wiki/File:Eminem_performing_in_2014.jpg), „Eminem performing in 2014", Flipped by Andrew Wood, https://creativecommons.org/licenses/by/2.0/legalcode

Albert Einstein, page 73
Unknown (https://commons.wikimedia.org/wiki/File:EinsteinZeemanEhrenfest.jpg), „EinsteinZeemanEhrenfest"

Marie Curie, page 73
Henri Manuel (died 1947) (https://commons.wikimedia.org/wiki/File:Marie_Curie_c._1920s.jpg), „Marie Curie c. 1920s", marked as public domain, more details on Wikimedia Commons: https://commons.wikimedia.org/wiki/Template:PD-1996

General George S. Patton, page 74
Photo by U.S. Army Signal Corps (https://commons.wikimedia.org/wiki/File:GeorgeSPatton.jpg), „GeorgeSPatton", Cropped by Andrew Wood, https://creativecommons.org/publicdomain/zero/1.0/legalcode

Kobe Bryant, page 78
Keith Allison from Baltimore, USA (https://commons.wikimedia.org/wiki/File:Kobe_Bryant_Washington_Full.jpg), „Kobe Bryant Washington Full", Cropped by Andrew Wood, https://creativecommons.org/licenses/by-sa/2.0/legalcode

George H.W. Bush, page 80
David Hume Kennerly creator QS:P170,Q2612206 (https://commons.wikimedia.org/wiki/File:CIA_Director_George_H.W._Bush_listens_at_a_meeting_following_the_assassinations_in_Beirut,_1976_-_NARA_-_7064954.jpg), „CIA Director George H.W. Bush listens at a meeting following the assassinations in Beirut, 1976 - NARA - 7064954", Cropped and flipped by Andrew Wood, https://creativecommons.org/publicdomain/zero/1.0/legalcode

Lee Iacocca and Bill Clinton, page 81
Ralph Answang for the White House; photo archived in Clinton Presidential Library (https://commons.wikimedia.org/wiki/File:President_Bill_Clinton_meets_with_Lee_Iacocca_in_1993.jpg), „President Bill Clinton meets with Lee Iacocca in 1993", marked as public domain, more details on Wikimedia Commons: https://commons.wikimedia.org/wiki/Template:PD-US

Malcolm Gladwell, page 81
© Laurence Agron | Dreamstime.com
File ID: 111683277
License: Editorial

The Beatles, page 81
Iberia Airlines (https://commons.wikimedia.org/wiki/File:Los_Beatles_(19266969775)_Recortado.jpg), „Los Beatles (19266969775) Recortado", https://creativecommons.org/licenses/by/2.0/legalcode

John Wayne, page 82
unknown (Universal) (https://commons.wikimedia.org/wiki/File:Conflict_(1936)_1.jpg), „Conflict (1936) 1", marked as public domain, more details on Wikimedia Commons: https://commons.wikimedia.org/wiki/Template:PD-US

John Ford, page 82
The original uploader was Tillman at English Wikipedia. (https://commons.wikimedia.org/wiki/File:John_Ford,_1946.jpg), „John Ford, 1946", Cropped by Andrew Wood, https://creativecommons.org/publicdomain/zero/1.0/legalcode

Wyatt Earp, page 83
unattributed (https://commons.wikimedia.org/wiki/File:Wyatt_Earp_portrait.png), „Wyatt Earp portrait", marked as public domain, more details on Wikimedia Commons: https://commons.wikimedia.org/wiki/Template:PD-US

John Wayne, page 84
A9Y734
Pictorial Press Ltd / Alamy Stock Photo

Robert De Niro, page 86
GianAngelo Pistoia (https://commons.wikimedia.org/wiki/File:Robert_De_Niro_-_GianAngelo_Pistoia.jpg), „Robert De Niro - GianAngelo Pistoia", https://creativecommons.org/licenses/by-sa/3.0/legalcode

Marlon Brando, page 86
Carl Van Vechten creator QS:P170,Q312851
(https://commons.wikimedia.org/wiki/File:Marlon_Brando_Streetcar_1948_e.jpg), „Marlon Brando Streetcar 1948 e", marked as public domain, more details on Wikimedia Commons:
https://commons.wikimedia.org/wiki/Template:Library of Congress-no known copyright restrictions

UCLA Basketball, page 87
Associated Students of the University of California at Los Angeles
(https://commons.wikimedia.org/wiki/File:UCLA_after_1971_NCAA_championship.png), „UCLA after 1971 NCAA championship", marked as public domain, more details on Wikimedia Commons:
https://commons.wikimedia.org/wiki/Template:PD-US

John Wooden, page 87
Associated Students of the University of California at Los Angeles
(https://commons.wikimedia.org/wiki/File:John_Wooden.JPG), „John Wooden", marked as public domain, more details on Wikimedia Commons:
https://commons.wikimedia.org/wiki/Template:PD-US

Michael Schumacher, page 90
F1 2005 - Michael Schumacher Ferrari
© Fabrice Gallou | Dreamstime.com
File ID: 10801740
License: Editorial

Bill Gates and Angela Merkel, page 92
Bil Gates, Angela Merkel
© Markwaters | Dreamstime.com
File ID: 8003460
License: Editorial

Billy Mays, page 96
Sharese Ann Frederick from Purchase, N.Y.
(https://commons.wikimedia.org/wiki/File:Billy_Mays_Portrait_Cropped.jpg), „Billy Mays Portrait Cropped",
https://creativecommons.org/licenses/by-sa/2.0/legalcode

Whoopi Goldberg, page 98
Whoopi Goldberg.
© Laurence Agron | Dreamstime.com
File ID: 106782205
License: Editorial

Chuck Connors, page 100
ABC Television-the back image has been rotated and altered to make it visible and legible enough to see the ABC information on it.
(https://commons.wikimedia.org/wiki/File:Chuck_Connors_The_Rifleman_1959.JPG), „Chuck Connors The Rifleman 1959", marked as public domain, more details on Wikimedia Commons:
https://commons.wikimedia.org/wiki/Template:PD-US

The Clash, page 101
Helge Øverås,
http://www.helgeoveras.com/concertphoto.shtml
(https://commons.wikimedia.org/wiki/File:Clash_21051980_12_800.jpg), „Clash 21051980 12 800",
https://creativecommons.org/licenses/by-sa/3.0/legalcode

Elvis Costello, page 102
Victor Diaz Lamich
(https://commons.wikimedia.org/wiki/File:Elvis_costello.jpg), „Elvis costello",
https://creativecommons.org/licenses/by-sa/3.0/legalcode

Marilyn Monroe, page 103
Dell Publications, Inc. New York, publisher of Modern Screen
(https://commons.wikimedia.org/wiki/File:Marilyn_Monroe_at_Ciro's.jpg), „Marilyn Monroe at Ciro's", marked as public domain, more details on Wikimedia Commons:
https://commons.wikimedia.org/wiki/Template:PD-US

Madonna, page 104
Madonna
© Laurence Agron | Dreamstime.com
File ID: 89403274
License: Editorial

MASH TV Cast, page 105
CBS Television
(https://commons.wikimedia.org/wiki/File:MASH_TV_cast_1975.JPG), „MASH TV cast 1975", marked as public domain, more details on Wikimedia Commons:
https://commons.wikimedia.org/wiki/Template:PD-US

Jay-Z, page 105
i am guilty (https://commons.wikimedia.org/wiki/File:Jay-Z_concert_(cropped).jpg), „Jay-Z concert (cropped)",
https://creativecommons.org/licenses/by-sa/2.0/legalcode

Pink, page 106
Pink
© Starstock | Dreamstime.com
File ID: 99080038
License: Editorial

Bono, page 106
Bono
© Simonemillward | Dreamstime.com
File ID: 35163636
License: Editorial

Michael Caine, page 106
Unknown
(https://commons.wikimedia.org/wiki/File:Behind-the-scenes-zulu-1964.jpg), „Behind-the-scenes-zulu-1964", marked as public domain, more details on Wikimedia Commons:
https://commons.wikimedia.org/wiki/Template:PD-US

Johnny Miller, page 107
Johnny Miller
© Jerry Coli | Dreamstime.com
File ID: 73982213
License: Editorial

Gene Sarazen, page 107
National Photo Company Collection
(https://commons.wikimedia.org/wiki/File:Gene_Sarazen_1922.jpg), „Gene Sarazen 1922", marked as public domain, more details on Wikimedia Commons:
https://commons.wikimedia.org/wiki/Template:PD-1923

Mark Twain, page 108
Unknown
(https://commons.wikimedia.org/wiki/File:MarkTwain.LOC.jpg), „MarkTwain.LOC", marked as public domain, more details on Wikimedia Commons:
https://commons.wikimedia.org/wiki/Template:PD-US

Evel Knievel, page 108
Unknown
(https://commons.wikimedia.org/wiki/File:Evel_Knievel_c1974cr.jpg), „Evel Knievel c1974cr", marked as public domain, more details on Wikimedia Commons:
https://commons.wikimedia.org/wiki/Template:PD-US

Stephen King, page 109
Pinguino Kolb
(https://commons.wikimedia.org/wiki/File:Stephen_King,_Comicon.jpg), „Stephen King, Comicon",
https://creativecommons.org/licenses/by/2.0/legalcode

John le Carré, page 110
German Embassy London
(https://commons.wikimedia.org/wiki/File:John_le_Carré_signing_books_after_the_ceremony_(35239522786).jpg), „John le Carré signing books after the ceremony (35239522786)",
https://creativecommons.org/licenses/by/2.0/legalcode

Rodney Dangerfield, page 112
Press photo, photographer unknown
(https://commons.wikimedia.org/wiki/File:Rodney_Danagerfield_1972-1.jpg), „Rodney Danagerfield 1972-1", Background Removed by Andrew Wood,
https://creativecommons.org/publicdomain/zero/1.0/legalcode

Bruce Springsteen, page 113
Bruce springsteen, the Boss in concert
© Juan Carlos Gomez Garcia | Dreamstime.com
File ID: 83473501
License: Editorial

Frank Sinatra, page 114
Frank Sinatra
(https://commons.wikimedia.org/wiki/File:Frank-sinatra-9484810-3-402.jpg),
https://creativecommons.org/licenses/by-sa/4.0/legalcode

Tiger Woods, page 114
Tiger Woods at Doral in Miami
© Michael Bush | Dreamstime.com
File ID: 128890739
License: Editorial

Magic Johnson, page 115
Magic Johnson
© Jerry Coli | Dreamstime.com
File ID: 78445804
License: Editorial

Babe Ruth, page 116
Unknown
(https://commons.wikimedia.org/wiki/File:Babe_Ruth_1922.jpeg), „Babe Ruth 1922", marked as public domain, more details on Wikimedia Commons:
https://commons.wikimedia.org/wiki/Template:PD-US

Robert Plant, page 117
Dina Regine (https://commons.wikimedia.org/wiki/File:Robert-Plant.jpg), „Robert-Plant", https://creativecommons.org/licenses/by-sa/2.0/legalcode

The Beatles, page 118
Eric Koch, Nationaal Archief, Den Haag, Rijksfotoarchief: Fotocollectie Algemeen Nederlands Fotopersbureau (ANEFO), 1945-1989 - negatiefstroken zwart/wit, nummer toegang 2.24.01.05, bestanddeelnummer 916-5098 (https://commons.wikimedia.org/wiki/File:The_Beatles_with_Jimmie_Nicol_916-5098.jpg), „The Beatles with Jimmie Nicol 916-5098", Cropped by Andrew Wood, https://creativecommons.org/licenses/by-sa/3.0/nl/deed.en

Stone Temple Pilots, page 119
Jeck M. (https://commons.wikimedia.org/wiki/File:Stone_Temple_Pilots_band_in_Manila.jpg), „Stone Temple Pilots band in Manila", https://creativecommons.org/licenses/by/2.0/legalcode

KISS, page 120
Alberto Cabello from Vitoria Gasteiz (https://commons.wikimedia.org/wiki/File:KISS_-_Azkena_Rock_Festival_2010_1.jpg), „KISS - Azkena Rock Festival 2010 1", https://creativecommons.org/licenses/by/2.0/legalcode

Hugh Hefner, page 121
Promifotos.de (https://commons.wikimedia.org/wiki/File:Hefner2006.jpg), „Hefner2006", https://creativecommons.org/licenses/by-sa/3.0/legalcode

Larry Page and Serge Brin, page 122
Joi Ito from Inbamura, Japan (https://commons.wikimedia.org/wiki/File:Schmidt-Brin-Page-20080520.jpg), „Schmidt-Brin-Page-20080520", Cropped by Andrew Wood, https://creativecommons.org/licenses/by/2.0/legalcode

Onitsuka Tiger, page 122
FRED (https://commons.wikimedia.org/wiki/File:ASICS.Onitsuka_Tiger.Mexico_66.White.Blue.Red.JPG), „ASICS.Onitsuka Tiger.Mexico 66.White.Blue.Red", https://creativecommons.org/licenses/by-sa/3.0/legalcode

Fred DeLuca, page 123
Subway (https://commons.wikimedia.org/wiki/File:Fred_De_Luca_2011-03-09_001.jpg), „Fred De Luca 2011-03-09 001", https://creativecommons.org/licenses/by/3.0/legalcode

Jeff Bezoz, page 124
Seattle City Council from Seattle (https://commons.wikimedia.org/wiki/File:Jeff_Bezos_at_Amazon_Spheres_Grand_Opening_in_Seattle_-_2018_(39074799225)_(cropped).jpg), „Jeff Bezos at Amazon Spheres Grand Opening in Seattle - 2018 (39074799225) (cropped)", https://creativecommons.org/licenses/by/2.0/legalcode

Apple logo, page 124
Original: Rob Janoff (https://commons.wikimedia.org/wiki/File:Apple_logo_black.svg), „Apple logo black", Color swap to white by Andrew Wood, https://creativecommons.org/publicdomain/zero/1.0/legalcode

Walter Cronkite, page 128
Rob Bogaerts / Anefo (https://commons.wikimedia.org/wiki/File:Walter_Cronkite_(1985).jpg), „Walter Cronkite (1985)", https://creativecommons.org/licenses/by-sa/3.0/nl/deed.en

Batman TV Series, page 129
Greenway Productions-producer of both the television series and the 1966 film. (https://commons.wikimedia.org/wiki/File:Batman_and_Robin_1966.JPG), „Batman and Robin 1966", marked as public domain, more details on Wikimedia Commons: https://commons.wikimedia.org/wiki/Template:PD-US

Ennio Morricone, page 133
LucaChp (https://commons.wikimedia.org/wiki/File:EnnioMorricone.jpg), „EnnioMorricone", https://creativecommons.org/licenses/by-sa/3.0/legalcode

Casey Jones, page 134
Casey Jones drives a train
PHOTO: Casey Jones Home and Railroad Museum

Clint Eastwood, page 136
movie studio (https://commons.wikimedia.org/wiki/File:Clint_Eastwood_-_1960s_(cropped).JPG), „Clint Eastwood - 1960s (cropped)", Background Removed by Andrew Wood, https://creativecommons.org/publicdomain/zero/1.0/legalcode

Greta Garbo, page 137
MGM (https://en.wikipedia.org/wiki/File:Greta_Garbo_-_1935.jpg), „Greta Garbo - 1935", marked as public domain, more details on Wikimedia Commons: https://commons.wikimedia.org/wiki/Template:PD-US

Michael Caine, page 139
Fred Ohert / Hufvudstadsbladet (https://commons.wikimedia.org/wiki/File:Michael-Caine-in-Helsinki-1967-c.jpg), „Michael-Caine-in-Helsinki-1967-c", marked as public domain, more details on Wikimedia Commons: https://commons.wikimedia.org/wiki/Template:PD-Finland

Gerald Ford, page 140
David Hume Kennerly creator QS:P170,Q2612206 (https://commons.wikimedia.org/wiki/File:President_Ford_campaigns_at_the_Nassau_County_Veterans_Coliseum_-_NARA_-_7027912.jpg), „President Ford campaigns at the Nassau County Veterans Coliseum - NARA - 7027912", marked as public domain, more details on Wikimedia Commons: https://commons.wikimedia.org/wiki/Template:PD-US

Rod Stewart, page 144
Rod Stewart
© Sbukley | Dreamstime.com
File ID: 30010500
License: Editorial

Audrey Hepburn, page 145
Audrey Hepburn (https://commons.wikimedia.org/wiki/File:Audrey_Hepburn_smokes.jpg), „Audrey Hepburn smokes", marked as public domain, more details on Wikimedia Commons: https://commons.wikimedia.org/wiki/Template:PD-1923

Lady Gaga, page 146
proacguy1 from Montreal, Canada (https://commons.wikimedia.org/wiki/File:Lady_Gaga,_ARTPOP_Ball_Tour,_Bell_Center,_Montréal,_2_July_2014_(47)_(14376657959).jpg), „Lady Gaga, ARTPOP Ball Tour, Bell Center, Montréal, 2 July 2014 (47) (14376657959)", https://creativecommons.org/licenses/by-sa/2.0/legalcode

Don King, page 147
Don King and Mike Tyson (cropped)
© Jerry Coli | Dreamstime.com
File ID: 22628211
License: Editorial

The Beatles, page 148
United Press International, photographer unknown (https://commons.wikimedia.org/wiki/File:The_Beatles_in_America.JPG), „The Beatles in America", Cropped by Andrew Wood, https://creativecommons.org/publicdomain/zero/1.0/legalcode

Josephine Baker, page 149
Walery, Polish-British, 1863-1929 (https://commons.wikimedia.org/wiki/File:Baker_Charleston.jpg), „Baker Charleston", marked as public domain, more details on Wikimedia Commons: https://commons.wikimedia.org/wiki/Template:PD-old

Farrah Fawcett, page 150
ABC Television (https://commons.wikimedia.org/wiki/File:Farrah_Fawcett_1977.JPG), „Farrah Fawcett 1977", marked as public domain, more details on Wikimedia Commons: https://commons.wikimedia.org/wiki/Template:PD-US

Brigitte Bardot, page 151
MGM (https://commons.wikimedia.org/wiki/File:Brigitte_Bardot_-_1962.jpg), „Brigitte Bardot - 1962", Flipped by Andrew Wood, https://creativecommons.org/publicdomain/zero/1.0/legalcode

Richard Branson, page 151
Sir Richard Branson
© Carrienelson1 | Dreamstime.com
File ID: 26490893
License: Editorial

Dolly Parton, page 151
Eva Rinaldi creator QS:P170,Q37885816 (https://commons.wikimedia.org/wiki/File:Dolly_Parton,_2011.jpg), „Dolly Parton, 2011", https://creativecommons.org/licenses/by-sa/2.0/legalcode

Telly Savalas, page 152
CBS Television (https://commons.wikimedia.org/wiki/File:Telly_Savalas_Kojak_1973.JPG), „Telly Savalas Kojak 1973", marked as public domain, more details on Wikimedia Commons: https://commons.wikimedia.org/wiki/Template:PD-US

Andre Agasi, page 153
Andre Agassi (background removed)
© Jerry Coli | Dreamstime.com
File ID: 74522177
License: Editorial

William Shatner, page 154
NBC Television
(https://commons.wikimedia.org/wiki/File:Captain_kirk_publicity_photo.jpg), „Captain kirk publicity photo", marked as public domain, more details on Wikimedia Commons:
https://commons.wikimedia.org/wiki/Template:PD-US

Sean Connery, page 155
photo by Alan Light
(https://commons.wikimedia.org/wiki/File:Sean_Connery.jpg), „Sean Connery",
https://creativecommons.org/licenses/by/2.0/legalcode

Slash, page 156
Slash
© Tudor Marian | Dreamstime.com
File ID: 47502426
License: Editorial

Devo, page 157
LivePict.com
(https://commons.wikimedia.org/wiki/File:Devo_2008.05.31_004.jpg), „Devo 2008.05.31 004",
https://creativecommons.org/licenses/by-sa/3.0/legalcode

Bob Marley, page 158
Paul Weinberg
(https://commons.wikimedia.org/wiki/File:Bob_marley_01.jpg), „Bob marley 01", https://creativecommons.org/licenses/by-sa/3.0/legalcode

Hulk Hogan, page 159
Hulk Hogan
© Starstock | Dreamstime.com
File ID: 77991345
License: Editorial

Oddjob, page 159
HEHFAP
AF Archive / Alamy Stock Photo

Richard Petty, page 160
Richard Petty
© Jerry Coli | Dreamstime.com
File ID: 74034446
License: Editorial

Che Guevara, page 161
Alberto Korda
(https://commons.wikimedia.org/wiki/File:CheHigh.jpg), „CheHigh", marked as public domain, more details on Wikimedia Commons:
https://commons.wikimedia.org/wiki/Template:PD-Cuba

Queen Elizabeth, page 162
www.nationalarchives.gov.uk/doc/open-government-licence/version/3/

John Lennon and Yoko Ono, page 164
Eric Koch / Anefo
(https://commons.wikimedia.org/wiki/File:John_Lennon_en_zijn_echtgenote_Yoko_Ono_op_huwelijksreis_in_Amsterdam._John_Lenn,_Bestanddeelnr_922-2305.jpg), „John Lennon en zijn echtgenote Yoko Ono op huwelijksreis in Amsterdam. John Lenn, Bestanddeelnr 922-2305",
https://creativecommons.org/publicdomain/zero/1.0/legalcode

Elton John, page 164
Elton John
© Featureflash | Dreamstime.com
File ID: 26491296
License: Editorial

Tom Cruise, page 164
Tom Cruise
© Featureflash | Dreamstime.com
File ID: 25588076
License: Editorial

Bono, page 165
Bono
© Simonemillward | Dreamstime.com
File ID: 35163659
License: Editorial

Buffalo Bill, page 167
Moffett, Chicago
(https://commons.wikimedia.org/wiki/File:Cody-Buffalo-Bill-LOC.jpg), „Cody-Buffalo-Bill-LOC", marked as public domain, more details on Wikimedia Commons:
https://commons.wikimedia.org/wiki/Template:PD-US

Tom Selleck, page 168
Tom Selleck
© Carrienelson1 | Dreamstime.com
File ID: 27156986
License: Editorial

ZZ Top, page 169
Ralph Arvesen
(https://commons.wikimedia.org/wiki/File:ZZ_Top_2015.jpg), „ZZ Top 2015",
https://creativecommons.org/licenses/by/2.0/legalcode

Mark Twain, page 170
Unknown
(https://commons.wikimedia.org/wiki/File:MarkTwain.LOC.jpg), „MarkTwain.LOC", marked as public domain, more details on Wikimedia Commons:
https://commons.wikimedia.org/wiki/Template:PD-US

Charlie Chaplin, page 171
Charlie Chaplin
© Martial Genest | Dreamstime.com
File ID: 36142761
License: Editorial

Rollie Fingers, page 173
Rubenstein
(https://commons.wikimedia.org/wiki/File:Flickr_-_Rubenstein_-_Rollie_Fingers.jpg), „Flickr - Rubenstein - Rollie Fingers",
https://creativecommons.org/licenses/by/2.0/legalcode

Peter Falk, page 174
Margie Korshak Associates-publicity agency-Falk was appearing at an awards dinner in Chicago.
(https://commons.wikimedia.org/wiki/File:Columbo_Peter_Falk_1973.JPG), „Columbo Peter Falk 1973", marked as public domain, more details on Wikimedia Commons:
https://commons.wikimedia.org/wiki/Template:PD-US

Leonard Nimoy, page 175
NBC Television
(https://commons.wikimedia.org/wiki/File:Leonard_Nimoy_Spock_1967.jpg), „Leonard Nimoy Spock 1967", marked as public domain, more details on Wikimedia Commons:
https://commons.wikimedia.org/wiki/Template:PD-US

Henry Winkler, page 176
ABC Television
(https://commons.wikimedia.org/wiki/File:Henry_Winkler_Fonzie_1977.JPG), „Henry Winkler Fonzie 1977", marked as public domain, more details on Wikimedia Commons:
https://commons.wikimedia.org/wiki/Template:PD-US

Marilyn Chambert, page 177
pinguino k from North Hollywood, USA
(https://commons.wikimedia.org/wiki/File:Chambers,_Marilyn_(2008).jpg), „Chambers, Marilyn (2008)", Cropped by Andrew Wood,
https://creativecommons.org/licenses/by/2.0/legalcode

John F. Kennedy, page 178
PD-USGOV
(https://commons.wikimedia.org/wiki/File:Jfk2.jpg), „Jfk2", marked as public domain, more details on Wikimedia Commons:
https://commons.wikimedia.org/wiki/Template:PD-US

Pierce Brosnan, page 179
Pierce Brosnan
© Denis Makarenko | Dreamstime.com
File ID: 13610188
License: Editorial

Johnny Cash, page 180
User:Johnnycash1950-2003
(https://commons.wikimedia.org/wiki/File:At_San_quentin_1969_2014-05-04_00-14.jpg), „At San quentin 1969 2014-05-04 00-14",
https://creativecommons.org/licenses/by-sa/3.0/legalcode

Gary Player, page 181
Lady 11390
(https://commons.wikimedia.org/wiki/File:All_Black.jpg), „All Black", marked as public domain, more details on Wikimedia Commons:
https://commons.wikimedia.org/wiki/Template:PD-self

Steve Jobs, page 182
Steve Jobs
© Featureflash | Dreamstime.com
File ID: 34830322
License: Editorial

Clint Eastwood, page 182
Unknown photographer
(https://commons.wikimedia.org/wiki/File:Eastwood_Publicity_Still_1960s.jpg), „Eastwood Publicity Still 1960s", marked as public domain, more details on Wikimedia Commons:
https://commons.wikimedia.org/wiki/Template:PD-US

Payne Stewart, page 183
Payne Stewart
© Jerry Coli | Dreamstime.com
File ID: 35108312
License: Editorial

Madonna, page 184
Madonna
© Alexandre DurÃ£o | Dreamstime.com
File ID: 104271834
License: Editorial

Muhammad Ali, page 186
Muhammad Ali v. Leon Spinks
© Jerry Coli | Dreamstime.com
File ID: 21169288
License: Editorial

Bruce Springsteen, page 187
SPRINGSTEEN
© Scott Anderson | Dreamstime.com
File ID: 22709158
License: Editorial

Bjorn Borg, page 189
Bjorn Borg
© Jerry Coli | Dreamstime.com
File ID: 74159758
License: Editorial

Evel Knievel, page 191
F6M13H
Entertainment Pictures / Alamy Stock Photo

Albert Einstein, page 193
Photograph by Orren Jack Turner, Princeton, N.J. Modified with Photoshop by PM_Poon and later by Dantadd.
(https://commons.wikimedia.org/wiki/File:Albert_Einstein_Head.jpg), „Albert Einstein Head", marked as public domain, more details on Wikimedia Commons:
https://commons.wikimedia.org/wiki/Template:PD-US

Barbra Streisand, page 193
Al Ravenna, World Telegram staff photographer
(https://commons.wikimedia.org/wiki/File:Barbra_Streisand_1962.jpg), „Barbra Streisand 1962", marked as public domain, more details on Wikimedia Commons:
https://commons.wikimedia.org/wiki/Template:Library of Congress-no known copyright restrictions

David Beckham, page 194
Brian MInkoff-London Pixels
(https://commons.wikimedia.org/wiki/File:Beckswimbledon.jpg), „Beckswimbledon", Flipped by Andrew Wood,
https://creativecommons.org/licenses/by-sa/3.0/legalcode

Vladimir Putin, page 196
Kremlin.ru
(https://commons.wikimedia.org/wiki/File:Pyotr_Velikiy_battlecruiser_4.jpg),
https://creativecommons.org/licenses/by/4.0/legalcode

Kremlin.ru
(https://commons.wikimedia.org/wiki/File:Vladimir_Putin_Cockpit_TU-160_Bomber.jpg),
https://creativecommons.org/licenses/by/4.0/legalcode

Kremlin.ru
(https://commons.wikimedia.org/wiki/File:2016_IIHF_World_Championship._Final_match_(2016-05-22)-08.jpg), Cropped by Andrew Wood,
https://creativecommons.org/licenses/by/4.0/legalcode

Kremlin.ru
(https://commons.wikimedia.org/wiki/File:Vladimir_Putin_2_April_2002-2.jpg),
https://creativecommons.org/licenses/by/4.0/legalcode

premier.gov.ru
(https://commons.wikimedia.org/wiki/File:Putin_drives_Formula_1.png), https://creativecommons.org/licenses/by/4.0/legalcode

Kremlin.ru
(https://commons.wikimedia.org/wiki/File:Vladimir_Putin_FIFA_World_Cup_Trophy_Tour_kick-off_ceremony.jpg),
https://creativecommons.org/licenses/by/4.0/legalcode

Barack Obama, page 197
MCC ERIC A. CLEMENT, USN
(https://commons.wikimedia.org/wiki/File:BarackObama-Basketball.JPEG), „BarackObama-Basketball", marked as public domain, more details on Wikimedia Commons:
https://commons.wikimedia.org/wiki/Template:PD-US

Winston Churchill, page 198
War Office official photographer, Horton (Capt)
(https://commons.wikimedia.org/wiki/File:Winston_Churchill_As_Prime_Minister_1940-1945_H2646A.jpg), „Winston Churchill As Prime Minister 1940-1945 H2646A", marked as public domain, more details on Wikimedia Commons:
https://commons.wikimedia.org/wiki/Template:PD-UKGov

Ernest Hemingway, pages 199-201

Not specified, owned by John F. Kennedy library
(https://commons.wikimedia.org/wiki/File:Hemingway_and_Marlins.jpg), „Hemingway and Marlins", marked as public domain, more details on Wikimedia Commons:
https://commons.wikimedia.org/wiki/Template:PD-US

Unknown photographer
(https://commons.wikimedia.org/wiki/File:Gellhorn_Hemingway_1941.jpg), „Gellhorn Hemingway 1941", marked as public domain, more details on Wikimedia Commons:
https://commons.wikimedia.org/wiki/Template:PD-because

unattributed
(https://commons.wikimedia.org/wiki/File:Ernest_Hemingway_skiing,_Switzerland,_1927.jpg), „Ernest Hemingway skiing, Switzerland, 1927", marked as public domain, more details on Wikimedia Commons:
https://commons.wikimedia.org/wiki/Template:PD-US

unattributed
(https://commons.wikimedia.org/wiki/File:Ernest_and_Mary_Hemingway_on_safari,_1953-54.jpg), „Ernest and Mary Hemingway on safari, 1953-54", marked as public domain, more details on Wikimedia Commons:
https://commons.wikimedia.org/wiki/Template:PD-US

unattributed
(https://commons.wikimedia.org/wiki/File:Ernest_Hemingway_and_Carlos_Gutierrez_aboard_Pilar,_Key_West,_1934.jpg), „Ernest Hemingway and Carlos Gutierrez aboard Pilar, Key West, 1934", marked as public domain, more details on Wikimedia Commons:
https://commons.wikimedia.org/wiki/Template:PD-US

unattributed
(https://commons.wikimedia.org/wiki/File:Ernest_Hemingway_and_Buck_Lanham,_1944.jpg), „Ernest Hemingway and Buck Lanham, 1944", marked as public domain, more details on Wikimedia Commons:
https://commons.wikimedia.org/wiki/Template:PD-US

unattributed
(https://commons.wikimedia.org/wiki/File:Ernest_Hemingway_at_the_Finca_Vigia,_Cuba_1946.png), „Ernest Hemingway at the Finca Vigia, Cuba 1946", marked as public domain, more details on Wikimedia Commons:
https://commons.wikimedia.org/wiki/Template:PD-US

unattributed
(https://commons.wikimedia.org/wiki/File:Ernest_Hemingway_on_safari,_1934.jpg), „Ernest Hemingway on safari, 1934", marked as public domain, more details on Wikimedia Commons:
https://commons.wikimedia.org/wiki/Template:PD-US

unattributed
(https://commons.wikimedia.org/wiki/File:Ernest_Hemingway_poses_with_water_buffalo,_Africa,_1953.jpg), „Ernest Hemingway poses with water buffalo, Africa, 1953", marked as public domain, more details on Wikimedia Commons:
https://commons.wikimedia.org/wiki/Template:PD-copyright holder

unattributed
(https://commons.wikimedia.org/wiki/File:Ernest_Hemingway_on_Safari_in_Africa_c1933.png), „Ernest Hemingway on Safari in Africa c1933", marked as public domain, more details on Wikimedia Commons:
https://commons.wikimedia.org/wiki/Template:PD-US

FDR and Churchill, page 202
US government photographer
(https://commons.wikimedia.org/wiki/File:Yalta_Conference_(Churchill,_Roosevelt,_Stalin)_(B&W).jpg), „Yalta Conference (Churchill, Roosevelt, Stalin) (B&W)", marked as public domain, more details on Wikimedia Commons:
https://commons.wikimedia.org/wiki/Template:PD-US

Ronald Reagan, page 203-204
White House Photographic Office
(https://commons.wikimedia.org/wiki/File:ReaganBerlinWall.jpg), „ReaganBerlinWall", marked as public domain, more details on Wikimedia Commons:
https://commons.wikimedia.org/wiki/Template:PD-US

Michael Evans creator QS:P170,Q13475480
(https://commons.wikimedia.org/wiki/File:President_Reagan_speaking_in_Minneapolis_1982.jpg), „President Reagan speaking in Minneapolis 1982", marked as public domain, more details on Wikimedia Commons:
https://commons.wikimedia.org/wiki/Template:PD-US

Bob Galbraith
(https://commons.wikimedia.org/wiki/File:Reagan_and_Gorbachev_in_western_hats_1992.jpg), „Reagan and Gorbachev in western hats 1992", marked as public domain, more details on Wikimedia Commons:
https://commons.wikimedia.org/wiki/Template:PD-US

Montparnasse derailment, page 205
Photo credited to the firm Levy & fils by this site. (It is credited to a photographer "Kuhn" by another publisher [1].)
(https://commons.wikimedia.org/wiki/File:Train_wreck_at_Montparnasse_1895.jpg), „Train wreck at Montparnasse 1895", marked as public domain, more details on Wikimedia Commons:
https://commons.wikimedia.org/wiki/Template:PD-1923

Gerald Ford, page 207
CP46TW
Everett Collection Inc / Alamy Stock Photo

Jane Fonda, page 209
Mieremet, Rob / Anefo
(https://commons.wikimedia.org/wiki/File:Jane_Fonda_1975d.jpg), „Jane Fonda 1975d",
https://creativecommons.org/licenses/by-sa/3.0/nl/deed.en

August Landmesser, page 208
Unknown
(https://commons.wikimedia.org/wiki/File:August-Landmesser-Almanya-1936.jpg), „August-Landmesser-Almanya-1936", marked as public domain, more details on Wikimedia Commons:
https://commons.wikimedia.org/wiki/Template:PD-anon-70

Elvis Presley with Richard Nixon, page 212
Ollie Atkins, chief White House photographer at the time. See ARC record. (https://commons.wikimedia.org/wiki/File:Elvis-nixon.jpg), „Elvis-nixon", Cropped by Andrew Wood, https://creativecommons.org/publicdomain/zero/1.0/legalcode

Ronald and Nancy Reagan with Prince Charles and Princess Diana, page 212
Courtesy Ronald Reagan Library [1] (https://commons.wikimedia.org/wiki/File:Prince_Charles,_Princess_Diana,_Nancy_Reagan,_and_Ronald_Reagan_(1985).jpg), „Prince Charles, Princess Diana, Nancy Reagan, and Ronald Reagan (1985)", marked as public domain, more details on Wikimedia Commons: https://commons.wikimedia.org/wiki/Template:PD-US

Dolly Parton with George and Laura Bush, page 212
White House photo by Eric Draper (https://commons.wikimedia.org/wiki/File:2006_Kennedy_Center_honorees.jpg), „2006 Kennedy Center honorees", marked as public domain, more details on Wikimedia Commons: https://commons.wikimedia.org/wiki/Template:PD-US

Donny Osmond, page 213
Rob Mieremet (ANEFO) (https://commons.wikimedia.org/wiki/File:Osmonds1973.jpg), „Osmonds1973", https://creativecommons.org/publicdomain/zero/1.0/legalcode

Angelyne, page 216
C9DMN3
Nik Wheeler / Alamy Stock Photo

Orville Redenbacher, page 220
Hunt-Wesson (https://commons.wikimedia.org/wiki/File:Orville_Redenbacher_1979.jpg), „Orville Redenbacher 1979", marked as public domain, more details on Wikimedia Commons: https://commons.wikimedia.org/wiki/Template:PD-US

Annie Leibovitz, page 222
Robert Scoble from Half Moon Bay, USA (https://commons.wikimedia.org/wiki/File:Annie_Leibovitz-SF-1-Crop.jpg), „Annie Leibovitz-SF-1-Crop", https://creativecommons.org/licenses/by/2.0/legalcode

Adriana Lima, page 223
Adriana Lima,Victoria's Secret
© Featureflash | Dreamstime.com
File ID: 36733160
License: Editorial

Abraham Lincoln, page 225
Archives New Zealand from New Zealand (https://commons.wikimedia.org/wiki/File:Abraham_Lincoln_(13552661785).jpg), „Abraham Lincoln (13552661785)", https://creativecommons.org/licenses/by-sa/2.0/legalcode

Steve McQueen, page 228
CBS Television (https://commons.wikimedia.org/wiki/File:Steve_McQueen_1960.JPG), „Steve McQueen 1960", marked as public domain, more details on Wikimedia Commons: https://commons.wikimedia.org/wiki/Template:PD-US

Naomi Campbell, page 229
The original uploader was Jgro888 at English Wikipedia. (https://commons.wikimedia.org/wiki/File:NaomiCampbell.jpg), „NaomiCampbell", https://creativecommons.org/licenses/by-sa/2.5/legalcode

Giesle Bundchen, page 229
Tiago Chediak (https://commons.wikimedia.org/wiki/File:Gisele_Bundchen2.jpg), „Gisele Bundchen2", https://creativecommons.org/licenses/by/2.0/legalcode

Steven Spielberg, page 230
Steven Spielberg
© Featureflash | Dreamstime.com
File ID: 32741289
License: Editorial

Banksy art, pages 231-233
Infrogmation of New Orleans (https://commons.wikimedia.org/wiki/File:Banksy_Swinger_Building_Detail.jpg), „Banksy Swinger Building Detail", https://creativecommons.org/licenses/by/2.0/legalcode

Markus Ortner (https://commons.wikimedia.org/wiki/File:Mauer-betlehem.jpg), „Mauer-betlehem", https://creativecommons.org/licenses/by-sa/2.5/legalcode

The original uploader was Ajuk at English Wikipedia.. The photographer's rights have been released under the following licences: (https://commons.wikimedia.org/wiki/File:Banksy-ps.jpg), „Banksy-ps", https://creativecommons.org/licenses/by-sa/3.0/legalcode

Marilyn Monroe, page 236
Published by Corpus Christi Caller-Times-photo from Associated Press (https://commons.wikimedia.org/wiki/File:Marilyn_Monroe_photo_pose_Seven_Year_Itch.jpg), „Marilyn Monroe photo pose Seven Year Itch", marked as public domain, more details on Wikimedia Commons: https://commons.wikimedia.org/wiki/Template:PD-US

Michael Jordan, page 238
Michael Jordan Chicago Bulls
© Jerry Coli | Dreamstime.com
File ID: 73480263
License: Editorial

John Wayne, page 241
EK3MHT
Glasshouse Images / Alamy Stock Photo

David Beckham, page 242
Beckham Shirtless
© Jingraham311 | Dreamstime.com
File ID: 24448651
License: Editorial

General George S. Patton, page 243
Uberti Patton Commemorative
© Ambopicinc | Dreamstime.com
File ID: 48066209
License: Editorial

James Bond Aston Martin from Goldfinger, page 245
Chilterngreen (https://commons.wikimedia.org/wiki/File:DB5-2.jpg), „DB5-2", https://creativecommons.org/licenses/by-sa/3.0/legalcode

John Lennon's Rolly Royce, page 246
Andrew Bone from Weymouth, England (https://commons.wikimedia.org/wiki/File:Rolls-Royce_Phantom_V_(1965)_Replica_of_John_Lennon's_car_(28447542675).jpg), „Rolls-Royce Phantom V (1965) Replica of John Lennon's car (28447542675)", https://creativecommons.org/licenses/by/2.0/legalcode

Pink Cadillac, page 247
Corkythehornetfan (https://commons.wikimedia.org/wiki/File:Elvis_Presley_Pink_Cadillac_on_display.png), Flipped by Andrew Wood, https://creativecommons.org/licenses/by-sa/4.0/legalcode

Steve Jobs car, page 249
Alison Cassidy (https://commons.wikimedia.org/wiki/File:Steves_Mercedes.jpg), „Steves Mercedes", Cropped by Andrew Wood, https://creativecommons.org/licenses/by-sa/3.0/legalcode

Haka, page 251
New Zealand Players- Haka
© Wesley Klue | Dreamstime.com
File ID: 28121071
License: Editorial

Lebron James, page 255
Keith Allison from Baltimore, USA (https://commons.wikimedia.org/wiki/File:LeBron_James'_pregame_ritual.jpg), „LeBron James' pregame ritual", https://creativecommons.org/licenses/by-sa/2.0/legalcode

Usain Bolt, page 256
Olympic Games Rio 2016
© Celso Pupo Rodrigues | Dreamstime.com
File ID: 97192513
License: Editorial

Dan Marino, page 260
Dan Marino
© Jerry Coli | Dreamstime.com
File ID: 78434228
License: Editorial

Taylor Swift, page 261
Taylor Swift. Premiere, grand.
© Starstock | Dreamstime.com
File ID: 117141087
License: Editorial

Francesco Baracca, page 262
Unknown (https://commons.wikimedia.org/wiki/File:FBaracca_1.jpg), „FBaracca 1", marked as public domain, more details on Wikimedia Commons: https://commons.wikimedia.org/wiki/Template:PD-HU-unknown

Tifosi, page 265
anonymous (https://en.wikipedia.org/wiki/File:Tifosi_Monza_2003.JPG), „Tifosi Monza 2003", https://creativecommons.org/licenses/by-sa/3.0/legalcode

Arnold Palmer, page 266
IowaDaughter (https://commons.wikimedia.org/wiki/File:PlayerFryRulePalmerLujackDriver.jpg), „PlayerFryRulePalmerLujackDriver", https://creativecommons.org/licenses/by-sa/3.0/legalcode

Lady Gaga, pages 268-269

proacguy1 from Montreal, Canada (https://commons.wikimedia.org/wiki/File:Lady_Gaga,_ARTPOP_Ball_Tour,_Bell_Center,_Montréal,_2_July_2014_(37)_(14563250345).jpg), „Lady Gaga, ARTPOP Ball Tour, Bell Center, Montréal, 2 July 2014 (37) (14563250345)", https://creativecommons.org/licenses/by-sa/2.0/legalcode

proacguy1 from Montreal, Canada (https://commons.wikimedia.org/wiki/File:Lady_Gaga,_ARTPOP_Ball_Tour,_Bell_Center,_Montréal,_2_July_2014_(43)_(14563249595).jpg), „Lady Gaga, ARTPOP Ball Tour, Bell Center, Montréal, 2 July 2014 (43) (14563249595)", https://creativecommons.org/licenses/by-sa/2.0/legalcode

proacguy1 from Montreal, Canada (https://commons.wikimedia.org/wiki/File:Lady_Gaga,_ARTPOP_Ball_Tour,_Bell_Center,_Montréal,_2_July_2014_(51)_(14561592524).jpg), „Lady Gaga, ARTPOP Ball Tour, Bell Center, Montréal, 2 July 2014 (51) (14561592524)", https://creativecommons.org/licenses/by-sa/2.0/legalcode

Packers cheesehead, page 269
Chris F (https://commons.wikimedia.org/wiki/File:Cheeseheads_in_Stadium_(14819823518).jpg), „Cheeseheads in Stadium (14819823518)", https://creativecommons.org/licenses/by/2.0/legalcode

Jimmy Buffett, page 270
Chief Mass Communication Specialist Michael W. Pendergrass (https://commons.wikimedia.org/wiki/File:Jimmy_Buffett_1.jpg), „Jimmy Buffett 1", marked as public domain, more details on Wikimedia Commons: https://commons.wikimedia.org/wiki/Template:PD-US

Grateful Dead, pages 271-273
Warner Bros. Records (https://commons.wikimedia.org/wiki/File:Grateful_Dead_(1970).png), „Grateful Dead (1970)", marked as public domain, more details on Wikimedia Commons: https://commons.wikimedia.org/wiki/Template:PD-US

Shelby Bell from Omaha, NE, US (https://commons.wikimedia.org/wiki/File:Grateful_Dead_-_Fare_Thee_Well_-_Soldier_Field_-_Chicago_-_2015.jpg), „Grateful Dead - Fare Thee Well - Soldier Field - Chicago - 2015", https://creativecommons.org/licenses/by/2.0/legalcode

Chris Stone https://cjstone.myportfolio.com/concert (https://commons.wikimedia.org/wiki/File:Grateful_Dead_at_the_Warfield-01.jpg), „Grateful Dead at the Warfield-01", https://creativecommons.org/licenses/by-sa/2.0/legalcode

Joe Montana, page 274
Joe Montana
© Jerry Coli | Dreamstime.com
File ID: 78434332
License: Editorial

Tom Cruise, page 276
Tom Cruise
© Carrienelson1 | Dreamstime.com
File ID: 26359187
License: Editorial

Winston Churchill, page 278
United Nations Information Office, New York (https://commons.wikimedia.org/wiki/File:Sir_Winston_S_Churchill.jpg), „Sir Winston S Churchill", marked as public domain, more details on Wikimedia Commons: https://commons.wikimedia.org/wiki/Template:PD-US

Giesle Bundchen, page 229
Tiago Chediak (https://commons.wikimedia.org/wiki/File:Gisele_Bundchen2.jpg), „Gisele Bundchen2", https://creativecommons.org/licenses/by/2.0/legalcode

Steven Spielberg, page 230
Steven Spielberg
© Featureflash | Dreamstime.com
File ID: 32741289
License: Editorial

Banksy art, pages 231-233
Infrogmation of New Orleans (https://commons.wikimedia.org/wiki/File:Banksy_Swinger_Building_Detail.jpg), „Banksy Swinger Building Detail", https://creativecommons.org/licenses/by/2.0/legalcode

Markus Ortner (https://commons.wikimedia.org/wiki/File:Mauer-betlehem.jpg), „Mauer-betlehem", https://creativecommons.org/licenses/by-sa/2.5/legalcode

The original uploader was Ajuk at English Wikipedia.. The photographer's rights have been released under the following licences: (https://commons.wikimedia.org/wiki/File:Banksy-ps.jpg), „Banksy-ps", https://creativecommons.org/licenses/by-sa/3.0/legalcode

Marilyn Monroe, page 236
Published by Corpus Christi Caller-Times-photo from Associated Press (https://commons.wikimedia.org/wiki/File:Marilyn_Monroe_photo_pose_Seven_Year_Itch.jpg), „Marilyn Monroe photo pose Seven Year Itch", marked as public domain, more details on Wikimedia Commons: https://commons.wikimedia.org/wiki/Template:PD-US

Michael Jordan, page 238
Michael Jordan Chicago Bulls
© Jerry Coli | Dreamstime.com
File ID: 73480263
License: Editorial

John Wayne, page 241
EK3MHT
Glasshouse Images / Alamy Stock Photo

David Beckham, page 242
Beckham Shirtless
© Jingraham311 | Dreamstime.com
File ID: 24448651
License: Editorial

General George S. Patton, page 243
Uberti Patton Commemorative
© Ambopicinc | Dreamstime.com
File ID: 48066209
License: Editorial

James Bond Aston Martin from Goldfinger, page 245
Chilterngreen (https://commons.wikimedia.org/wiki/File:DB5-2.jpg), „DB5-2", https://creativecommons.org/licenses/by-sa/3.0/legalcode

Benjamin Disraeli, page 289
anonymous (https://commons.wikimedia.org/wiki/File:Disraeli.jpg), „Disraeli", marked as public domain, more details on Wikimedia Commons: https://commons.wikimedia.org/wiki/Template:PD-old

Harry Truman, page 290
Greta Kempton creator QS:P170,Q5607652 (https://commons.wikimedia.org/wiki/File:HarryTruman.jpg), „HarryTruman", Cropped by Andrew Wood, https://creativecommons.org/publicdomain/zero/1.0/legalcode

Bruce Springsteen, page 292
Bruce Springsteen Cork 2013
© Simon Peare | Dreamstime.com
File ID: 37036996
License: Editorial

Napoleon Bonaparte, page 293
Jacques-Louis David creator QS:P170,Q83155 Unknown (https://commons.wikimedia.org/wiki/File:Jacques-Louis_David_-_The_Emperor_Napoleon_in_His_Study_at_the_Tuileries_-_Google_Art_Project_2.jpg), „Jacques-Louis David - The Emperor Napoleon in His Study at the Tuileries - Google Art Project 2", marked as public domain, more details on Wikimedia Commons: https://commons.wikimedia.org/wiki/Template:PD-old

Princess Diana, pages 294-295
Rick (https://commons.wikimedia.org/wiki/File:Princess_Diana,_Bristol_1987-2.jpg), „Princess Diana, Bristol 1987-2", https://creativecommons.org/licenses/by/2.0/legalcode

John Mathew Smith (https://commons.wikimedia.org/wiki/File:Diana,_Princess_of_Wales_1997_(2).jpg), „Diana, Princess of Wales 1997 (2)", https://creativecommons.org/licenses/by-sa/2.0/legalcode

Fran Tarkenton, page 296
© Jerry Coli | Dreamstime.com
File ID: 74893010
License: Editorial

Voice of America (https://commons.wikimedia.org/wiki/File:Fran_Tarkenton_2016_RNC.jpg), „Fran Tarkenton 2016 RNC", marked as public domain, more details on Wikimedia Commons: https://commons.wikimedia.org/wiki/Template:PD-US

Unknown (https://commons.wikimedia.org/wiki/File:Fran_Tarkenton.png), „Fran Tarkenton", Flipped by Andrew Wood, https://creativecommons.org/publicdomain/zero/1.0/legalcode

Walter Hagen, page 298
Bundesarchiv, Bild 102-07807 / CC-BY-SA 3.0 (https://commons.wikimedia.org/wiki/File:Bundesarchiv_Bild_102-07807,_Berlin,_Golfmeisterschaften.jpg), „Bundesarchiv Bild 102-07807, Berlin, Golfmeisterschaften", https://creativecommons.org/licenses/by-sa/3.0/de/legalcode

Princess Diana, page 299
United States Federal Government (https://commons.wikimedia.org/wiki/File:John_Travolta_and_Princess_Diana.jpg), „John Travolta and Princess Diana", marked as public domain, more details on Wikimedia Commons: https://commons.wikimedia.org/wiki/Template:PD-US

George Clooney, page 300
George Clooney attends the `Money Monster`
© Denis Makarenko | Dreamstime.com
File ID: 83416433
License: Editorial

Seve Ballestros, page 301
© Jerry Coli | Dreamstime.com
File ID: 74069788
License: Editorial

Julia Roberts, page 302
Julia Roberts attends the `Money Monster`
© Denis Makarenko | Dreamstime.com
File ID: 83229376
License: Editorial

Ronald Reagan, page 303
Unknown (https://commons.wikimedia.org/wiki/File:Official_Portrait_of_President_Reagan_1981.jpg), „Official Portrait of President Reagan 1981", marked as public domain, more details on Wikimedia Commons: https://commons.wikimedia.org/wiki/Template:PD-US

Tom Hanks, page 305
© Featureflash | Dreamstime.com
File ID: 30078160
License: Editorial

Martin Luther King Jr., page 306
Herman Hiller / New York World-Telegram & Sun (https://commons.wikimedia.org/wiki/File:Martin_Luther_King_Jr_NYWTS_5.jpg), „Martin Luther King Jr NYWTS 5", marked as public domain, more details on Wikimedia Commons: https://commons.wikimedia.org/wiki/Template:Library of Congress-no known copyright restrictions

Bill Clinton, pages 307-308

The U.S. National Archives (https://commons.wikimedia.org/wiki/File:Photograph_of_President_William_Jefferson_Clinton_Greeting_People_in_a_Large_Crowd_at_a_"Get_Out_the_Vote"_Rally_in_Los_Angeles,_California,_11_02_2000.jpg), „Photograph of President William Jefferson Clinton Greeting People in a Large Crowd at a "Get Out the Vote" Rally in Los Angeles, California, 11 02 2000", marked as public domain, more details on Wikimedia Commons: https://commons.wikimedia.org/wiki/Template:PD-US

TSGT Victor Trisvan (https://commons.wikimedia.org/wiki/File:President_Clinton_greets_the_crowd_at_Spangdahlem_Air_Base.jpg), „President Clinton greets the crowd at Spangdahlem Air Base", marked as public domain, more details on Wikimedia Commons: https://commons.wikimedia.org/wiki/Template:PD-US

Bob McNeely and White House Photograph Office (https://commons.wikimedia.org/wiki/File:Bill_Clinton_in_the_White_House_Music_Room_(cropped1).jpg), „Bill Clinton in the White House Music Room (cropped1)", marked as public domain, more details on Wikimedia Commons: https://commons.wikimedia.org/wiki/Template:PD-US

White House Photograph Office (https://commons.wikimedia.org/wiki/File:Clinton_Yeltsin_1995.jpg), „Clinton Yeltsin 1995", marked as public domain, more details on Wikimedia Commons: https://commons.wikimedia.org/wiki/Template:PD-US

Gage Skidmore (https://commons.wikimedia.org/wiki/File:Bill_Clinton_by_Gage_Skidmore.jpg), „Bill Clinton by Gage Skidmore", https://creativecommons.org/licenses/by-sa/3.0/legalcode

Jack Nicklaus, pages 309-310
GADD7P
PA Images / Alamy Stock Photo

Jack Nicklaus, PGA Golfer
© Jerry Coli | Dreamstime.com
File ID: 76434167
License: Editorial

Billy Casper, page 312
Unknown (Associated Press) (https://commons.wikimedia.org/wiki/File:Billy_Casper_and_Gene_Littler_1970.jpg), „Billy Casper and Gene Littler 1970", marked as public domain, more details on Wikimedia Commons: https://commons.wikimedia.org/wiki/Template:PD-US

Jack Nicholson, page 314
Jack Nicholson and Lara Flynn Boyle
© Denis Makarenko | Dreamstime.com
File ID: 13902657
License: Editorial

Donald Trump, page 316
OCTOBER 15, 2016, EDISON, NJ - Donald Trump speaks at Edison New Jersey Hindu Indian-American rally for 'Humanity United Against T
© Joe Sohm | Dreamstime.com
File ID: 84990718
License: Editorial

Hillary Clinton, page 316
Hillary Clinton rally
© Joe Tabb | Dreamstime.com
File ID: 72349804
License: Editorial

Sid Viscious, page 319
Koen Suyk; Nationaal Archief, Den Haag, Rijksfotoarchief: Fotocollectie Algemeen Nederlands Fotopersbureau (ANEFO), 1945-1989 - negatiefstroken zwart/wit, nummer toegang 2.24.01.05, bestanddeelnummer 928-9662 (https://commons.wikimedia.org/wiki/File:Sex_Pistols_in_Paradiso_-_Johnny_Rotten_2.jpg), „Sex Pistols in Paradiso - Johnny Rotten 2", https://creativecommons.org/publicdomain/zero/1.0/legalcode

Sex Pistols, page 320
frankiboi (Bruno Ehrs) (https://commons.wikimedia.org/wiki/File:Tdpe_0002_xs_Thomas_Dellert_and_the_Sex_Pistols_1978.jpg), „Tdpe 0002 xs Thomas Dellert and the Sex Pistols 1978", https://creativecommons.org/licenses/by-sa/3.0/legalcode

Punk rock music vinyl records
© Dimitris Kolyris | Dreamstime.com
File ID: 38695777
License: Editorial

Richard Branson, page 322

Enzo Ferrari, page 324
Rainer W. Schlegelmilch (https://commons.wikimedia.org/wiki/File:Enzo_Ferrari_-_Monza,_1967.jpg), „Enzo Ferrari - Monza, 1967", marked as public domain, more details on Wikimedia Commons: https://commons.wikimedia.org/wiki/Template:PD-1996

Ferruccio Lamborghini, page 324
ignoto (https://it.wikipedia.org/wiki/File:Ferruccio_lamborghini.jpg) , „Ferruccio lamborghini"

Lamborghini Miura, page 325
Ed CallowCropped by uploader Mr.choppers (https://commons.wikimedia.org/wiki/File:Lamborghini_Miura_SVJ.jpg), „Lamborghini Miura SVJ", https://creativecommons.org/licenses/by/2.0/legalcode

Richard Simmons, page 327
DNXNFY
Zuma Press, Inc. / Alamy Stock Photo

Frederick Douglas, pages 328-329

Walter Smalling for the Historic American Buildings Survey (https://commons.wikimedia.org/wiki/File:Frederick_Douglass_House.jpg), „Frederick Douglass House", marked as public domain, more details on Wikimedia Commons: https://commons.wikimedia.org/wiki/Template:PD-US

George Kendall Warren creator QS:P170,Q30303227 (https://commons.wikimedia.org/wiki/File:Frederick_Douglass_(circa_1879).jpg), „Frederick Douglass (circa 1879)", marked as public domain, more details on Wikimedia Commons: https://commons.wikimedia.org/wiki/Template:PD-old

Eva Peron, pages 330-331
I am the author of this work (https://commons.wikimedia.org/wiki/File:Evita_La_Prensa_cuatro_rostros.jpg), „Evita La Prensa cuatro rostros", marked as public domain, more details on Wikimedia Commons: https://commons.wikimedia.org/wiki/Template:PD-self

Unknown (https://commons.wikimedia.org/wiki/File:Evita_(foto).JPG), „Evita (foto)", marked as public domain, more details on Wikimedia Commons: https://commons.wikimedia.org/wiki/Template:PD-AR-Photo

Bruce Lee, page 333
ABC Television, restore by BevinKacon (https://commons.wikimedia.org/wiki/File:Bruce_Lee_as_Kato_1967.jpg), „Bruce Lee as Kato 1967", marked as public domain, more details on Wikimedia Commons: https://commons.wikimedia.org/wiki/Template:PD-US

UFO, page 334
Fliing UFO
© Emoke Kupai | Dreamstime.com
File ID: 75432920
License: Royalty Free

Eminem, page 336
Mika-photography (https://commons.wikimedia.org/wiki/File:Eminem-01-mika.jpg), „Eminem-01-mika", https://creativecommons.org/licenses/by-sa/3.0/legalcode

Niki Lauda, page 337
Anefo / Croes, R.C. / neg. stroken, 1945-1989, 2.24.01.05, item number 928-0061 (https://commons.wikimedia.org/wiki/File:Podium_at_1975_Dutch_Grand_Prix.jpg), „Podium at 1975 Dutch Grand Prix", https://creativecommons.org/licenses/by-sa/3.0/nl/deed.en

Muhammad Ali, page 339
PA (https://commons.wikimedia.org/wiki/File:Muhammad_Ali_and_Henry_Cooper_following_their_fight_on_June_18,_1963.jpg), „Muhammad Ali and Henry Cooper following their fight on June 18, 1963", marked as public domain, more details on Wikimedia Commons: https://commons.wikimedia.org/wiki/Template:PD-old

Harry Houdini, page 342
Bain News Service (https://commons.wikimedia.org/wiki/File:HoudiniSubmergedCrate.jpg), „HoudiniSubmergedCrate", marked as public domain, more details on Wikimedia Commons: https://commons.wikimedia.org/wiki/Template:PD-US

Jesse Owens, page 345-346
Library of Congress

Bundesarchiv, Bild 183-G00630 / Unknown / CC-BY-SA 3.0 (https://commons.wikimedia.org/wiki/File:Bundesarchiv_Bild_183-G00630,_Sommerolympiade,_Siegerehrung_Weitsprung.jpg), „Bundesarchiv Bild 183-G00630, Sommerolympiade, Siegerehrung Weitsprung", https://creativecommons.org/licenses/by-sa/3.0/de/legalcode

Johan Cruyff, pages 347-348

Bert Verhoeff / Anefo (https://commons.wikimedia.org/wiki/File:Johan_Cruijff_krijgt_in_Amstelveen_Ballon_dor_(onderscheiding_voor_Europees_vo,_Bestanddeelnr_925-5239.jpg), „Johan Cruijff krijgt in Amstelveen Ballon dor (onderscheiding voor Europees vo, Bestanddeelnr 925-5239", https://creativecommons.org/publicdomain/zero/1.0/legalcode

Bundesarchiv, Bild 183-N0716-0314 / Mittelstädt, Rainer / CC-BY-SA 3.0 (https://commons.wikimedia.org/wiki/File:Bundesarchiv_Bild_183-N0716-0314,_Fußball-WM,_BRD_-_Niederlande_2-1.jpg), „Bundesarchiv Bild 183-N0716-0314, Fußball-WM, BRD - Niederlande 2-1", https://creativecommons.org/licenses/by-sa/3.0/de/legalcode

Elvis Presley, page 350
Unknown (https://commons.wikimedia.org/wiki/File:Elvis_Presley_and_Colonel_Tom_Parker_1969.jpg), „Elvis Presley and Colonel Tom Parker 1969", marked as public domain, more details on Wikimedia Commons: https://commons.wikimedia.org/wiki/Template:PD-US

Nelson Mandela, page 354
NELSON MANDELA WITH UFFE ELLEMANN-JSEN_DK
© Deanpictures | Dreamstime.com
File ID: 111738898
License: Editorial

White House Photograph Office (https://commons.wikimedia.org/wiki/File:Clinton_Yeltsin_1995.jpg), „Clinton Yeltsin 1995", marked as public domain, more details on Wikimedia Commons: https://commons.wikimedia.org/wiki/Template:PD-US

Gage Skidmore (https://commons.wikimedia.org/wiki/File:Bill_Clinton_by_Gage_Skidmore.jpg), „Bill Clinton by Gage Skidmore", https://creativecommons.org/licenses/by-sa/3.0/legalcode

Jack Nicklaus, pages 309-310
GADD7P
PA Images / Alamy Stock Photo

Jack Nicklaus, PGA Golfer
© Jerry Coli | Dreamstime.com
File ID: 76434167
License: Editorial

Billy Casper, page 312
Unknown (Associated Press) (https://commons.wikimedia.org/wiki/File:Billy_Casper_and_Gene_Littler_1970.jpg), „Billy Casper and Gene Littler 1970", marked as public domain, more details on Wikimedia Commons: https://commons.wikimedia.org/wiki/Template:PD-US

Jack Nicholson, page 314
Jack Nicholson and Lara Flynn Boyle
© Denis Makarenko | Dreamstime.com
File ID: 13902657
License: Editorial

Donald Trump, page 316
OCTOBER 15, 2016, EDISON, NJ - Donald Trump speaks at Edison New Jersey Hindu Indian-American rally for 'Humanity United Against T
© Joe Sohm | Dreamstime.com
File ID: 84990718
License: Editorial

Hillary Clinton, page 316
Hillary Clinton rally
© Joe Tabb | Dreamstime.com
File ID: 72349804
License: Editorial

Sid Viscious, page 319
Koen Suyk; Nationaal Archief, Den Haag, Rijksfotoarchief: Fotocollectie Algemeen Nederlands Fotopersbureau (ANEFO), 1945-1989 - negatiefstroken zwart/wit, nummer toegang 2.24.01.05, bestanddeelnummer 928-9662 (https://commons.wikimedia.org/wiki/File:Sex_Pistols_in_Paradiso_-_Johnny_Rotten_2.jpg), „Sex Pistols in Paradiso - Johnny Rotten 2", https://creativecommons.org/publicdomain/zero/1.0/legalcode

Sex Pistols, page 320
frankiboi (Bruno Ehrs) (https://commons.wikimedia.org/wiki/File:Tdpe_0002_xs_Thomas_Dellert_and_the_Sex_Pistols_1978.jpg), „Tdpe 0002 xs Thomas Dellert and the Sex Pistols 1978", https://creativecommons.org/licenses/by-sa/3.0/legalcode

Lady Gaga, page 393
Brian Allen/Voice of America (https://commons.wikimedia.org/wiki/File:Super_Bowl_LI_halftime_show_02_(cropped1).jpg), „Super Bowl LI halftime show 02 (cropped1)", marked as public domain, more details on Wikimedia Commons: https://commons.wikimedia.org/wiki/Template:PD-US

John F. Kennedy, page 396
Walt Cisco, Dallas Morning News (https://commons.wikimedia.org/wiki/File:JFK_limousine.png), „JFK limousine", marked as public domain, more details on Wikimedia Commons: https://commons.wikimedia.org/wiki/Template:PD-US

Buzz Aldrin, page 397
NASA (https://commons.wikimedia.org/wiki/File:Aldrin_Apollo_11_original.jpg), „Aldrin Apollo 11 original", marked as public domain, more details on Wikimedia Commons: https://commons.wikimedia.org/wiki/Template:PD-US

Berlin Wall, page 398
Bundesarchiv, Bild 183-1990-0105-029 / Reiche, Hartmut / CC-BY-SA 3.0 (https://commons.wikimedia.org/wiki/File:Bundesarchiv_Bild_183-1990-0105-029,_Berlin,_Loch_in_Mauer_am_Reichstag.jpg), „Bundesarchiv Bild 183-1990-0105-029, Berlin, Loch in Mauer am Reichstag", https://creativecommons.org/licenses/by-sa/3.0/de/legalcode

Frank Sinatra, page 399
Frank Sinatra
© Laurence Agron | Dreamstime.com
File ID: 51117095
License: Editorial

Tony Robbins, page 400
Randy Stewart (https://commons.wikimedia.org/wiki/File:Tony_Robbins.jpg), „Tony Robbins", https://creativecommons.org/licenses/by-sa/2.0/legalcode

Steve Jobs and Bill Gates, page 403
Joi Ito from Inbamura, Japan (https://commons.wikimedia.org/wiki/File:Steve_Jobs_and_Bill_Gates_(522695099).jpg), „Steve Jobs and Bill Gates (522695099)", https://creativecommons.org/licenses/by/2.0/legalcode

Ralph Waldo Emerson, page 405
User:Scewing derivative work: 2009 (https://commons.wikimedia.org/wiki/File:Ralph_Waldo_Emerson_ca1857_retouched.jpg), „Ralph Waldo Emerson ca1857 retouched", marked as public domain, more details on Wikimedia Commons: https://commons.wikimedia.org/wiki/Template:PD-old

Pablo Picasso, page 407
Paolo Monti creator QS:P170,Q18169099 (https://commons.wikimedia.org/wiki/File:Paolo_Monti_-_Servizio_fotografico_(Milano,_1953)_-_BEIC_6356204.jpg), https://creativecommons.org/licenses/by-sa/4.0/legalcode

John Wayne, page 408
(https://commons.wikimedia.org/wiki/File:John_Wayne_Publicity_Photo_1952.jpg), „John Wayne Publicity Photo 1952", Cropped by Andrew Wood, https://creativecommons.org/publicdomain/zero/1.0/legalcode

Don McLean, page 409
Egghead06
(https://commons.wikimedia.org/wiki/File:Don_McLean_in_2012.jpg), „Don McLean in 2012",
https://creativecommons.org/licenses/by-sa/3.0/legalcode

Emmylou Harris, page 411
jess hodge (digboston)
(https://commons.wikimedia.org/wiki/File:Emmylou_Harris_Newport_Folk_Festival_2011.jpg), „Emmylou Harris Newport Folk Festival 2011",
https://creativecommons.org/licenses/by/2.0/legalcode

Elvis Presley, page 413
Metro-Goldwyn-Mayer, Inc.
(https://commons.wikimedia.org/wiki/File:Elvis_Presley_Jailhouse_Rock.jpg), „Elvis Presley Jailhouse Rock", marked as public domain, more details on Wikimedia Commons:
https://commons.wikimedia.org/wiki/Template:PD-US

Frank Sinatra, page 414
Unknown
(https://commons.wikimedia.org/wiki/File:Frank_Sinatra_Billboard.jpg), „Frank Sinatra Billboard", marked as public domain, more details on Wikimedia Commons:
https://commons.wikimedia.org/wiki/Template:PD-US

Mick Jagger, page 415
Gorupdebesanez
(https://commons.wikimedia.org/wiki/File:Rolling_Stones_33.jpg), „Rolling Stones 33", https://creativecommons.org/licenses/by-sa/3.0/legalcode

Jimmy Hendrix, page 418
Warner/Reprise Records Uploaded by We hope at en.wikipedia
(https://commons.wikimedia.org/wiki/File:Jimi_Hendrix_experience_1968.jpg), „Jimi Hendrix experience 1968", marked as public domain, more details on Wikimedia Commons:
https://commons.wikimedia.org/wiki/Template:PD-US

Niki Lauda, page 422
Dijk, Hans van / Anefo / neg. stroken, 1945-1989, 2.24.01.05, item number 932-2315
(https://commons.wikimedia.org/wiki/File:Lauda_at_1982_Dutch_Grand_Prix.jpg), „Lauda at 1982 Dutch Grand Prix",
https://creativecommons.org/licenses/by-sa/3.0/nl/deed.en

Kevin Costner, page 424
F6H85G
Entertainment Pictures / Alamy Stock Photo

Harry Potter books, page 426
Harry Potter shop
© Siempreverde22 | Dreamstime.com
File ID: 105860823
License: Editorial

JK Rowling, page 427
Daniel Ogren
(https://commons.wikimedia.org/wiki/File:J._K._Rowling_2010.jpg), „J. K. Rowling 2010",
https://creativecommons.org/licenses/by/2.0/legalcode

Thomas Edison, page 429
Levin C. Handy (per http://hdl.loc.gov/loc.pnp/cwpbh.04326)
(https://commons.wikimedia.org/wiki/File:Edison_and_phonograph_edit1.jpg), „Edison and phonograph edit1", marked as public domain, more details on Wikimedia Commons:
https://commons.wikimedia.org/wiki/Template:PD-old

Ronald Reagan, pages 431-432
White House Photographic Office
(https://commons.wikimedia.org/wiki/File:The_Reagans_waving_from_the_limousine_during_the_Inaugural_Parade_1981.jpg), „The Reagans waving from the limousine during the Inaugural Parade 1981", marked as public domain, more details on Wikimedia Commons:
https://commons.wikimedia.org/wiki/Template:PD-US

Warner Bros.
(https://commons.wikimedia.org/wiki/File:Ronald_Reagan_in_Knute_Rockne-All_American_1940.jpg), „Ronald Reagan in Knute Rockne-All American 1940", marked as public domain, more details on Wikimedia Commons:
https://commons.wikimedia.org/wiki/Template:PD-because

The Beatles, page 434
PRESSENS BILD (Mikael J. Nordström)
(https://commons.wikimedia.org/wiki/File:The_Beatles_and_Lill-Babs_1963.jpg), „The Beatles and Lill-Babs 1963", Cropped by Andrew Wood,
https://creativecommons.org/publicdomain/zero/1.0/legalcode

Sir James Dyson, page 435
The Royal Society
(https://commons.wikimedia.org/wiki/File:Sir_James_Dyson_CBE_FREng_FRS.jpg),
https://creativecommons.org/licenses/by-sa/4.0/legalcode

Jay-Z, page 436
Jay-Z in Concert
© Artofchriz | Dreamstime.com
File ID: 14680929
License: Editorial

Jim Carrey, page 437
Jean-François Gornet
(https://commons.wikimedia.org/wiki/File:Jim_Carrey.jpg), „Jim Carrey", https://creativecommons.org/licenses/by-sa/2.0/legalcode

Sylvester Stallone, pages 438, 440
Towpilot
(https://commons.wikimedia.org/wiki/File:Sylvester_Stallone.jpg), „Sylvester Stallone",
https://creativecommons.org/licenses/by-sa/3.0/legalcode

photo by Alan Light
(https://commons.wikimedia.org/wiki/File:Sylvester_Stallone_1978.jpg), „Sylvester Stallone 1978",
https://creativecommons.org/licenses/by/2.0/legalcode

Ronald Reagan assassination attempt, page 441
anonymous
(https://commons.wikimedia.org/wiki/File:Reagan_assassination_attempt_4.jpg), „Reagan assassination attempt 4", marked as public domain, more details on Wikimedia Commons:
https://commons.wikimedia.org/wiki/Template:PD-US

Ronald Reagan, page 442
anonymous
(https://commons.wikimedia.org/wiki/File:Reagans_wave_after_returning_from_WH_1981.jpg), „Reagans wave after returning from WH 1981", marked as public domain, more details on Wikimedia Commons:
https://commons.wikimedia.org/wiki/Template:PD-US

Fred Astaire, page 445
Studio publicity still
(https://commons.wikimedia.org/wiki/File:Astaire,_Fred_-_Daddy.jpg), „Astaire, Fred - Daddy", Flipped by Andrew Wood,
https://creativecommons.org/publicdomain/zero/1.0/legalcode

Vera Wang, page 449
Christopher Peterson
(https://commons.wikimedia.org/wiki/File:Vera_Wang.jpg), „Vera Wang",
https://creativecommons.org/licenses/by/2.0/legalcode

Niki Lauda, page 450
Lothar Spurzem
(https://commons.wikimedia.org/wiki/File:LaudaNiki19760731Ferrari312T2.jpg), „LaudaNiki19760731Ferrari312T2",
https://creativecommons.org/licenses/by-sa/2.0/de/legalcode

Walt Disney, page 452
Boy Scouts of America
(https://commons.wikimedia.org/wiki/File:Walt_Disney_1946.JPG), „Walt Disney 1946", marked as public domain, more details on Wikimedia Commons:
https://commons.wikimedia.org/wiki/Template:PD-US

Howard Schulz, page 454
Gage Skidmore
(https://commons.wikimedia.org/wiki/File:Howard_Schultz_by_Gage_Skidmore.jpg), „Howard Schultz by Gage Skidmore", https://creativecommons.org/licenses/by-sa/3.0/legalcode

Made in the USA
Monee, IL
07 May 2022

96033945R00260